A CAVALRYMAN'S STORY

Memoirs of a
Twentieth-Century
Army General

A CAVALRYMAN'S STORY

HAMILTON H. HOWZE

SMITHSONIAN INSTITUTION PRESS
Washington and London

This book was edited by Initial Cap Editorial Services and designed by Janice Wheeler.

EDITOR'S NOTE: Special thanks are due to General Williams and to Bill Harris, editor of *Army Aviation* magazine, for their generous and steadfast support in the advance to accuracy.

Library of Congress Cataloging-in-Publication Data

Howze, Hamilton H. (Hamilton Hawkins), 1908– .
    A calvaryman's story : memoirs of a twentieth-century Army general / Hamilton H. Howze.
        p.   cm.
    Includes index.
    ISBN 1-56098-664-6 (alk. paper)
    1. Howze, Hamilton H. (Hamilton Hawkins), 1908– . 2. Generals—United States—Biography. 3. United States. Army—Officers—Biography. 4. United States. Army—Aviation—History. 5. Military helicopters—United States—History. I. Title.
U53.H68A3 1996
355`.0092—dc20
[B]
                                                                            95-47501
                                                                                CIP

The paper used in this publication meets the minimum requirements of the American National Standard for Permanence of Paper for Printed Library Materials Z39.48-1984.

Printed in the United States of America

10 9 8 7 6 5 4 3 2 1   02 01 00 99 98 97 96

CONTENTS

FOREWORD

A Cavalryman's Story narrates how Hamilton H. Howze brought to vigorous life in the U.S. Army the concept of replacing many ground vehicles and weapons systems with helicopters. General Howze accomplished this through a tremendous force of will alloyed with superb organizational skills and a genteel but direct ability to express himself.

Each of his names—Hamilton, Hawkins, and Howze—conjures up images of great men of the past and a proud Army. General Howze's father was a famous general and winner of the Congressional Medal of Honor. You will read in the next few pages how his link to Army aristocracy goes back even further.

Born into and reared in the old "Horse Army" between the wars, Hamilton Howze was a visionary who participated in the transformation of the Army of the 1930s to the mechanized Army of the 1940s to the highly mobile, air-minded Army of today. As a junior cavalry officer for more than ten years, he was among the first to see the promise of a mechanized Army in tank warfare. After proving himself in combat in World War II, when he spoke about tactics and organization for a future Army the Army leadership listened.

Ideas on ways to employ helicopters in various combat missions were espoused by many, including such great American leaders as Gen. Jim Gavin, before Howze came on the Army Aviation scene. However, it remained for the young Brigadier General Howze to move the concept forward. As the first Director of Army Aviation, General Howze guided the aircraft development programs that later produced the great fixed-wing and rotary-wing aircraft needed for air mobility. Then, as Commanding General of the 82nd Airborne Division, he took every opportunity to persuade the Army's leaders to test the concept of actually replacing ground vehicles with helicopters.

Before the Army and the Department of Defense would make the big investment in "Air Mobility," however, many tasks had to be accomplished. As a member of the Rogers Board, General Howze clearly described the concept of air mobility. And when that concept had to be developed in detail and demonstrated, the Howze Board took over.

Howze's chairmanship of the now-famous Howze Board in 1962 led to the implementation of modern heliborne warfare, an innovation that has characterized every conflict from Vietnam to Desert Storm and beyond. In heliborne warfare, helicopters are integrated into the Army forces to carry out maneuver, fire support, intelligence, air defense, logistics, and battle command. The concept has been known as Air Cavalry and as Air Mobility, but the most popular title in use today is the title General Howze gave it in 1962: Air Assault. Although this may be his greatest accomplishment, there is much, much more to this man's story.

This is the story of a different Army and, in some respects, a different United States of America than we see today. It is a cautionary and evolutionary tale told with an abiding affection for this country and its institutions, but with some very strong implications for today's military, and, indeed, the nation.

Robert R. Williams
Lieutenant General, U.S. Army (Ret.)

PREFACE

Autobiography is traditionally the province of the famous and the powerful, of those who have had major influence on the lives of many others. I have not managed to do that, yet I persist in the belief that there may be something worth recording in the lives of the relatively unknown. I have lived in America for a long time—for considerably more than one-third of the years since the American colonists revolted against the British crown.

I acknowledge not only affection for the United States but also a special sensitivity in its regard, a certain proprietary feeling that, I suspect, is shared by all who have devoted most of their lives to its service, particularly if that service were military. My wife and I grew up in military and therefore "conservative" (in the current lingo) families; and after our marriage, with her help and concurrence, I pursued a full military career.

While some might argue that long government service must have shielded us from some of the more important facts of life in America I don't think so: as children we lived in many places, and always, until I left for West Point, I attended public schools. As adults we lived in several parts of the country and for twelve years overseas, in Europe and the Far East. Since retirement we have dwelt for thirty years in Fort Worth—civilian life in a civilian community—and all of our daily contacts are with civilian men and women. For the first ten of those years I was an officer, and then a consultant, with Bell Helicopter Textron. In those capacities I had extensive business travel in Europe, the Middle East, and on the periphery of Asia.

Of course a military upbringing does condition one's reactions in more ways than one, and military service continues the process. I hope that the reader will regard this revelation without undue alarm, and in that hope devote the first chapter of this volume to very brief biographical summaries of our antecedents.

In the account of my participation in World War II I have made no attempt at presenting a consecutive outline of what occurred to me or anyone else, confining myself simply to impressions of what went on in my general vicinity. Some of the incidents I describe are important, some tragic, some altogether trivial. Perhaps their description will serve in some way to help illuminate the war era—in which trivia and humor, and sometimes the ridiculous, played a part. But that era, one should know, was one in which these United States, through unity and enormous effort, generosity and self-sacrifice, rose to very great heights.

A CAVALRYMAN'S STORY

A VERY WELCOME ADDITION

1 My mother, at the age of 36, and my father at 45 were not enthusiastic about my predicted arrival; one girl and one boy already on hand seemed quite enough. In later years, however, my mother was kind enough to say that I was a very welcome addition. On this subject my father, Robert Lee Howze, was noncommittal, no doubt on the basis that my care and upbringing were obvious obligations he fully intended to fulfill and that earlier sentiments were therefore of no moment. However that may sound, with my brother and sister I had the great good fortune of growing up in a close and loving family with much emphasis on the military tradition. It was never a rich family, but never lacked in the essentials. My wife's family was also military, and may be similarly described.

From 1904 to 1908 my father was Commandant of Cadets at the Military Academy. From what I was told much later, he was considered a strict disciplinarian, but he introduced polo as a sport for the cadets, for which reason Howze Field is still to be found at West Point—up near the football stadium.

I was born in the quarters, which are still standing and regularly assigned to the incumbent Commandant. Four weeks later I journeyed to San Juan, Porto (now Puerto) Rico, making the trip, before the invention of fancier accommodations for traveling infants, in a clothesbasket. By virtue of my father's new assignment as commander of what was then known as the Porto Rico Regiment of Infantry, we lived in Casa

1

Blanca, a most substantial residence overlooking San Juan Harbor. It was built, remarkably, by Ponce de Leon in 1570, thirty-eight years before the establishment of Jamestown, Virginia, the first permanent English colony in North America. I don't know how long de Leon dwelt in the house. It is now a Puerto Rico state park.

My family lived in relative luxury for the next three years, with a suitable staff of servants and, I was told, the services of a milch cow brought down from New York State. My mother was able to take her three children to Fort Preble, Maine, each year during the hot season in Porto Rico.

In San Juan my sister Harriot, nine years older than I, had as one of her constant playmates Gloria Swanson, of precisely the same age. In her book, *Swanson on Swanson* the actress speaks of my sister, spelling both her first and last names incorrectly. The daughter of an Army warrant officer (then, I'm told, known as a "field clerk"), Gloria grew up to become a multi-husbanded, super-glamorous lady, known wherever on this earth a movie screen could be found. My sister, who lived in what Gloria called the "Pink Palace" (it was big but not pink), married a West Pointer who retired as a colonel. Her life has been a most worthwhile one with a devoted family and countless friends, but like the rest of us she was neither famous nor rich. The contrast between her life and Gloria's illustrates the vagaries—but also, of course, the opportunities—of life in America.

My mother was Anne Chifelle Hawkins, a daughter of Brig. Gen. Hamilton Smith Hawkins of the Army. Of five children, she and a younger brother and sister survived, about the usual percentage for the times. She was the granddaughter of an Army surgeon (the title once conferred on all Army doctors), also named Hamilton S. Hawkins, who lies buried somewhere near Vera Cruz, Mexico. He lost his life in 1847 during the Mexican War—presumably from yellow fever, then a scourge of all military forces operating in the tropics.

Some years ago I sent to the library at West Point an 1852 letter to my mother's grandmother written in very legible script by Robert E. Lee, then Superintendent of the Military Academy. She had remarried to a Lorenzo Draper, then U.S. Consul in Havre, France. Lee apparently knew the lady well, telling her in the most sympathetic terms that her cadet son was incurring too many demerits for various infractions of military discipline; he was also not applying himself properly to his studies. These were reasons that Lee could not allow her son to attend his sister's wedding; more important, however, it was becoming apparent that unless the young man studied harder he was very likely to be found academically deficient and dismissed from the Academy. My grandfather did not improve and was thrown out. Although he considered himself a Virginian, and might have resented his expulsion from the Military Academy, he reentered service on the Union side during the Civil War, much later becoming the only Commandant of Cadets in the history of the Academy to have failed in his own effort to graduate. (Lee's letter, with others to Mrs. Draper by General Sherman and her son, my grandfather, are reproduced in appendix A.)

My mother had very little formal schooling by reason of her father's repeated posting to various Army garrisons in the far west during the Indian wars. Fortunately her very literate soldier-father kept her supplied with books and tutored her faithfully when he wasn't in the field, and when he became Commandant of Cadets at the Military Academy (as her husband did later) her father exposed her to the influence and very generous guidance of one Dr. Holt, then a distinguished civilian professor, I think of history, at West Point. In any event, despite her lack of formal education my mother became a knowledgeable, charming, eminently interesting conversationalist with a quick wit, a sense of the ridiculous, and a great talent as a hostess. Her pictures as a girl and young woman show a lovely, gentle face and a clear fresh skin; she developed into a handsome, extremely popular woman, known throughout the Army. Her children loved her dearly, and found, for as long as she lived, the greatest pleasure in her company.

My paternal grandfather did his military service as a captain of Confederate infantry, settling thereafter as a farmer in the small town of Overton, in east Texas. On one occasion my father (christened Robert Lee, which in the South must have been almost obligatory at the time) journeyed alone at the age of 12 from Overton to New York, his railroad ticket allegedly bought from his savings as a helper to his father and other farmers. On this adventure my father found his pleasure mainly by riding the horsecars up and down Fifth Avenue, marveling at the wonders of the big city. But on one occasion he took passage on the Hudson River Day Boat, which stopped at several river towns—and West Point. The Military Academy enthralled him, imbuing this young son of an ex-Rebel with the resolve to attend, a resolve reinforced perhaps by the limitations of the night life in Overton.

He should have graduated from West Point in 1887, but as a cadet he was given a year's leave to recuperate from a severe case of typhoid fever. On commission in 1888, his first assignment was to the Fifth Cavalry Regiment at Fort Wingate, New Mexico, where he fought in what I believe was the last campaign against the Apaches. He was transferred thereafter to the Sixth Cavalry, then at the Pine Ridge Agency in South Dakota. The Sioux were still hostile, and very active. For one battle, in which he was in command of a small isolated detachment of soldiers under heavy Sioux attack, he was awarded the Congressional Medal of Honor.

He served as the adjutant of a regular cavalry regiment in Cuba during the Spanish American War. I don't know what the regiment did by way of fighting, but I know something of what my father did because he is mentioned frequently—in a most complimentary way, I'm happy to report—by Teddy Roosevelt in *The Rough Riders*. In the same book Roosevelt also speaks admiringly of my mother's father, then a brigadier general commanding a regular infantry brigade whose mission it was to take San Juan Hill.

Roosevelt, incidentally, did not "lead the charge on San Juan Hill," as the history books say—my mother's father, Hamilton Hawkins, the one who didn't make it at West Point, did. The Rough Rider regiment took Kettle Hill, alongside San Juan Hill. The letters by Mr. Roosevelt to my father and grandfather, reproduced in the appendix, do not altogether bear out this contention, though one of them, written on "Feby. 5th, 1900" from the Executive Chamber, State of New York, to my grandfather, tends to support it.

Some years after the war my father was appointed military aide at the White House when Teddy Roosevelt was president. Roosevelt told him that of course he knew that he and his regiment were on Kettle Hill, not San Juan, but the news dispatches had put him firmly on San Juan and the tale stuck. For some months he attempted to correct the record, but the perception was by then so ingrained in the public mind that he gave up the effort. The distinction, it should be said, is inconsequential.

Almost as soon as he was back from Cuba, my father, by then brevetted as a lieutenant colonel, was entrusted with the raising and training of a regiment of volunteer infantry, the 34th, in Colorado for service in the Philippine Islands. He was much impressed with his recruits, mostly outdoorsmen—hunters, trappers, and cowhands—experienced in the handling of firearms. In only about six weeks the regiment was declared fit for field service, and was embarked on a ship for the Philippines. The enemy were the Insurrectos—armed Filipinos in rebellion against the authority of the United States soon after the treaty ending the Spanish American War ceded the Philippine Islands to this country.

The 34th Volunteer Infantry was commanded by a Colonel Hare, but my father's incomplete notes rarely acknowledge that fact, for reasons I do not pretend to understand. My father, as the regimental lieutenant colonel, was given command of a force of several companies that not long after disembarkation fought a bloody but enormously successful action against the Insurrectos in the hills bordering the Lingayen Plain. Almost immediately thereafter he led (according to his detailed account of the event, though other evidence indicates that Hare also was along for part of the time) a protracted, incredibly difficult and, for a time, famous action in the wild, jungle-covered mountains of northern Luzon, the main island, to rescue Lieutenant Commander Gilmore, U.S. Navy, and a number of sailors and soldiers held prisoner by the Insurrectos. At that time the area was occupied, literally, only by savages. The expedition, lasting about six weeks, almost failed due to terrible hardship and the near-starvation of its participants, but all the prisoners were safely recovered. Governor Roosevelt cabled his congratulations from Albany:

> My dear Colonel Howze,
>
> Just a line to say how pleased and proud Mrs. Roosevelt and I are over your triumph. I have been watching your career with the utmost eagerness, and now comes news of your striking triumph. I congratulate you more than heartily.
>
> Please present my regards to Colonel Hare also.
>
> Faithfully yours,
>
> Theodore Roosevelt

In 1916 my father, then only a major in the Regular Army despite his earlier higher "volunteer" ranks, commanded what was known as the "flying squadron" of the 11th Cavalry in the Punitive Expedition into Mexico. Neither he nor anyone else managed to catch sight of Pancho Villa, the quarry, in the primitive vastness of northern Mexico.

By 1918 he was a major general commanding the 38th Infantry Division in the American Expeditionary Force in France. To his dismay the division arrived too late to participate more than very briefly in the fighting. He however was moved to the command of the veteran 3rd Infantry Division, and in that post served more than a year in the Army of Occupation, with station at Andernach, on the Rhine River.

As a major general and the fifth ranking officer in the Army my father died in 1926—on an operating table in Columbus, Ohio, when his heart stopped in the course of removal of his gallbladder. He was only 62, to all appearances still a vigorous man. The event is indicative, I believe, of the amazing progress in medicine. If the same operation were done today, on the same man with the same problem, he might have lived another 20 years.

My wife entered this world at Fort Riley, Kansas. Mary Rogers Henry, her mother, had been a spectacular beauty as a girl in Chestertown, Maryland, on the eastern shore of the Chesapeake Bay, and her looks persisted throughout most of her lifetime. My wife's father, Guy V. Henry Jr., at the time of her birth an instructor in horsemanship at the Cavalry School, was graduated from West Point in the class of 1898. Though slight, gentle in manner, and rather esthetic in appearance he became one of the country's outstanding horsemen and the captain of the Olympic equestrian team in the 1912 (Stockholm) Olympics. He later became Commandant of Cadets at West Point. (Since so many of our family managed to hold that title, I should explain that the "Com" commands the corps of cadets under the overall command of the Superintendent, who runs the whole shebang. When Robert E. Lee wrote my great-grandmother, he was the Superintendent.)

Guy Henry became a major general and Chief of Cavalry, and then and later was very instrumental in converting the horse cavalry into the branch now called Armor—the tank forces that were so vital to the winning of World War II. He retired from service in 1939 at the age of 64, but was recalled to duty during World War II, serving first as a member and then as Chief of the InterAmerican Defense Board. His second retirement, after an extraordinary total of nearly 51 years of military service, was celebrated at the White House, President Truman and General Eisenhower officiating.

My wife's grandfather, the first Guy Vernor Henry, graduated from the Military Academy in 1861, and for "conspicuous gallantry in action" won the Medal of Honor at Cold Harbor during the Civil War. Thereafter he became one of the best-known figures on the western frontier, mentioned in virtually every book devoted to the Indian Wars.

One incident bears reiteration. In the Battle of Rosebud Creek, against the Oglala Sioux, an Indian bullet penetrated both cheekbones and his sinus cavities, removing in the process some of his upper teeth and blinding, permanently, one eye; he tried unsuccessfully to stay aboard his horse, and was thereafter overrun by the attacking Indians.

The cavalry force he commanded rallied and retook the ground where he lay. After the battle he was placed, by this time close to death from blood loss, on a litter strapped to the back of a mule (one account) or tied to a travois carried between two mules in tandem (another account)—from which, from time to time, he fell off (both accounts). The mule or mules carried him for 200 miles, or, I would guess, at least eight days, before arrival at a frontier post and what passed in those days as a hospital. Once, during this ordeal, a fellow officer expressed his sympathy and concern; Henry replied, according to one author, "It is nothing. For this we are soldiers." We might surmise that the writer dressed up the language a bit; however, the remark, as written, has been much quoted since.

One book, *Indian Fights and Fighters* by Cyrus Townsend Brady, devotes its entire final chapter to this extraordinary, utterly courageous soldier, veteran of countless savage battles in the Civil War and the Indian Wars: Guy V. Henry, "Captain of the Brave."

His father, William Seaton Henry, also graduated from the Military Academy, in 1835, but we know very little about him. We have however what may be the last surviving copy of the *Register of the Officers of the Army of the United States,* dated August 1836; it is a green paperback, tattered, eight inches long by five inches wide, and less than an eighth of an inch thick. It contains the names, many more than once, of all Army officers on active duty in 1836, and the names of all the cadets at West Point. Not a very big Army. The name of William S. Henry, my wife's great-grandfather, is listed as a second lieutenant of the Third Regiment of Infantry, the location of which is not shown; *my* great-grandfather, Hamilton S. Hawkins, is listed as a surgeon, stationed in Florida, probably in connection with the Seminole Wars. Hawkins, as said before, was destined to die in Mexico.

FORT BLISS TO WEST POINT

2 Mine was an undistinguished childhood marked by much
travel among the several stations to which my father was
posted: Porto Rico, Fort Oglethorpe (Georgia), El Paso
(while Father was chasing Pancho Villa in Mexico), Washington, D.C., Boston, more Washington (while he was in Europe), Fort
Bliss (near El Paso), and finally Fort Hayes in downtown Columbus,
Ohio—from which I left for West Point, and where he died. I attended
public grammar schools in Washington, Boston, and El Paso—skipping
two grades, as then permitted—and El Paso High School, from which
I was graduated at 16.

My recollections of an Army childhood center on Fort Bliss, about
five miles northeast of El Paso, where my father commanded the 1st
Cavalry Division. We lived in a large, two-story frame house centrally
located in the row of officers' quarters bordering the very long parade
ground. For our five and a half years in that house I slept always on the
upstairs screened porch. In winter some nights were very cold, and
sandstorms sometimes laid a generous layer of sand on my top blanket
or sheet—and my face. With the other Army children I went to school
in El Paso, riding to and from on the hard wooden benches in the back
end of an old four-cylinder, three-ton Liberty truck of World War I vintage. It had solid rubber tires.

Great advantages were then available for children living on an Army
post: lots to do, lots of room to play, horses to ride if a child was so in-

clined—which I rarely was. As a boy I had a long-barreled .22 special rifle of amazing accuracy with which I occasionally shot, at very impressive ranges, my father's pigeons, being careful afterwards, like any prudent criminal, to clean up the blood and feathers. My playmates and I also devised single-band slingshots from old tire tubes and, using the shot mold of a set of prime silver dueling pistols my father had brought back from Europe we made, from scrap lead small boys are always able to find somewhere, perfectly spherical, shiny-bright projectiles. With these, I'm ashamed to say, we could kill a stray cat at fifty paces. For lesser game, like sparrows, we used ordinary pebbles launched from a smaller Y-shaped slingshot of conventional design.

My father never heard of the responsibility of a father to be a companion to his son, and wouldn't have paid any attention to it if he had. I loved and admired him greatly, but we moved on different levels. Although not at all a martinet he was a disciplinarian: never, for example, was I allowed outside after supper on school nights, never could I do less than three hours work on my lessons, and never was I forgiven for poor grades in school.

Mother had a magnificent fat cook, name of Netty. She was half Mexican, half black, and gave me a good deal of trouble. One Christmas she gave Mother a ghastly foot-high blue-and-white ceramic statue of a boy and a goat—I think it was a goat—that she had bought in Juarez, Mexico, just across the border. In making the presentation, on Christmas day, Netty took the thing up to the parlor mantel, moved candlesticks and other things right and left, and, announcing that she had just the place for it, placed her present at dead center. Mother blanched, but had the wisdom to make no objection—Netty was the best cook in Texas.

I was about 11 at the time and had no love for Netty, so, knowing Mother's sentiments I contrived one day to break the statue. The household went into a state of crisis: Netty nearly quit and my parents were very severe with me, but of course Mother was secretly relieved. I'm not sure how she managed to keep Netty from replacing the thing—perhaps it was with a bribe.

Our house at Bliss was supported by concrete piers about two feet high. One afternoon I was on the front lawn shooting at sparrows with my beloved slingshot when a sergeant drove by in his open Model-T

Ford. Very unwisely I took a shot at him, and caught him on the side of his nose. Screeching to a halt, he piled out of the car in pursuit. Naturally I went under the house—way under. No more than a minute later, unfortunately, my father appeared, walking across the parade ground from his office. He was formally dressed, as always, in breeches and cavalry boots and a high-collar blouse.

Huddled in the darkness underneath the house I was quickly reduced to a state of terror by the sight of my parent, on his hands and knees, bellowing "Hamilton!" at me while the highly indignant (and bleeding) sergeant, hands on hips, stood over him. I knew that this constituted a sort of role-reversal that my father, a traditionalist, was not likely to relish. I have forgotten what my punishment was, but it quite apparently did not involve execution. At the time I thought it might.

We had many distinguished visitors in the big old house. Among others I remember Marshal Foch, the supreme commander of the enormous French Army during World War I and the great hero of contemporary France, and General of the Army John J. Pershing. I recall seeing each of them, on separate occasions, paddling down our back upstairs hall in pajamas and bathrobe, toothbrush in hand, on the way to what I considered to be my bathroom, but from which of course I was temporarily barred.

One day my father told Mother that General Obregon, then president of Mexico, was to visit Juarez, and with his party would come across the river a week hence to have lunch at our quarters. "General Obregon says his party will be about 25 strong," said my father, "but I know Mexican politicians and you better prepare for 50." "I know them better than you do," said Mother, "so I'll prepare for 75." Actually about 150 showed up, some clad in overalls; they filled the house and porches and covered much of the lawn. Mother, the cook, and the maid manufactured sandwiches as fast as they could and had them passed around, but my mother finally said the hell with it and gave up. Some guests wondered why they came and so did Mother.

One of our visitors was Col. Billy Mitchell, now immortalized as the great-granddaddy and prophet of airpower. It's going to take me some time to deal with Billy Mitchell because the president of the court-martial that tried and convicted him a few years later was my father.

Mitchell was a welcome guest, my dad having known him during the U.S. military occupation of Germany in 1918–20. During a discussion in our living room between the two men (both in uniform, civilian clothes being rarely worn by professional officers in those days) I was, quite unusually, allowed to sit in the background and listen.

In demonstration of his advocacy of airpower, Mitchell's aircrews had already sunk, with heavy bombs, some old U.S. battleships off the Virginia coast. As he talked that evening he was full of ardor and enthusiasm. I remember, in particular, two statements. One was that a single 2,000-pound bomb burst 16 feet under water 500 yards abeam of a modern battleship would sink it. One may doubt that I remember those long-ago figures, but I do. And of course the statement was totally wrong, wrong by so large a margin as to make it absurd.

He also said that the Navy was obsolete as a fighting force—modern land-based airpower would take over its function completely. Well, this was partly right in that surface gunbattle between capital ships is probably passé, being supplanted by the action of carriers and their aircraft and (a new development) by missile-firing surface ships. Even so, at this writing the United States has put back in service two battleships, and all modern navies deploy many attack submarines, cruisers, destroyers, and frigates; and atomic-powered submarines carrying missiles with atomic warheads constitute a major part of our overall strategic force. All in all, I'm glad we didn't abolish our Navy as Mitchell, from what he said that evening (and wrote, later, in a series of articles published in the old *Liberty* magazine), would have had us do.

The point is that though Mitchell was farsighted and very correct in many of his forecasts as respects airpower, it would have been a tragic error for the United States to have followed his counsel in all respects.

Mitchell was tried by court-martial in 1925. My father was not the original president of the court: Gen. Charles P. Summerall was, but he was successfully challenged by the defense and removed, making my father, the next senior, president. According to the papers the court was "perhaps the highest ranking board that ever sat at any trial" and included, among others, Maj. Gen. Douglas MacArthur. Some journalists and authors have since painted the court with the same brush they did those who disputed Mitchell's claim of the supremacy of airpower; actually, however, the court was composed of different people and its duty was simply to determine whether Mitchell was or was not guilty of violating prescribed military law.

For my father, the worst moment came in the middle of the trial, which was conducted in an old, badly deteriorated Washington, D.C., warehouse. My mother, an interested spectator, was seated alongside an old steam radiator, which got so hot that she, for the first time in her life, fainted. Billy Mitchell, in the defendant's dock, was the first to see her keel over. He leapt to his feet, vaulted an intervening rail, and, kneeling on the floor, cradled Mother's head in his arms and called for water and smelling salts as he patted her head and stroked her brow in the most solicitous possible manner. During this melodrama my father sat, speechless with embarrassment and indignation, behind the elevated bench.

Mitchell was charged not for his efforts on behalf of airpower but for "insubordination and conduct prejudicial to the service"—standard language in the manual for court-martial. He had accused Navy—particularly Navy—and Army leadership of "almost treasonable" behavior and "criminal negligence," terms not likely to endear him to the high command of either service.

Clayton Bissell, a fellow airman of Mitchell's, was a member of Billy's defense staff. He is quoted as saying that, before the trial, "we quickly decided that Mitchell was guilty as charged. We even convinced him that he would be found guilty. . . . We agreed that the trial had to be used to educate the American people on aviation, to make national defense mean something. It was the only way left. To do that we knew we had to stay on the front pages of the newspapers."

Well, the point is simply that Col. Billy Mitchell was legitimately found guilty of a breach of discipline; the court did not address, in any way, the legitimacy of his ideas about airpower. Even so, the trial served his crusade well, providing a gigantic sounding board for his theories and doctrine. The court heard several weeks of thoroughly publicized testimony on the revolutionary effect of airpower, but its decision had to be made largely in disregard of that element of the matter: it could not have acquitted the defendant of the specific charges against him unless it chose, in violation of its oath, to disregard the law.

In the court's sentence Billy was not thrown out of the Army, but was "suspended from rank, command and duty with the forfeiture of all pay and allowances for five years." Quite naturally, he resigned.

Mitchell, of course, gained very wide national prominence and proceeded to make more money on the lecture circuit and to receive greater acclaim than he ever could have done by remaining in active service. More important he had, to the benefit of America, advanced greatly the development and employment of modern military aircraft. The military services took a beating because of their conservatism, but the court-martial proceedings, despite the publicity that attended them, were a matter altogether separate from Billy Mitchell's advocacy of airpower. This point is totally disregarded by every modern writer commenting on the matter.

Well, so much for my family's old quarters at Fort Bliss, at which Billy Mitchell and so many others had been welcome guests. One day I accidentally fired a .45-caliber pistol through two floors of the house, very narrowly missing the Mexican maid, Lupe, who was dusting the furniture in the downstairs hallway. It caused her to retreat to her room for a total of three days. She was a dear person; we would have missed her if I hadn't missed her. The holes in the two hardwood floors and the hallway ceiling were quickly repaired and to the benefit of my reputation are no longer visible.

My father's last assignment was as commander of the IV Corps Area, with station in Columbus, Ohio. I entered Ohio State University, marking time there until I became 17 and could enter West Point.

I well remember the shock of my first impression of OSU—how unbelievably impersonal it was, with more than 8,000 students, none of whom seemed to know any of the others. I found that bigness profoundly distasteful. At this writing its enrollment is about 44,000.

Among my subjects I chose French, of which I had already three years in high school. There were more than 50 other students in that French class. The semester started just after Labor Day, but it was nearly Thanksgiving before I was first called upon to say, in class, my first words in French. Because of this and not too dissimilar experiences in other classes I secretly elected for that year to major in billiards and pool, and in those pursuits became reasonably proficient. But to my shame, I learned very little else. My disgust with OSU apparently overcame any pangs of conscience at wasting the money my father paid for tuition, and my eventual acceptance as a cadet diverted his attention from my deplorable grades at the monstrous university.

The Military Academy is an educational and disciplinary institution, and in my day stuck strictly to its mission. My four years there were not an unalloyed joy, for along with 1,200 other cadets I didn't like all that close-order drill and the four weekly parades; moreover, despite an Army upbringing I had incessant trouble with the tactical officers, or "tacs." These were commissioned officers, under the Commandant of Cadets, who administered the disciplinary system with the assistance of cadet officers of the second and first (meaning junior and senior) classes. Tacs, one to a company, inspected our rooms each day wearing white gloves, the gloves serving to discover the presence of dust. My dusting was rarely up to standard, and the way I folded the underwear in my wall locker and the condition of my soap dish weren't either. Cadet officers also found frequent fault with various aspects of my deportment, such as being on time, awarding me additional demerits. All in all, though my crimes were innocent and minor, I was listed almost at the bottom of my class in discipline. On this account I managed to become no more than a lowly cadet sergeant in my first class (senior) year, most of my classmates by then being cadet lieutenants and captains—glorious creatures with prominent gold chevrons, red sashes, and swords instead of rifles as they marched at the head of the platoons and companies at parade.

Actually, just before graduation I was promoted to cadet lieutenant because my roommate, who held that rank, came to see me after visiting hours as I languished in the Cadet Hospital; he was caught and busted and I was given his rank. At Graduation Parade I marched, for the first and last time, sword, red sash, and all, at the head of a platoon.

I would have liked to have been a member of several corps (varsity) athletic teams, but I am put together improperly: as I face due north my left knee points northwest and my right knee northeast. Before it was corrected surgically, many years later, if my left knee were subjected to a sudden strain it would "go out of joint" (more accurately, I believe, the cartilage would tear) and I would hit the ground, hard, and thereafter suffer great pain.

In consequence, I was of no account in any sport requiring legs. Plebes, soon after they arrive at the Academy, are tested in all sorts of physical exercises—push-ups, pull-ups, and various track events. I suspect I hold the permanent Academy record for slowness in the 100-yard dash—something like 18 seconds.

But I was a fair swimmer, and managed to make the corps "squad," or team. Even in the water, however, my legs didn't do well: what little I accomplished was altogether to the credit of my arms. Being one of the less formidable competitors I was assigned to the quarter-mile swim—then the longest, most exhausting, and least popular in collegiate competition. Moreover, a classmate assigned to the same event was better than I, and so was at least one member of every opposing team. During the winter season, therefore, I swam and swam and swam each weekday for practice and on Saturdays swam an unending quarter-mile against Yale or Harvard or whatever to see whether I would garner for my alma mater third place and one lousy point—or nothing at all.

Curiously, my mediocre ability at swimming would have won for me, 20 years earlier, the academy record in nearly every intercollegiate swimming event; by the same token, my teammates broke every Academy record while I was a team member, and the records they established have been broken again and again since. Today's collegiate athletic teams are, across the board, amazingly better than their predecessors—such, obviously, is the effect of more skillful conditioning and coaching—and, I would guess, better nutrition.

I didn't like them better, but I did better in academics, graduating as number 62 in my class, which started at a strength of a little more than 400 and ended at 240. The remainder had been "found deficient" and dismissed from the Academy. I did well in math, and math is prime at West Point.

However the great recompense for being a cadet was one's classmates: they were, with exceptions, a fine lot, and since one was practically locked up with them for four years we formed very close friendships. The "bull session" under our confined and regulated circumstances became the prime relaxation, a release without which cadet life would have been hard to tolerate. The bull session generated tremendous humor and goodwill, comradeship that has lasted for a lifetime. The Greek letter fraternity as an institution is not permitted at West Point, but the fraternity among classmates is very significant.

Despite its great strengths in the formulation of character, West Point had a weakness then, and I suppose now, in getting rid of the unsuitable. Operating on the basis of hard, provable fact, it is good at eliminating the academically and physically incompetent, the ones lacking in honor and the unneat—it almost got rid of me—but it doesn't weed out some few that, for any of a number of reasons, are not good officer material. My good friends and I decided, by long, earnest discussion, that if the *least suitable* 10 percent of our classmates could be drowned in the Hudson the remaining 90 percent would constitute an extraordinarily fine body of young men that would greatly benefit the Army it was to serve; with the 10 percent still aboard, however, the benefit would be considerably mitigated. I'm sure that we were correct, and would recommend the policy to the present authorities at West Point—with the caution, however, that the 10 percent should be selected, say, at the end of the yearling year, not by the tactical department but by the class itself, in secret ballot. And perhaps the 10 percent need not be drowned—simple departure would do.

I'll close discussion of the Military Academy with some words on honor. The honor system has broken down twice in history; in both cases, the breach has been within the football squad and took the form of cheating in academics; in both cases, the violation caused profound dismay not only at West Point but for all living graduates, and the dead ones may be assumed to have turned in their graves. The honor system rests on the individual cadet and his word: as one example in a thousand, if a cadet crosses a sentinel post and is challenged, his "All Right, Sir" is taken as incontrovertible proof that he is authorized, under the regulations or possibly by special permission, to cross it. As a second example, he is trusted absolutely, without supervision, not to cheat in academics.

The honor systems is fundamental; without it West Point would be nothing at all. When it failed, twice, the institution and the Army itself suffered badly. Its failure is indicative of an overemphasis on football: the scandal, in each case, resulted in the dismissal, from the Academy, of most of the football squad. There followed a long succession of years in which Army football teams were of pretty low caliber—in football, not character—because professional football had become a highly lucrative business, and the super-players shunned the military academies because graduates are committed for four years of military service after graduation. A super-player would obviously prefer the glory and emoluments of the NFL.

Of far more importance, however, is the fact that subsequent Army teams have been composed of young men of honor whose primary interest has been in becoming officers, not pro football players. But since these teams are not likely to compete successfully against big "football universities" whose squads are in large part proving grounds for the NFL, the three military academies might be wise to select as opponents universities and colleges that still regard college football as an amateur sport.

A CAVALRYMAN

3 I graduated from West Point in 1930, serving my first four years in the 7th Cavalry at Fort Bliss, Texas, near El Paso. My close friends at Bliss were all young West Pointers. The uniform of a cavalryman was a good-looking one, with well-cut breeches, shirt or blouse, and extremely expensive English-made Peal or Maxwell boots, shined to a mirror finish. Theoretically, a young cavalry officer's training encouraged him to act boldly and independently when necessary. Polo, jump-riding, and occasional steeple-chasing served to inure him to danger—twice I played in polo matches in which a player was killed—and injuries were fairly frequent. These sports also taught a young man to think quickly. It should be admitted, however, that our lives at Bliss included the sometimes injudicious imbibing of liquor, facilitated, in those days of Prohibition, by easy access to the bars and cheap whiskey (it had to be very cheap near the end of the month) of Juarez, just across the Rio Grande.

With occasional exception, an officer's life could not be called very intellectual; neither were we greatly inspired, in those days of apparently everlasting peace, by the Army's function or importance. War seemed impossible; indeed, with most of my fellows I expected to retire at 64 as a lieutenant colonel or colonel. The Army was pitifully small—about 130,000 officers and men—and woefully ill-equipped: in my regiment we had not a single gasoline-driven vehicle, and for our resupply in the field we depended in part on a Quartermaster muletrain. Our equipment was outdated, and individual items were old and frequently unserviceable. As a small example, the EE-8 binoculars issued to officers, especially to lieutenants, usually provided a view that was either grossly distorted or altogether opaque—nothing visible. The natural consequence of this was that the binocular case, attached to each officer's field Sam Browne belt during maneuvers, regularly carried a sandwich, not the Double-E Eight. I vividly remember our much heralded modernization in 1933: cavalry line troops, for the first time, were provided with six Browning light machine guns. Up to then the Browning automatic rifle—the "Bar"—was our most potent weapon.

Demands for housekeeping were such, and our strength so meager, that we rarely had enough men available in a rifle troop to engage in more than the smallest and simplest tactical exercises; often, indeed, what few men were available for drill could do no more than give the horses a modicum of exercise, each trooper riding one horse and leading three others. This, and the ensuing routine of grooming all those horses, was not an inspiring procedure for the soldiers to do or for a young officer to supervise. On the other hand, saber training (the spearing of straw-packed gunnysack "saber heads" from the back of a hard-charging horse) was great sport; also good was mounted pistol training. But both prepared us for the execution of—what? The cavalry charge, that's what, and that maneuver, however exciting in practice, did not promise to decide the outcome of the next war.

Such was my dismay at this state of affairs that after three years I was tempted to resign my commission. But before doing so, I elected to motor down to Fort Clark, near Bracketville, Texas, about 300 miles southeast, to talk to my mother's brother, my Uncle Ham Hawkins. Of the West Point class of 1894, Uncle Ham was a brigadier general commanding the 1st Cavalry Brigade. A tall, erect, dedicated professional, he was shocked and seriously concerned by my disillusionment, but talked me out of resignation. Later I became glad that he had.

The professional highlight of each year was the annual "division" maneuvers. They weren't that, really, because the Army never had enough money to assemble the whole division from its several posts down along the Rio Grande. So the annual event was usually just the 8th Cavalry maneuvering against the 7th Cavalry, with the batteries of the 82nd Field Artillery (Horse) divided between the two sides. But everyone was mounted and thereby provided the maximum in individual mobility. Trucks, tanks, and helicopters now give the Army far greater group mobility, of course, but nothing ever has, or perhaps ever will again, offer the individual battlefield mobility provided by the soldier's horse. Anyway, we just played a grown-up (and very vigorous, I must say) variety of Cowboys and Indians in the vast area of desert and low, barren mountains stretching north, forever, from El Paso into New Mexico. But there were great opportunities for young lieutenants full of beans to lead their platoons on night raids, surprise attacks, and other feats of harmless derring-do.

Our drinking-water supply on these maneuvers was abysmal. If we were lucky the Southern Pacific Railroad would spot a tank car full of water on a siding of the track that ran down the length of the maneuver area; after a week or so in the sun that water had a metallic taste and was almost too hot to shave with, but at least you could see through it. Frequently we had recourse to the same water the cattle (such few as the desert could sustain) drank. The better part of this second deal was when we could find a windmill-supplied open metal tank, however rusty; less attractive were the not-infrequent occasions when a troop's or a platoon's supply was limited to an open cattle tank with a foot or so of greenish, muddy water. It was quite obvious where the green came from.

If he had managed, with his spring wagon, to find us, the troop cook was encouraged to fill his thirty-gallon canvas water bag before the horses were led into the tank to drink. He then put in a generous helping of powdered chlorine, and in another 30 minutes added about a quart of root-beer extract, which diluted, slightly, the taste of all the other ingredients and added a purple tinge. But the water remained totally opaque because of suspended matter, and its taste was indescribable. I am unable to explain why it didn't kill us all.

The Chief of Cavalry usually came down from Washington to visit these grand maneuvers. On one occasion the Chief, accompanied by a staff officer and orderly, came riding across the desert to encounter the bugler sergeant of the 7th Cavalry, afoot. The sergeant, who despite his title was quite deaf, had just seen a very large rattlesnake disappear down a hole in a "boondock," that being one of millions of four- or five-foot hummocks formed by sand building up around mesquite bushes. The following deathless dialogue ensued.

"Tell me, my good man," said the general, "where is the 7th Cavalry Regimental Headquarters?"

"Right down this hole, sir!" said the sergeant, pointing.

"Sergeant, what's the matter with you? Are you crazy?"

But the sergeant triumphed: "Yezzir," he said, "the boondocks are full of 'em."

During these years I took my turn at serving as a member of a court-martial and at other times as the defense advocate, whose duty it was to represent the accused at trial. I wish to record the opinion that trial under the old Manual of Court Martial came closer to providing real justice than any other American system of jurisprudence: the accused was brought promptly to trial, while the memory of witnesses were fresh; court routines were simple and quickly accomplished, which resulted in trials themselves being short and to the point; the rules of evidence, while eminently fair to the accused, served to allow the truth to become known; and the court itself was composed of officers with a good understanding of the law. I agree with the statement, I believe by the eminent Elihu Root, that if I as the accused were innocent of a crime I would rather be tried by a military court than by any other tribunal; but if guilty I would wish to be tried by any tribunal other than a military one.

At the Cavalry School at Fort Riley, Kansas, I attended the Troop Officers Class and then the Advanced Equitation Class, the latter for young officers (ten per class) demonstrating special aptitude in horsemanship. This was a delightful year devoted altogether to the training and showing of four fine thoroughbreds in various stages of development as chargers, jumpers, and polo ponies; we were also instructed in hippology and the principles of pathological horseshoeing.

In the course of the year I began courting Miss Mary Ingraham Henry, a most attractive and desirable young lady, warding off the occasional inference of my classmates that her desirability was not lessened by her father's rank and position: he was then a major general and Commandant of the Cavalry School. She was, so to speak, the boss's daughter.

We were married in the post chapel, a small religious structure halfway down the block between my bachelor apartment and her family's quarters—another manifest convenience. The ceremony took place as scheduled even though, at the engagement party a month or so earlier, she had appeared in a low-cut dress with her skin covered with large purply-blue spots of methyln blue—a medication applied not by a doctor but by the post veterinarian to whom she had appealed, characteristically, to rid her of a ringworm infection. Her father's charger, Grey Falcon, which she rode occasionally, also had ringworm very badly, and for a time it spoiled his looks also. It was a recurrent subject of debate among Mary's friends whether he gave it to her or she gave it to him.

My bride's father further endangered the wedding by repeatedly asking his daughter, as they came down the aisle, if she really wanted to go through with it. The wedding night was spent in the bridal suite of the best and only hotel of Salina, Kansas, in which the drapes, carpeting, chairs, and bedspread were all in a brilliant shade of red appropriate only to the popular conception of an old-fashioned Western bawdy house.

Our return to Fort Riley, on a bitterly cold day in March, found my four assigned horses the willing conspirators in an obvious plot on the part of my classmates: the horses had gone unexercised for the last couple of days and were full of oats. The next day, as I mounted them under the studiously casual observation of my fellow officers, they threw me all over that part of Kansas.

I should now make a record that when I married Mary Henry I also married her dog, Barney; I wasn't told so specifically, but it was obvious that the two came as a package. Barney was a handsome Irish setter, a superb athlete with a long running stride, great to behold as he ran with our horses. Barney accepted me with tolerance and grace and was perfectly obedient to my commands, but there was no doubt to whom he belonged.

The Assistant Commandant of the school, Lt. Col. "Skinny" Wainwright (later the lieutenant general whose fate it was, in 1942, to surrender the almost starving, grossly undersupplied U.S. forces in the Philippines to the Japanese), had a luncheon for the members of the Advanced Equitation Class and their wives immediately after the brief graduation ceremonies. It was a very hot June day; luncheon was held outside under the big trees alongside the Wainwright quarters. Barney was there as a matter of course, and the dessert was green pistachio ice cream. Not all the guests finished their ice cream and, of course, put their half-empty cups on the grass. Barney cleaned them all up.

When luncheon was finished, Mary and I said goodbye to everybody and, with Barney and several suitcases in the back seat of our aging Chevrolet, we took off for Fort Oglethorpe, Georgia, our new station. After about half an hour it became apparent that Barney was suffering acute indigestion: he was vomiting, and everything, all over the back cushions and the suitcases. We ground to a halt and threw open the back door, far too late, of course. By this time Barney had gotten rid of everything that was bothering him and bounded happily out the car and into an adjoining pasture, where he found a large, fresh cow-pie to roll in. At this point the situation could be perceived as not a good way for a young couple to start for a new station—the *first* station away from the bride's family.

I said that this was it—Barney was staying right there, forever, as far as I was concerned. Mary said in that case she was staying there, too, and we proceeded to debate the pros and cons of that. Eventually it was decided that everybody would go, and Barney reentered, with obvious distaste, the disaster that had been a back seat.

A few miles down the road the car, emitting the most frightful odor, crossed a creek—a typical east-Kansas creek with almost vertical sides descending about eight feet to a muddy stream just a few inches deep. Barney ignored my request to enter the creek; in desperation I finally picked him up in my arms, thereby putting a number of unattractive deposits on my front elevation, and tried to throw him in. But my feet slipped: in I went, upside down, the back of my neck reaching the water first. I looked up to see Barney on top of the bank, wagging his tail as he looked down at me.

But our marriage is still intact, 59 years later.

Compared to Fort Bliss and Fort Riley, the two biggest and most active cavalry posts, Oglethorpe seemed more appropriate to the nineteenth century. Only one regiment, the 6th Cavalry, was there. We had polo, of course—I would have resisted going anywhere there was no polo— and horse shows and a post fox hunt, pink coats and all. For training as well as sport we had use of the beautiful wooded acreage of Chicamauga National Park adjoining the military reservation. Some fine officers—lieutenants and captains—were in the regiment, and we became fast friends with them and their wives. Life was pleasant and relaxed, but didn't seem to lead anywhere.

Relaxed, I just said it was: life for a while was jazzed up by my receiving, in exchange for a check for $156, a private mount in the shape of a 16:3-hand, four-year-old thoroughbred from the Reno Remount Depot. A gorgeous thing he was: a bay with a shiny black mane and tail, beautiful dark eyes, three white feet, and a star-and-run on his forehead. Col. Hap Gay, the remount depot commander (as a major general, later, he was George Patton's Chief of Staff in World War II), sent me through the mail a small slip of paper transferring to me, for my 156 bucks, the horse, named Reno Hopeful. On the paper Colonel Gay had written, paraphrasing the language then common on a sales slip for a new Ford or Chevrolet, "Walk for the first 500 miles." I tried that, on a 1,200-pound coiled spring that had never been saddled. It almost killed me, but love can conquer any horse if you just keep getting back on. In the end he became a lamb, one my wife loved to ride.

At Oglethorpe, for six weeks, I had my first experience at breaking and training, with the aid of perhaps 50 men, about 150 "remounts"— those being, like my Reno Hopeful, unbroken four-year-olds either raised at one of the remount deposits or bought from farms or ranches. It was (both at Oglethorpe and at my next station) a great job, filled with action and all kinds of incidents—some of them delightfully funny. A hard-bucking horse is always worth watching if only because it is capable of initiating all sorts of ancillary activity—like making most of the others start bucking, too.

In 1938 Mary and I departed for the Philippine Islands, leaving our gallant Barney in a kennel with a huge outdoor run at Fort Oglethorpe. One old Army transport of 7,500 tons took us from New York to San Francisco, taking nearly two weeks; another, the *Grant*, slightly larger but even more venerable, used 28 days (cruise speed, 11 knots) to take us to Manila. Our cabin was cramped, the days passed slowly, and the saltwater showers left our bodies sticky and unrefreshed. Honolulu and Guam were welcome respites, however, and the meals served on all the old lumbering transports featured best-quality roast beef and were uniformly excellent. We got what exercise we could with calisthenics on the top deck. A welcome party, with rum cocktails and exotic fruits, awaited us in the old Army and Navy Club in Manila.

We were posted to the 26th Cavalry (Philippine Scouts) at Fort Stotsenberg, about 65 miles north of Manila. Philippine Scout regiments had native Filipino enlisted men with American officers in charge. Service in those regiments approximated that of the English in prewar British India; in the vernacular, those were "the days of the Empire." Except for the times we were in the field on extended maneuvers, regimental officers went to the troop barracks at 7:30 A.M.; the mornings we occupied with various small tactical exercises, marksmanship, saber drill, and similar training, after which came "stables," when the horses were groomed, watered, and fed. At 11:30 we attended Officers Call, presided over by the regimental commander, during which the business of the day (there wasn't much) was discussed. And that was the workday.

Lest anyone think this represented a neglect of duty I should explain that the enlisted men's afternoons were devoted to individual training and housekeeping, which were quite adequately supervised by the experienced and competent NCOs. Our sergeants averaged 22 years of service, our corporals about 15.

As is still true, most Filipinos were poor, so service in U.S. Army Philippine Scout units was very popular. The regiment had a long waiting list, allowing us to pick and choose among applicants for enlistment. Rarely did a soldier fail to apply for reenlistment, and discipline was no problem at all. Soldiers occasionally would complain, very politely, that the Army fed them only brown, unpolished rice. Rice was and is the staple of all oriental diets, but polished rice lacks some of the nutrients of brown, which is why the Army gave them brown rice.

An officer's afternoons were occupied by working polo ponies or jumpers, or by polo practice scrimmages, or by tennis or golf. Tough life. On Sundays we sometimes had informal jumping competitions, sometimes more formal horse shows, and, nearly always, formal polo games—the last quite often in Manila because that's where most of the military and all of the civilian teams were located. Some of the younger ladies, my wife among them, participated in all save the polo.

I was still a first lieutenant, with a monthly pay of $173 plus about another $40 in allowances. From this we paid (and fed) a cook, a houseboy, and a lavandera, or washwoman, all full-time; we also had a Filipino soldier horse orderly, and the services of gardeners provided by the post. All were excellent, extremely loyal, and trustworthy servants, partly because such employment was much in demand, partly because Filipinos were such good people.

We lived in a tropical bungalow without, of course, air conditioning. It was delightful, despite the intense tropical heat. The front and one side of each bungalow had large screened porches, and under the wide overhang of the roof hung a string of broad droopy-leafed air plants, providing shade without seriously impeding air flow. The windows were perhaps eight feet wide and six high, and were never closed except during the occasional typhoons of the two-month rainy season, when the rain sometimes blew horizontally. Each window could be closed by a single sliding panel consisting of barely translucent seashell set in a wooden matrix. There was not a pane of window glass in the house. Although the bungalows stood on low concrete piers with metal troughs filled with oil at their tops, bugs still made their way in. It was a standing joke that when the typhoons blew the termites had to hold hands to keep the house together.

When one arrived in his bungalow from drill or tennis or polo, he simply threw his clothes on the floor and popped in the shower; the houseboy immediately scooped up the clothing and delivered it to the lavandera. She returned it, washed, starched as appropriate, and ironed, the next day. Because of the humidity one never hung up a damp garment: it would mildew within 24 hours, even though we kept an electric bulb glowing in every closet. An unattended sweaty pair of boots would turn green almost as one looked at them.

A very few quarters had constrictors of modest size in the attics; ours didn't, and we didn't miss that amenity, though the snakes were said to be good for rats. But we had no rats. Every household was occasionally visited by a bat or two, upon which a regular drill was put in motion. Ladies having strong objections to bats climbed on a bed and lowered over it, using a light rope and pulley, a large mosquito netting. This netting, for reasons of health, not of bats, was a mandatory arrangement for every bed. The lady being thus safely enclosed, the man of the household, joined by his delighted children or perhaps by a neighbor, armed themselves with tennis rackets and made a game out of removing the offending bat. Sometimes the players would also remove the chandelier.

When we arrived in 1938 the Philippines had been a commonwealth for three years, with a Filipino president, Manuel Quezon, and an American governor general. In Manila the American presence was very apparent and dominant; and everywhere, whatever the official arrangement, we were still the colonists and the Filipinos the colonials. So far as I could determine, there was no antipathy between the two; in contrast with what obtains today, we could go anywhere without danger of any unpleasantness, except perhaps for the *very* remote areas inhabited by what were known as the tribes: people in breech-clouts who hunted with bows and arrows, and who had very recently graduated from the status of headhunters.

A tribe of negritos, the Balugas, lived in the hills just behind Fort Stotsenberg. Pygmies clad only in loincloths, the men rarely reached the height of four feet, six inches. Quite harmless, they seemed always covered with ash and smelled awful, living on camotes (a wild sweet potato) and the deer and wild chicken they killed with their arrows. I occasionally rode up into those hills (the lower slopes covered with cogan grass, often six feet high, the high elevations with jungle), sometimes with Mary along; only once or twice did we see any sign of cultivation, and those few were confined to perhaps six or eight square yards cultivated with a sharp stick and planted in camotes.

I think we Americans were good colonists. We had much trade with the Philippines to the benefit of both countries, but we operated the territory at a net loss to ourselves; there was essentially no exploitation of a subject people. Our greatest favor to the islands lay in our establishment of a good, country-wide school system that taught English as a mandatory subject, for the archipelago contains some 7,000 islands of which many hundred are occupied, and the people use perhaps 100 mutually unintelligible dialects. Without English, the Philippines would be impossible to govern—and, of course, even with English the government is currently having much difficulty.

There were and still are many aristocratic Spanish families in Manila. Residents in the islands for many generations, their big old-fashioned houses lined Dewey Boulevard, bordering the harbor. Many Spanish were enormously wealthy and moved in a society of their own, though there had obviously been some intermarriage with Filipinos. They got along well enough with most Americans, but at one point were sufficiently unhappy with their treatment at the old Manila Polo Club that they built another, grander club nearby, called the Tamarao Club. "Tamarao" is the native word for the wild water buffalo; called the carabao in its domesticated state, the water buffalo plows the rice paddies and is therefore essential to life in the islands.

Manila had fine horse shows yearly, in which my wife and I regularly competed. We were lucky enough to have the use of two excellent jumpers, Nick Toney and Speed King, and won much silver and many ribbons. Usually as a member of the 26th Cavalry team, of which I was the captain, but sometimes with a civilian one, I played lots of polo in Manila, at both clubs.

The Tamarao Club had been financed largely by the four polo-playing brothers of the Spanish Elizalde family. The eldest, "Mike," was then the ambassador to the United States, so he was not on the island. The other three were Angel, Manuel, and Manolo. Angel (pronounced "Anhel") and Manuel were very formidable players; Manolo, the youngest, only fair. But all were mounted beautifully on extremely expensive horses imported from abroad. When the three Elizaldes and a fourth player, all superbly mounted, were on the field no other civilian team and no Army regimental team (on much slower horses) could beat them.

For competition the Elizaldes imported the "Californians," who remained in Manila for several years. The Californians were high-goal players: Peter Perkins, Bill Andrews, Lewis Brown, and for awhile Earle

Hopping. The story was that the large Chinese population of Manila used to like to see Earle Hopping play; they called him Ho-Ping, and thought he was Chinese. The Californians were, of course, beneficially employed in various Elizalde businesses. One of them described his function as that of visiting the rope factory once a month to make sure the clock hadn't fallen off the wall.

Although no Army regimental team could do it, an Army-picked team could and did occasionally give the Elizaldes or the Californians a run for their money. I was a member of such teams, having by then a four-goal handicap. For me this was great polo and a great thrill. I also umpired a number of games between the Californians and the Tamarao Club (meaning the Elizaldes), because I wasn't afraid of Angel, a good player with a foul temper, a contempt for the rules of polo, and a profound dislike of umpires.

Perhaps my greatest satisfaction in polo came from play on the 26th Cavalry team that came within an inch of winning the Ten Goal Championship of the Philippines—the biggest tournament of the two years of our service there, in which virtually every club had one or more teams. Our other players were Capt. Thomas Trapnell and Lieutenants James Alger and Ralph Haines. Many years later, two of our four achieved four-star rank; the two that didn't had been captured, one in the Philippines and one in Africa—being thus deprived of the rapid promotion that came during the war. Even so, they each ultimately achieved the three stars of a lieutenant general.

During our tour in the Islands, Gen. Douglas MacArthur, already retired from the U.S. Army but still relatively young, was the commander of the armed forces of the Philippines, then being expanded and modernized under his direction. He was very highly regarded by President Quezon, the U.S. governor general, and other high officials. He lived with his handsome young wife and small son in a suite embracing an entire floor of the Manila Hotel, on the Luneta—a tremendous public area of lawn and flowers near the harbor—across from the Army-Navy Club. I was not exactly on his level of society, so I never laid eyes on him.

But I came to know, very casually, an odd sort of fellow of Spanish blood who amused himself by dressing up as an Indian maharaja. Thus caparisoned he would loaf around the bar at the Tamarao Club awaiting introduction, by his co-conspirators, to visitors or new members, to whom he'd tell tall tales of the current life and times of a maharaja. I'm quite unable to explain why he derived pleasure from this charade. That's just the way it was.

One day this bogus maharaja, in his most elaborate robes, called at MacArthur's office. Much impressed by his grand appearance, MacArthur's secretary told the general that the maharaja was visiting from India, and the general told her to let him right in. We don't know further details of this encounter, but when MacArthur's American military aide appeared, somewhat later, the general told him to find out where the Indian potentate was staying in Manila and to arrange a return call on him by the general.

The aide, of course, knew all about this clown at the Tamarao Club and under the circumstances of this new dilemma, we may assume, seriously contemplated resignation from the Army. I think the matter was resolved by a fortuitously early departure of a ship bound for Calcutta.

Just before our two-year Philippine tour was up my wife and I made a delightful trip, by the Dutch ship *Tjinigara,* to the Dutch East Indies, now Indonesia. This was October 1940; the Germans had already overrun much of Europe.

In Batavia (now Djakarta) we called on Ambassador Foote, an experienced U.S. professional foreign service officer. Mr. Foote told us in some detail of a Nazi-managed plot among the substantial local German population in the Dutch Indies, with the aid of some disaffected Malays, to overthrow the Dutch colonial government. One holiday morning about a week or so before the opening German attack on Western Europe, a native cable clerk in Batavia received a long coded message from Berlin addressed to the senior German diplomatic officer. The clerk was suspicious, and tried to get in touch with his own government, but could find no one, during the holiday, in the government offices. On his own hook, then, this man simply filed the message without delivery—an obviously illegal act.

It turned out that the message contained elaborate last-minute instructions for an intended German coup in the Dutch colony, a coup that was to be triggered by a signal: the mispronunciation of the name

"Berlin" on German-language radio broadcasts heard in the Indies. Ambassador Foote—not foreseeing the overrun of the Dutch Indies by the Japanese Army a few years later—was full of praise for the cable clerk. It might have been easier on the Dutch living in the Indies had the German coup succeeded.

However that may be, it is interesting now, many years later, to speculate on the impact on history if that unknown cable clerk had not held the message. If in 1940 a German coup had overturned the presiding government in the Dutch East Indies—an enormous area rich in natural resources—how would the Japanese have reacted to such a European incursion into what they chose to call their "East-Asian Co-Prosperity Sphere"? This "sphere," of course, the Japanese empire planned to dominate altogether for its own purposes; it was not something to share with Hitler and might have interfered with the later (1941) alliance of German and Japan.

In 1940, also, the United States generally looked on the new European war as something from which we'd vastly prefer to stand aside. Our alarm at a German intrusion into the South Pacific, the cruising area of our Asiatic fleet, might have resulted in our earlier rearming and possibly our earlier entry into World War II.

But the little cable clerk preempted all that.

My wife and I enjoyed service in the Philippines so much that we would almost certainly have "extended"—that is, have elected to remain a third year—were it not for our Irish setter, Barney, awaiting our return in the pen at Fort Oglethorpe. So we came home on the last boat carrying Army officers—thereafter, the officers stayed put, while their wives and children were evacuated in the face of an increasing possibility of Japanese invasion. Because we came home I was not in the 26th Cavalry when the Japanese invaded; because we came home I missed an appalling, hopeless, very inadequately supplied campaign against the Japanese forces, and a 50 percent chance of being killed or dying (from starvation, or drowning at sea in a destroyed Japanese prison ship, or outright execution) while a prisoner of the Japanese. Many close friends, in the 26th Cavalry and in other units, had one or more of those experiences, including my West Point roommate, Harry Packard, who died in the stinking hold of a sinking Japanese prison ship on the way to Japan. I missed all that because of Barney.

I am still saddened when I read or think about the campaign that killed so many of my close friends, so many classmates, and so many of the gallant troopers that fought so valiantly in the 26th United States Cavalry, Philippine Scouts.

We returned for station with the 3rd Cavalry at Fort Myer, Virginia, just across the Potomac from Washington. The regiment was being expanded by adding all of two troops: two troops of *horse cavalry* to the already existing six. The Soviet Union had already concluded its cynical alliance with Germany and had participated with Germany in the quick, brutal overrun, with tanks and armored infantry supported by dive bombers, of Poland—whose defenses, incidentally, depended heavily on horse cavalry. Horses don't thrive in competition with tanks.

I commanded one of the newly formed troops. In a world promising to come unstuck at the seams, my troopers and I were engaged in paving, with jagged sections of concrete scavenged from the sidewalks of the just-abandoned Experimental Farm down by the Potomac River, the saddle room of my new troop stables; up to then it had only a dirt floor.

We had good polo, and I fell heir to a magnificent little mare, Black Beauty, which won lots of ribbons and silver in military and civilian horse shows for her jumping ability. This was all great in a way, but a bit later, when I was offered the command of a troop in the mechanized reconnaissance squadron of the 1st Cavalry Division, at Fort Bliss, Texas, I took the offer.

Mind you, the First Cav, though composed of fine officers and men and recently expanded in strength, still had all its horses; the squadron I joined was the only mechanized combat unit in the entire division. My new troop, part of the squadron, also was the only one in the world equipped with jeeps as its primary means of locomotion. This gave us uncommon mobility, and since there was no precedent to our organization we were privileged to invent our own tactics and techniques.

We were also required to test various new jeep types developed for the Army. On one occasion I was driving an experimental type that had not only four-wheel drive but also four-wheel steer, the latter giving the driver the ability to turn the vehicle bottom-side-up, with the great possibility of killing himself and his passengers, with a mere flip of his wrist.

I didn't do that, but on this occasion, out in the desert, I went roaring across a high boondock and onto a large, uncovered, double-bed spring that some criminal bum had dumped out there. My rapidly turning drive shaft, its universal joints, and the steering mechanism all wound themselves up in that mass of coiled spring-steel wire in a way impossible to describe: my jeep and that bedspring locked one another into a single melded, indivisible unit—nothing, not the engine, not even the steering wheel, would budge. It had to be brought home, bedspring and all, suspended ignominiously on the boom of a wrecker. In the meanwhile I had a long walk across the desert.

Every elderly American remembers where he was when the Japanese hit Pearl Harbor. My wife and I were picnicking, by ourselves, on the edge of Kilbourne's Hole—an enormous crater out in the New Mexico desert, formed by some ancient meteor.

And the "Special Troops" team, of which I was a member, won the 1st Cavalry Division polo championship, even though all the regimental teams had been strengthened by the addition of a number of good college players—now newly added reserve officers. Oddly enough, our Number 4, Maj. Eddie Doyle, was the only man killed in the essentially unopposed British-American landings at Algiers, in North Africa, before a year was out.

1ST ARMORED DIVISION

4 One day in March of 1942 a call from the Chief of Cavalry's office asked me if I'd like assignment to the newly forming 8th Armored Division at Fort Knox. By that time I had given up on my beloved Cavalry—I thought it would spend the war at home. The facts, of course, are that all nondivisional cavalry regiments were converted to armored cavalry and fought very effectively in Europe; and that the 1st Cavalry Division fought brilliantly, without its horses, as infantry in the Pacific Theater—MacArthur once identified it as his finest combat division. This compliment was earned in part, I've been told, by the service of the young officers receiving their reserve commissions at four fine schools: Texas A&M, New Mexico Military Institute, and the Universities of Arizona and Oklahoma—the men who led many of the troops and platoons of the division. Many had taken Cavalry ROTC training in school because of its association with polo.

I leapt at the chance of assignment to an armored division, even though that division existed mostly on paper. Actually, I left Fort Bliss before receipt of orders—I was legally AWOL for a couple of days, but no one seemed to notice. At Fort Knox I was promoted to major and assigned command of the division's reconnaissance battalion which, at the time, consisted of only a cadre of officers and NCOs transferred from other divisions farther along in training. And my battalion had no equipment at all. The war still seemed to be very far away.

But then to my amazement, I was offered the job of G-3 (the Operations Officer) on the staff of the 1st Armored Division, then fully manned, equipped, and in preparation for movement overseas. I knew nothing about tank tactics and nothing about staff work—I had not so much as ridden in a tank, and had not been near the Army's Staff College at Fort Leavenworth.

The offer came from Maj. Gen. Orlando Ward, recently transferred from command of the 8th to command of the 1st Armored Division. Although distantly related to him by marriage I had met him only a week or so previously. General Ward had a fine reputation as a tactician and commander; if he was willing to take a chance on me, despite my total lack of experience with tank forces, I could not object.

The 1st Armored was built around three regular regiments: the 1st and 13th Cavalries (by then the 1st and 13th Armored Regiments) and the 6th (by then Armored) Infantry. The division was packing up to leave Fort Knox; among the excess baggage it discarded was a quantity of harness for four-mule wagon teams.

For shipment to Europe the division was split into two categories: equipment, accompanied by drivers and maintenance personnel, which via numerous freight trains was shipped for loading at several East Coast ports; and the rest of the officers and men, who initially went by passenger trains during March and April to a staging area at Fort Dix, New Jersey. We who went to Dix spent about a month there. Thereafter, in increments, we moved by train to New York. For purposes of "security," the troop trains had blinds drawn over the windows, and in New York port we boarded the *Queen Mary* at night.

So we rather sneaked off to war. I thought that was silly: we should have gone off with the bands playing and the flags flying, which would have made us feel a whole lot better about things. I was very much aware, believe me, of the threat posed by German submarines, but equally aware that the massive movement of our men and equipment could hardly be kept secret from German intelligence, no matter how tightly we drew the trains' window blinds.

Our equipment, which was very heavy, crossed the Atlantic in a variety of cargo ships, of which the most remarkable were the "Maracaibos"—vessels developed and used by American oil companies in Maracaibo Bay, Venezuela, in the exploitation of the oil fields there. The Maracaibos had one special feature: the ship bows, on giant hinges, could be let down by winches and cables to serve as ramps for the oil trucks and drilling equipment to disembark directly from the ship's hold onto a beach. This arrangement served admirably for military vehicles and became a standard feature of all the thousands of beach-assault boats and ships built for American and English forces in World War II.

Such was her speed, the *Queen Mary* took only six days to cross. We had to make ready, of course, for possible sinking by an enemy submarine. I was appointed the officer whose duty it was to coordinate the U.S. Army part—getting everybody to the proper spots—in case of emergency evacuation of the ship. We had daily practice, each an improvement over the previous one, but our best time was 45 minutes from the initial practice alarm to the time the last man was on deck. It took a lot to get ten thousand men up eight, nine, or ten decks from where they started.

An interesting feature of this exercise was what would have happened next. The North Atlantic in May is rough as a cob and the water a temperature that will allow a man to survive for about 20 minutes. There was lifeboat room for about 4,000, as I remember, packing each to the gunwales—everyone else would depend on rubber rafts and life-jackets. Among my large number of associates in working out and supervising ship evacuation we had a macabre little joke: in the interest of fairness the officer controlling entry to each of the lifeboats would let one man aboard, shoot the next one (we had pistols), let another aboard, shoot the next, etcetera, etcetera. And then shoot himself.

Our destination was the north of Ireland, but the *Queen Mary* went into the River Clyde, in Scotland, transferring us to what the British chose to call "butterflies" for ferry across the Irish Sea to Belfast. From there we moved by road to what used to be British Army garrisons in County Down. Our heavy equipment, including several hundred 35-ton tanks, was delivered to North of Ireland ports, upon which the vehicles were launched on winding, narrow, lightly paved Irish country roads for movement to their several destinations. The effect on those roads, and on the little Irish cottages that sometimes lay too close to those roads, was pretty dreadful: here and there an entire bedroom or sitting room or kitchen would be exposed to the Irish wind and rain, and some roads, at the bends, disintegrated altogether.

The *Queen Mary*, among many other passenger ships, did yeoman service. With her sister ship, the *Queen Elizabeth*, she was the biggest and fastest afloat. She would remain in the Clyde only long enough to disgorge her load, but on each trip spent three or four days in New York, where she was boarded immediately by the first of three shifts of several hundred workmen that tore out more of her palatial accommodations in favor of hammocks or bunks to accommodate soldiers. She carried only 10,000 on our trip, but (I was told) eventually reached a capacity of almost 20,000 troops.

In October of 1942 the load included a few replacements for our division. I happened to encounter two of these on their arrival in Ireland— young officers from Oklahoma, neither of whom had seen before so much as a drop of seawater. They seemed a bit dazed: a not-surprising effect, I thought, of their first sight of the turbulent North Atlantic, and that from the deck of one of the world's two biggest ships. Quite a thrill. Then they told me their story.

The *Queen Mary* habitually navigated the confined waters near New York under the escort of two or three American destroyers, but because of her speed (which exceeded that of the destroyers and, by a wide margin, that of any submarine) it was deemed safer for her to make the rest of the crossing unescorted, on a zig-zag course, at 29 knots. When she was a few hours out of the Clyde a British escort picked her up. All of this impressed the two young Oklahomans on their initial trip at sea.

On their last day aboard they watched, fascinated, the British escort fall into position. But after an hour or so they saw a light cruiser make a turn; other accounts say the *Mary* did the turning, but which ship turned makes little difference. The *Queen Mary*, at 85,000 tons and tearing through the water, went through the middle of the other ship, the cruiser's bow coming down one side of the *Mary*, the stern down the other.

The *Mary* slowed her engines, but only momentarily; she could not afford to, in dangerous waters, with thousands of men aboard. The crew threw over life-rafts and life-rings, but they could have been of no help. Some of the other escort ships attempted rescue, but not all—the job was still to protect the huge, vulnerable, uniquely valuable passenger ship and her cargo.

My subsequent research identifies the cruiser as HMS *Curacao,* and indicates that 338 of her crew perished, 72 survived. *Queen Mary* stayed in the Clyde, at the shipyard that built her, only long enough for what remained of her front end to be made reasonably watertight—with concrete. She then limped back to the Boston Naval Yard, where only a few weeks of frantic endeavor were necessary to fit her with a gigantic new steel bow. In World War II one got the sense that America and Great Britain could do anything. A great feeling, believe me, one no longer to be experienced.

Two full U.S. divisions, plus a lot of ancillary troops, spent several months in North Ireland—to their distinct disadvantage. But it was a matter of getting over to somewhere in Europe troops that were fully equipped and presumably close to being ready for combat, a matter of using precious sealift to begin the movement of power across the Atlantic, even though its use was not imminent.

But Ulster was a poor place to train, especially for an armored division. I was the staff officer responsible, under the direction of the division commander, for the training of the combat elements of the division, and saw at once that the greatest favor I could do them would be to get more area in which they could maneuver. Tank and armored infantry battalions need lots of space to shoot and move in.

In my search for land I was aided by locally available British officers of World War I vintage recalled to active service. With one or another of them I called on many Irish farmers, asking for the use, by our tanks, of pasture land; their response was sometimes sympathetic but always negative. Quite often it was hostile, causing me to say, "Now look! We're Americans over here to help Great Britain hold off Hitler. If we can't train, someday you may see German infantry and tanks in Ireland!" To which the response (particularly if the farmer was Catholic) was sometimes, "Let 'em come! They'll be no worse than the *#&%$##@* British!" I found this altogether shocking, not at all the way things should be. But I was learning.

We had one "grand maneuver" while in the north of Ireland, or Ulster, under general British direction. Our units—tanks, armored infantry, and artillery—simply drove down the roads to various places at which the troop commander and the local maneuver umpire would agree that *if* we could get off the road, which we couldn't, the tanks and half-tracks would go across that field and attack that position over there that the enemy was presumed to be in.

If this exercise did us any good it was not apparent to me. But it was really no one's fault. We couldn't expect poor Irish farmers to let us chew up their land in a country suffering, courtesy of the German fleet of U-boats, a chronic shortage of food. However, the net result was that our state of training deteriorated, day by day.

One day we learned that the British monarch, King George VI, would visit the division, and General Ward designated me as the king's escort officer. Of course, I knew that Ward himself would have to escort the king; though I would certainly meet him, my job would be to lay out the itinerary and deal with lesser luminaries as the visiting party went around. I nevertheless thought this was great stuff, partly because I hadn't met any kings. King George came, but I was in bed with a great cast on my leg: my damnable left knee had gone out of joint while I was running a pistol firing course (of my own devising) with other officers of the division headquarters a few days before the arrival of the royal party.

The king offered to "give" the British armored force beret to the division; this was a compliment that in the British tradition meant that our division, and only our division of the increasingly large American Army, would be authorized to wear a black beret of that special design. We were absolutely delighted at this prospect—it would give us a unique status and be great for morale. But Washington, for reasons I thought very unsatisfactory, disapproved: we never got it.

Our stay in County Down was at least interesting, despite the fact that when it wasn't raining it was about to. Our latitude was that of northern Canada: in midsummer it was still light at midnight. We worked approximately an eleven-hour day, seven-day week, but found time occasionally for spectacularly good mackerel fishing in the Bay of Dundrum, where the tide was about 14 feet. And fresh live lobsters cost us 50 cents apiece; a large box of delicious strawberries, two bits. The offices and many of the personnel of our Division Headquarters were ensconced in the castle at Castlewellan, an enormous stone pile of countless rooms with fireplaces—no other heat in that wintry climate—and a very few primitive bathrooms, obviously an afterthought. Rhinoceros, elephant, and cape buffalo heads decorated the front hall and the wide staircase. The grounds and gardens were magnificent, including a lovely deep lake with lots of swans. We had little time to enjoy all this.

On one occasion we were visited by a party of three British generals and, after showing them about, had a dinner in their honor in the enormous formal dining room of Castlewellan. General Ward, the division CG, didn't like any Britisher—an unfortunate trait in an otherwise splendid soldier: the British were our allies and it was important that we got along with them. Anyway, about thirty of us dined at one big table. The English officers in their formal red dinner jackets were all clustered around General Ward and his Chief of Staff at the head; I was sitting with my fellow staff officers below the salt.

Percy Brown, my classmate and the division G-4, or logistics officer, and one of the world's most amusing people, told a joke—not a slimy joke but still pretty improper—and we at our end burst into laughter.

General Ward at the other end of the table was apparently having a poor time with his British guests, whom he didn't like anyway: when he heard the uproar, he called down, "That sounds good, Brown! Tell us the story!" Percy had just taken a gulp of his coffee: this he spat in one convulsive burst all over the table. This was unintentional, but I think it saved his life—that joke would never do for the distinguished visitors. Feigning illness, Brown clutched a napkin to his mouth and fled in the direction of the bathroom, never to return. The rest of us at the lower end of the table dissolved into paroxysms of laughter, but no longer at the joke. All very embarrassing to our general.

The attitude of the local populace varied from friendly to darkly suspicious, the latter stemming probably from the congenital Irish suspicion of any and all constituted authority. A couple of my pals and I, driving what was known as a command car, once stopped at a country pub for a beer. An American military policeman stopped his motorcycle, quite properly, to have a look at our car. We at the bar were instantly approached by a couple of Irishmen who informed us of the MP's activity and then asked, quite pointedly, "Is there anything we can *do* for you?" We got the impression that, had we said the word, the two would have gladly garroted the MP and thrown his body into the bushes.

In October we started a move, in many echelons of men and equipment, to England; this took a few months. We settled near Chester, close to the Welsh border and not far from Liverpool. Our 14,000 officers and men were billeted in a wild variety of accommodations ranging from sorry abandoned military billets to enormous country estates once occupied by British nobility. This stay lasted from one to two months, depending on what unit of the division one was in. There was no possibility of doing any useful tactical training.

At a chapel of the Church of England, near Chester, I heard a puzzling and shocking sermon: the priest said, in effect, that the English government was asking the British people to fight for a system that was criminally unfair to the underclasses. Let it be warned, therefore, that this was the last time unless major social reforms were enacted. This was my first inkling of the socialism that would eventually become so strong in postwar Britain.

Now let me digress.

The 1st Armored was ostensibly a Regular Army division, but it had had most of its experienced officers and NCOs cadre'd. "Cadre" had become a verb: when a unit was "cadre'd" it meant that, once again, more of its best, most experienced people were removed for reassignment to other, newer units of a frantically expanding Army. As a result of repeated cadre-ing, the regular officers remaining in our division were lieutenant colonels and above, and with few exceptions the regular NCOs were master sergeants. Like other divisions, we were no longer regulars but a part of a citizen Army.

But unlike most other divisions, the 1st Armored was not long from its initial commitment to battle, battle in which, at first, much of the division did poorly. I was the G-3 of the division, the staff officer responsible (always under the division commander) for movement, training, and combat operations. I would have to say, then, that our initial lack of success could be laid in part at my door. I have no complaint: this did not stop my subsequent promotion to high rank, and perhaps a prudent man, in the interest of his own reputation, wouldn't raise the issue now. But let me explain.

A combat organization, like a football team, requires repeated hard-working practice if it is to do well. The 1st Armored Division (1AD) spent March of 1942 turning in peacetime gear and packing the rest for departure from Fort Knox; almost a month in moving to Fort Dix; a month at Dix, waiting, without equipment to train with; a month getting to and settling in Ireland; five months in Ireland, with totally inadequate terrain on which to do more than very limited gunnery practice—the maneuvering of tank and armored infantry battalions being out of the question; two months getting to and waiting around in England, without equipment or training area; and some weeks in preparation and movement, as we shall see, to North Africa. Our sharpness, our cutting edge, was about that of a broom handle.

And what did we meet, by way of enemy, in North Africa? The highly skilled, war-tested German Army—including Rommel's Afrika Korps, perhaps the most skillful, experienced, battle-hardened tank force on earth. And we—a major part of the division—were clobbered. The situation was not far different from a football game between a team of *potentially* good players, almost a year out of practice, and a team that a week before had played in the Super Bowl.

There is a moral, of course, to the foregoing sad tale. I hope that the civilian and military leadership of this country remains aware of it as it contemplates the problem of dispatching forces overseas for combat.

On one occasion, in October of 1942, I accompanied the division commander, General Ward, and his Chief of Staff to a major British-American command meeting in a large stone building on Grosvenor Square, London, very near the American Embassy. On the wall of the conference room were huge maps of the environs of Oran and Algiers, both port cities in what was then the French-African colony of Algeria.

The Germans, one may remember, had overrun the Low Countries and the largest part of France itself. In the autumn of 1940, France had surrendered, but by the terms of the surrender had retained control—

but only at the sufferance of the Germans—of the southern part of France proper, the provisional capital being at the city of Vichy. "Vichy France," as it came to be called, was in turn allowed to retain control of the French-African colonies, and allowed to maintain a substantial quantity of troops and some naval forces (including at least one battleship) there. The rest of the surviving French Navy was gathered in the French Mediterranean port of Toulon.

Charles de Gaulle, then only a brigadier general, had with British concurrence set himself up in London as the leader of the "Free French"—totally disassociated from the Vichy French. The Free French, as I remember, had forces only in Syria and perhaps in the Far East—none in Africa.

We learned later that the American generals Lyman Lemnitzer and Mark Clark had made a clandestine trip by submarine to a midnight rendezvous with representatives of the French military headquarters in North Africa, arriving at some sort of accommodation with them. The intelligence given us at the conference, however, was ambiguous: the degree of French resistance to be expected was unknown, but one was invited to hope for the best while preparing for the worst.

Green blobs on the enormous wall map showed known French military locations, and large blue arrows indicated the landing beaches and subsequent movements and objectives planned for execution by British and American troops. The sight of all this, believe me, got me pretty excited, an excitement soon quashed by the realization that only about a third of our division—a third not including the headquarters—would participate. As it happened, the British and American landings at Algiers were essentially unopposed, and the American ones at Oran fairly lightly opposed, except in one instance which I'll address a bit later. The American landings on Morocco's Atlantic coast, by forces mounted from ports on the eastern seaboard of the United States, were for a time pretty vigorously resisted. No U.S. Marine units were involved in any of the operations.

At mid-morning a short recess in the briefing was announced by the British master of ceremonies—I've quite forgotten who he was. In any case, three tall English serving women, each clad from neck to shoetops in white cotton dresses, appeared with trays of tea and biscuits. The Americans were aghast—there on the wall, uncovered for all to see, were the maps of the North African coast showing the complete plan of the forthcoming operation. I nudged a nearby British officer, pointing out the obvious breach of security. "Oh no," he said, "they're just bringing in the *tea!*" In the old days the British gentry really didn't see servants as individuals capable of independent or even hostile action. They were just "there"—depersonalized creatures, in this case "just bringing in the tea."

The participating third of our division, and parts of the 1st Infantry Division, landed in early December on beaches east and west of Oran, about 40 miles or so from the city; opposed only sporadically, they circled inland, occupied the French military airfield at Tafaraoui, south of Oran, and then went into town. There were some glitches and French forces put up some resistance: a fair number of men were killed and wounded on both sides, but the operation was deemed a success. However, in an associated endeavor a part of our division suffered disaster.

Admiral Lord Mountbatten, a member of the British royal family, had a long naval background; he ultimately became commander of the British China-India-Burma theater, and later still was the last British viceroy of India. In his then-current post as Chief of "Special Operations" on the British General Staff he had originated the famous, gallantly executed (but in the opinion of many, futile and unduly costly) British-Canadian commando raid on Dieppe, a small German-occupied port on the French Atlantic coast.

After the basic plan for taking Oran was complete and set, Lord Mountbatten, we were told, decided that it would be very unfortunate if the harbor machinery in the port (the anchorage for several French men-of-war) were blown up by the French before the port could be occupied by our enveloping forces. At his instigation, therefore, and in spite of objection by General Ward, a special operation to capture that machinery intact was added to the plan, and the 3rd Battalion, 6th Armored Infantry, of our division was selected to execute it. To carry the battalion (actually just its forward combat personnel, and none of its vehicles) directly into the inner harbor were two ex–U.S. Coast Guard cut-ters, the *Walney* and the *Hartland,* manned by the British navy but with thirty-two U.S. Navy personnel also aboard.

A young West Pointer, Lt. Col. George F. Marshall (no kin to the then–Chief of Staff of the Army), was our battalion's commander. Just before he left England he had dinner with a close friend of mine, to whom he said that because of his assignment and mission he considered himself the luckiest of men; he would trade places with no one alive.

H-hour for the forces landing on the beaches flanking Oran was set at 1:00 A.M. It was desired that nothing serve to alert the French to those landings, so the cutters' approach to the inner harbor was set an hour later, at 2:00 A.M. One wonders what the British planners thought would happen to soft vessels, mounting only tiny deck guns, as they ap-proached a harbor whose defenses would, by then, be fully alerted by the beach landings.

As the cutters, flying large American flags, made their approach to the antisubmarine boom protecting the inner harbor the French were at their posts and ready. Searchlights on the shore suddenly illuminated the little ships, allowing French shore batteries to take them under fire, and sirens were heard sounding in the city. *Walney* managed to get through a narrow gap in the harbor boom, but was thereupon engaged by the heavy guns of a French cruiser and one or more destroyers. Its bridge blown away, it went out of control, drifting through a holocaust of fire; *Hartland* was in similar circumstances, burning and sinking, in the outer harbor. A few officers and men managed to swim ashore, many of them wounded; only forty-seven survived unhurt. George Marshall was killed on the bridge of the *Walney.*

The 1st Armored Division had initially three armored infantry bat-talions; before the war really began, from our point of view, one was al-ready destroyed, to no purpose. The French had no plans or intent to disable the harbor machinery.

WORLD WAR II

5 I begin now some loose and very incomplete accounts, with no great historical value, of what befell me and those around me in World War II. I would call my perspective in that war as "upper middle." I served altogether in one combat division, but in the ranks of lieutenant colonel and colonel enjoyed certain small comforts not available to lower ranks.

My class at West Point graduated at a strength of 240, but some resigned or otherwise left the service in the eleven years before the war started. Of those remaining, 20 were killed in action or died in prison camps: our fatality rate was thus about 9.5 percent. The World Almanac tells us that the United States had 16,112,586 men, all told, "in" World War II for varying lengths of time; of these 357,116 were killed, or 2.2 percent of the total. But of course that's only part of the story: many combat units suffered great hardship and incurred very heavy losses. But even in those units, higher ranking officers, most of whom were career professionals, were killed less frequently and suffered far less hardship than did junior officers and enlisted men, most of the latter being draftees.

The Israeli Army boasts that its officers "lead from the front"; indeed, that army is a fine one and its junior officers suffer many casualties, but the statement, nevertheless, is true only in part. The facts in any army are that officers are posted to positions of control according to their perceived level of competence: the more experienced and therefore the higher ranking the officer, the larger the unit he is designated to command. If a high-ranking officer elects to operate at the very front of the action, he may theoretically give to the squad or the tank he finds there a highly refined brand of leadership, but in the meanwhile the other thousands of men whose efforts he is supposed to coordinate will go uncoordinated—and may possibly come unstuck on that account. This does not mean that a good commander does not from time to time find it necessary and desirable to expose himself to danger—several U.S. two- and three-star generals were killed in World War II.

My intention, however, in this aside, is to acknowledge that I spent the war at a comparatively comfortable level, usually in no great danger and missing few meals. I saw many dead soldiers, German and American, and some of other nationalities, but I did not become one; indeed, I was never hit at all.

I thought this should be acknowledged at the beginning.

By far the most professionally intriguing series of events of my life was that of participation, in the course of a bit more than three years abroad, in World War II. But a recitation of all the events of that war, as those events touched me, would go on forever. Moreover, as a lieutenant colonel and colonel, I was at the middle level, not where the big history-making decisions were made and, for most of my days and nights, not where the hardship was, not where the dying was done. So, to reinforce what was said in the preface, what follows in the next several chapters is neither an inclusive chronological recitation of events nor a serious contribution to history: it is no more than a series of observations of a sort not to be found in more academic works—an endeavor to give the flavor of the war at the middle level of command. I would however hope that it might help the officers of the Army, should war come again, to anticipate some of the difficulties they will face as participants—though that is not the main purpose of this part of the book.

A bit deflated at having missed the landings against the French, the rest of the division sailed in a convoy of twenty-odd troop ships and escorting destroyers for North Africa in December 1942. Landlubbers are never terribly happy at sea in wartime, for the ocean seems hostile and very likely to harbor submarines. Soldiers are presumably conditioned by training and doctrine to face up to danger on land—danger they can usually avert or counter by their own action—but not to the threat of a silent foe lurking under the surface of the sea. Submarines are viewed by the soldier as dreadful, malevolent things.

The trip was uneventful, however. We went through the narrow Straits of Gibraltar at night, presumably for good reason, though the lights of Tangiers, Spanish Morocco, on the south shore were shining brightly. This was a Spanish right of neutrality, but it made it easy for a German submarine, if it lay near the north shore at periscope depth, to see a ship outlined against the lights and sink it. But none did.

Although there was no attack, there was a near collision between our ship and another moving considerably faster than ours. Both were running without lights of any kind—great hulking shapes rushing through the night—but both, of course, were going in the same general direction. I happened to witness this, standing with only one or two others on the deck: there was a great slapping, splashing sound as the bow wave of each ship collided with that of the other, and the pounding of the two ships' engines built to a crescendo. For a short time I thought we'd bought the farm, and indeed I don't think we missed collision by more than 100 feet.

Once through the Straits the convoy broke into parts. Ostensibly we were bound for Oran, but our ship took us to Algiers. We arrived at anchorage, out in the harbor, after dark. Unable to get a good explanation for our situation from the British skipper, General Ward sent me ashore about 9 P.M. to investigate and, incidentally, to see if we might debark there inasmuch as it was much closer to our ultimate destination, Tunisia.

The city was completely blacked out, and there was no moon. I went in the captain's boat, the bow waves and wake a bright electric blue from the phosphorus in the water, and was put ashore at the foot of a narrow stairway cut into the face of a concrete landing quay at the water's edge. I had never been to Africa, to me a continent of great mystery, and this was an eerie beginning. In the darkness of the blackout I walked down the quay in what I considered a promising direction, and was startled by the challenge of a British sentry with a rifle pointed at my middle. I was equipped, fortunately, with a password, and was able to make my peace with him.

Nearby, just visible in the starlight, I noticed a great V-shaped scar penetrating the concrete and its underlying rock—perhaps 15 feet horizontally, and vertically about 20 feet down to the water line. The sentry, by now a friendly chap, explained that a British destroyer in the course of the landings a few weeks previously had suffered a little confusion in the transmission of signals from the bridge to the engine room, in result of which the ship had hit the concrete—the north shore of Africa— at flank speed and a 90-degree angle. The casualties to the crew must have been frightful. I later confirmed the story, and then, consulting a map, reckoned that in the direction the destroyer was going the next stretch of navigable water was 5,000 miles away, due south.

With the help of my new friend and his guard telephone I found transportation to take me to the St. George Hotel, by then occupied by Eisenhower's headquarters, NATOUSA (North African Theater of Operations, U.S. Army). Somebody had to awaken the Chief of Staff, Gen. Beetle Smith. He was sympathetic neither with being awakened, nor with the British Navy for having brought us to the wrong spot, nor with our desire to stay there. He told us to go back to Oran. I said, "Yessir" (which is sometimes one word) and departed. We sailed before sun-up.

Enemy forces in North Africa, both those in Tunisia and those under Feldmarschal Erwin Rommel in Libya, were German and Italian, subordinated to a joint German-Italian command in Rome. But though American forces in Tunisia occasionally encountered Italian combat elements, those elements were by that time thoroughly disenchanted with their association with the Germans, showed little enthusiasm for combat, and surrendered easily. In what follows, therefore, I don't speak of "German-Italian" forces but simply of the Germans. Indeed, any American veteran of the campaign in Tunisia will hardly remember the Italians as an enemy—it was the Germans we fought in bloody and sometimes disastrous battle.

The Allied landings in Morocco and Algeria had apparently surprised the Germans both as to timing and location, this being accomplished at least partly by a clever deception scheme involving a dead body, wearing the uniform of a British Army captain, allowed to wash ashore where the Germans would find it. In its pockets were elaborately faked orders and maps indicating a very different operation at a different spot.

To cope with the new threat from the west, the Germans were necessarily in a state of urgent rearrangement of forces. Fortunately (for them), combat reinforcements originally destined for Marshal Rommel's field army (the Afrika Korps plus some Italian divisions), now withdrawing before Montgomery's victorious Eighth Army in Libya, were near southern Italy's ports and thus ideally located for quick movement across the Med into northern Tunisia. Combat Command B (CCB) of our division, shortly after its arrival in Tunisia after the fall of Oran, inadvertently demonstrated the enemy need for that reinforcement: one of its kitchen trucks, lost and unescorted, had gotten within six miles of the capital city of Tunis, the ultimate goal of the Allied campaign in Africa, before discovering that all the military road signs were in German. It reversed course and got away, but it took the combined efforts of several hundred-thousand American, British, and French-Colonial troops almost five months of hard fighting to get that far again.

In late November 1942 CCB entered heavy combat against the Germans in northern Tunisia. Its battalions had some successes, some severe reverses, but for troops new to battle they acquitted themselves well in most cases. That Command became a battle-experienced force very quickly, and for some months this had a slightly divisive effect within the division, particularly because some other division elements, in their first battle experience, were soundly beaten. For their part, German forces in northern Tunisia reacted with impressive speed and professionalism to the sudden presence of new Allied forces in North Africa.

While the remaining two-thirds of the division unloaded at Oran, my division commander, Gen. Orlando Ward, took his aide and me for a quick look at what was transpiring in Tunisia. Central Tunisia is a vast area of mountain and desert—some of the former high enough to support a little timber, a little of the latter irrigated enough for meager cultivation. Most of the flat is simple desert of rock or sand broken by occasional large patches of prickly-pear cactus, some of it 10 feet high.

One of the less attractive local sights was that of camels feasting on the juicy leaves of the cactus, apparently with relish, in disregard of the bloody green slime pouring from the corners of their mouths.

Because forces on both sides were small as compared to the area, we, our allies, the Germans and the Italians fought what I'd describe as a loose maneuvering war with tanks and motorized or armored infantry based on key terrain features (mountain passes, in most instances) with long stretches of rough terrain, unoccupied and only lightly patrolled, between those positions.

We were in Tunisia only a few days, mostly to touch base with the elements of our division which had made the landings at Oran and thereafter come east. On the way back to Oran we celebrated Christmas Eve sitting alongside our pup tents, out in the desert. Next day we called at the Allied Headquarters in Algiers. I was not admitted to any important meetings, but I remember a luncheon in the officers' mess in the St. George Hotel. General Ward and I were invited to sit at General Eisenhower's table, seating about twelve in the large main dining room of the hotel. Initially Eisenhower wasn't there, but we were invited to sit. When he did arrive we all rose, and were then reseated. He had just come from a thoroughly irritating and frustrating conference with Admiral Darlan, then the senior French military commander in North Africa.

Ike was not happy. He called down to then–Brig. Gen. Al Gruenther (later to become very prominent in the Army) who was sitting at the foot of the table. "Al," he said, "call everybody to attention." Gruenther got to his feet.

"And be sure," said Eisenhower, "that all the waiters are present. And tell everybody here that anyone who wants my job command of the North African Theater of Operations can damned well have it!" I'm sure that made him feel better.

It is worth noting that German weapons in World War II were, in general, better than ours. It is quite true that the pronounced Allied advantage in quantity—weapons and manpower—more than made up the difference and assured our eventual victory, but this truth was often of no consolation to the individual American soldier fighting at the risk of his life. If, for example, his tank and a German tank were shooting at one another, to him the *pertinent* facts were that the German's basic tank (in Africa the Mark IV) was more agile, had a lower silhouette and was therefore much harder to hit, and had a much better gun (with greater velocity, more penetration, and far better sight) than our tank.

And as our tanks gradually improved, the Germans' did, too. It was in Africa that we first encountered the gigantic 60-ton Mark VI Tiger tank, which carried an 88mm gun (ours was 75mm, later 76mm) and thick frontal armor that none of our guns could hope to penetrate. The German Mark V Panther, which appeared later in Italy and France, was the finest tank of the war.

German antitank guns, both in 88- and 75mm calibers, were also far better than ours—faster, which gave them better penetration, and more accurate. German machine guns (and many would contend that the machine gun was, and may still be, the basic weapon of ground warfare) had a much faster rate of fire and were generally more reliable than ours. German artillery was good, but in that we had an edge in quality, I would say, and certainly in quantity. As a matter of very small consequence, I once tested a German Luger pistol (which I always carried, once I got my hands on one) and an American .45 against a German helmet and an American helmet: the smaller Luger went cleanly through both, the larger American Colt through neither.

The division (less CCB), arriving in Tunisia by bits and pieces because of varying modes of transport, was greeted by a most difficult and disheartening command situation. To our very great disappointment we remained split into widely separated parts: General Ward did not regain control of CCB, which remained detached in the northern area; and, to add insult to injury, an additional tank battalion was detached from the division to beef up the separate CCB.

Let me now speak parenthetically of an event that didn't happen, though it might have and perhaps should have. In January 1943 Rommel's field army had been defeated by the British Eighth Army at El Alamein, in Egypt, not far from Alexandria, and was falling back across Libya in the direction of Tunisia. In *The Rommel Papers,* the Feldmarschal speaks of the terrible danger he faced because of the new presence, in

Tunisia, of American and British forces brought into that area after landings in Algeria and Morocco: he refers to a German "front" or "flank" of some 400 miles which, penetrated anywhere, would cut his line of supply and force his surrender. His situation may be appreciated by a look at Map 1.

The situation was, of course, equally apparent to Allied Headquarters in Algiers, which developed Plan SATIN for an operation in which our 1st Armored Division, reunited in Tunisia and reinforced with additional infantry, would attack (as per arrow) in the direction of Sfax, a port on the Mediterranean coast. Although we recognized that Rommel would pull all the stops to defeat such a plan we were (in our innocence, perhaps) anxious to give it a try, and indeed it was the tactically sound thing to do—assuming our ability to pull it off. And we thought we could, if the attack was initiated very promptly, before the Germans could reinforce the target area.

Our first disappointment came with the news that General Ward, initially the designated commander for the operation, would be subordinated to the commander of the American II Corps, a Lieutenant General Fredendall. And eventually General Eisenhower, no doubt in consultation with General Anderson, the commander of the British First Army, abandoned the whole idea, believing apparently that the greater wisdom lay in the adoption of a defensive posture in central and north Tunisia pending the arrival of the German and Italian (and the following British) forces still in Libya.

It is interesting to speculate on what might have happened had SATIN been attempted. The possibilities range from spectacular success and an earlier end to the Tunisian campaign and perhaps even World War II—to tragic failure, involving, as a matter only of personal interest, my own demise or over two years in a German prison camp.

Notwithstanding the cancellation of SATIN, the 1AD was subordinated to II Corps. A tragic quarrel erupted between Ward and the Corps Commander, General Fredendall. I'll omit the details of the quarrel; it is enough to say that each distrusted the other, with the result that Fredendall specified in very improper and, I'd say, deliberately insulting detail how Ward was to dispose and maneuver the troops remaining to him. Fredendall's judgment was based solely on his staff officers' very

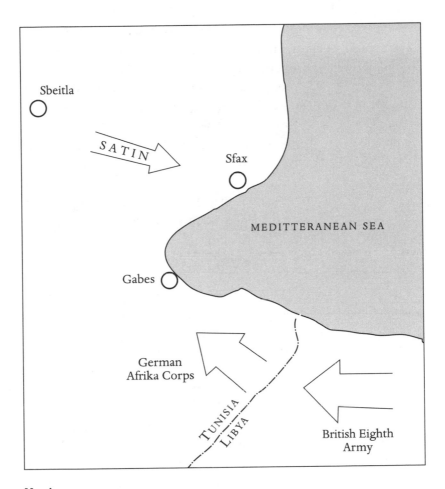

Map 1.

infrequent visits to the forward area, which he never visited himself; he also suffered from a manifest lack of understanding of the tactics of mobile warfare. I was then and remain now convinced that the right lay altogether with Ward, though I make no attempt here to prove it. The result of the quarrel was the effectual removal of Ward and his division headquarters from the tactical chain of command.

I would guess that Allied timidity (in not attempting to cut the enemy in two at Sfax) must have struck Rommel, the Desert Fox, as a gift from God. Even so, he apparently thought the gap between our lines and the sea too narrow for comfort, so he eventually attacked us, initially at a pass, known as Faid, through a low range of barren desert mountains. The first phase of the attack cleared the pass, held by a regiment of French Colonials, the Zouavves. The German success put Combat Command A, a task force of our CCB under Col. Johnny Waters, and a substantial force of misplaced infantry and artillery from another division (these, of course, not under command of our CCA, as it should have been) in a perilous position—having to defend against a powerful, highly professional, and experienced enemy already holding the key terrain—this disadvantage being reinforced by the strictures imposed on us and CCA by a corps commandeer from his underground office 100 or so miles to the rear.

I should note here that the Tunisian campaign was fought mostly in a state of German air superiority. The Luftwaffe employed a generous quantity of slow but ominous-looking and very effective dive bombers, the Stukas, which came down on you vertically, scaring your pants off; and two classes of fighters, the Messerschmidt 109 and the new Focke-Wulf 190, and a light bomber, the Junkers 88.

Our Air Force—then still part of the Army—had the P-39 Airacobra, which carried, unbelievably, a 37mm cannon in its nose; this afforded it some limited value as a ground attack aircraft but the slow old bird was a sucker for an enemy fighter—when it was used it had to be given top cover by other fighters. We also had P-40s, of only moderate ability against German fighters, and P-38s Lightnings, twin-boom twin-engine aircraft good for high-altitude deep penetration reconnaissance missions, but of no great shakes in a dogfight. Our counterair strength in the early days lay mostly in British Spitfires borrowed and flown by our Air Force, but there were not many of those. And in the last few weeks of Tunisia American P-51 Mustang fighters arrived—fine ships, greatly welcomed, though for a while their pronounced similarity to the German fighters caused us on the ground to shoot at them—sometimes, I regret to say, successfully. Soon our Air Force put three wide white stripes on each wing of the P-51 to distinguish it.

One U.S. P-40 fighter base I visited had gotten hold of an American magazine, which contained an American aircraft company's brightly colored ad that asked, in the supremely confident words of an advertising copywriter safe in his New York office, "Who's Afraid of the Big Focke-Wulf?" Some wag had put the ad on the pilots' bulletin board with the admonition "Sign below." Every pilot in the squadron put his name down.

In Tunisia, anyway, from our point of view the sky belonged to the Germans. We were wont to remark that the day was divided into two parts: Spitfire time, when German aircraft preferred to be elsewhere, but Spitfire time was only one half-hour, or sometimes two half-hours, each day; the other twenty-three or twenty-three-and-a-half hours were Messerschmidt, Focke-Wulf, and Stuka time.

One reason for this was that our ground forces were east of a range of mountains often topped by heavy layers of cloud, while almost all our airfields were west of those mountains and far from the combat area. The other reason was that a decision had been made that our fighters' greatest contribution would come from the intercept of German air and ocean supply traffic across the Mediterranean. In retrospect one cannot dispute the wisdom of that decision; I know, however, that the American soldier in Tunisia thought he was getting precious little help from the Air Forces. Fighter response to our calls for reconnaissance or fire support was slow, infrequent, and unreliable.

The Spitfire, when it did appear, was the darling of the ground soldier, partly because of its beauty and the grace of its flight, mostly because when they did find German fighters in the vicinity the Spitfires tore into them. There are few shows more gripping than the dogfight, the planes arcing beautifully, if desperately, through the sky; and a stricken plane evokes instant sympathy on the part of the ground observer because he often can't tell at first whether it's friend or foe. When it approaches the ground and can be identified the groans are heartfelt, or the cheers of triumph and relief uproarious. Over several months we saw many craft shot down, sometimes trailing fire, sometimes ejecting a parachute, crashing usually in a great ball of flame and black smoke.

The Luftwaffe, usually unbothered by aerial opposition, was good at punishing us on the ground. The first experience of hostile air attack is quite terrifying: I remember trying to take advantage of the cover afforded by a tire rut no deeper than an inch or two. I remember also the admiration I felt for an American antiaircraft battery commander, on the same occasion, standing on the armored hood—the highest spot—of the most exposed vehicle during that attack, thus encouraging his men to stick to their weapons. Which they did.

Results of air attack in Tunisia were extremely variable: sometimes a single German fighter, whose 20mm machine guns fired an explosive bullet, could tear up a small ground column; on the other hand I've seen units, totally exposed, absolutely disappear in the towering black smoke of bombs, only to reappear without damage.

But massive attack by tactical aircraft, of the sort that did not occur at all in Tunisia but which was often inflicted on enemy forces in subsequent campaigns in Italy and France, can be devastating, particularly if units can be caught moving on a road. The American troops that fought in Tunisia and in the first part of the Italian campaign are the last Americans that experienced battle under local enemy tactical air superiority. In the 1944–45 battle for Western Europe, and in the Korea and Vietnam wars, our forces enjoyed dominance in the sky over the battlefield.

The British helped us prepare for attack by hostile aircraft by a little booklet, "How to Be Bombed." The booklet didn't downplay the shock of one's first bombing or strafing, but by the citation of many statistics it reassured the reader as to his chances of survival, which in usual circumstances were really rather good. In my job as G-3 I took pains to get one of those booklets for issue to each man in the division. Unquestionably, it served to cushion the first shock. Our Army today should have a supply of such booklets in stock, ready for issue.

In February our elements in the vicinity of Sidi bou Zid, on our side of Faid Pass, were hit by the German 10th and 21st Panzer Divisions, both understrength but still powerful. I make no attempt to describe the infinitely complicated series of battle actions that resulted from that savage, professionally skillful German attack. It is enough to say, first, that a terribly ineffectual system of aerial reconnaissance gave us no warning of the German concentration of assault forces, and fighter aircraft gave us little help in thwarting their attack; second, we faced a foe with vastly greater experience and much better (and in the immediate area, larger numbers of) tanks and antitank guns. So we took a bad licking, with many tanks set afire and many men killed. Some large units, including a major part of a regiment of National Guard infantry, cut off in isolated positions on the desert hills, were forced to surrender.

Other surviving elements were scattered: one story was of an American maintenance crew, separated from its parent unit, joining a mess line they came onto in the desert after dark. The Americans withdrew, without challenge, when they found that the chow line was not American but German.

General Fredendall reacted to the debacle by releasing to division control a single tank battalion earlier detached from it, and directing that that battalion be made the nucleus of a counterattack to drive the Germans from the vicinity of Sidi bou Zid. This was insanity: we could build no adequate force from the few resources left to us, after all the earlier detachments and our new losses, to contest major elements of two German panzer divisions waiting for us in the desert. General Ward didn't like it and neither did I, but this does not relieve the sense of shame I feel, to this day, for not contesting the order more strongly, even at the cost of my commission.

If there is an excuse to be found it would lie in our ignorance, because of our lack of air reconnaissance, of the real strength of the German tank force. The tank battalion newly restored to us was married up with an armored infantry battalion and an armored artillery battalion. This force, in deployed battle formation, took off across the desert. Somewhat surprisingly, in retrospect, it had some initial successes, maneuvering skillfully and destroying several German outlying tanks while losing some of its own. But eventually it entered the maw formed by a quantity of German tanks and antitank guns dug into the terrain undulations and wadis (dry creekbeds) near Sidi bou Zid, and encountered as well the fire of other tanks enveloping its flanks. The armored infantry and artillery battalions, following the tanks, were not greatly hurt, but the tank battalion was destroyed, utterly, its surviving officers and men, including the battalion commander, spending the rest of the war as prisoners.

After their defeat of our counterattack at Sidi bou Zid and their overrun of the garrison at Gafsa to the south, German troops (now rein-forced) began, on Rommel's orders, methodical advance westward. The whole Allied line in central Tunisia was ordered to withdraw to hill po-sitions to the west.

Our division headquarters had for some weeks been just west of Sbeitla, in a huge prickly pear cactus patch. This was not quite as undig-nified and impracticable as it sounds: the plants were some 10 feet high, providing considerable cover in the bare flat terrain and minor protec-tion, I suppose, against bomb fragments. The plants would also, on oc-casion, stab you.

We were still in place in the cactus patch when German tank forces made a coordinated attack on our delaying forces (CCB had finally been restored to the division) east of Sbeitla. By dusk the enemy had begun its entry into the town, and by this time the fighting had become heavy. The noise of tank and artillery fire was enhanced by the U.S. Ordnance detachment responsible for the ammunition depot near the town—it commenced demolition of the ammunition stacks. It looked and sounded as though the whole damned world was blowing up. And en-tering this spectacular milieu was a French narrow-gauge railroad train loaded with ammunition: it moved slowly, unchallenged and to all ap-pearances undisturbed, through our lines, the village of Sbeitla, and the German lines, enroute to a French garrison once located in the town of Hadjeb el Aioun, a destination by then in the hands of the enemy.

The lesson derived from all this confirmed what we'd already learned from the book: a military retreat is terribly expensive. As one example of a thousand, a vehicle (truck, tank, self-propelled gun—whatever) with no more wrong with it than a dirty carburetor or a flat tire may be lost to the enemy, and a major portion of your supplies almost in-evitably will be.

One of our staff officers, to his dismay, had to abandon his crippled jeep, and with it his beloved bedding roll. He consoled himself, however, with the belief that he exacted due retribution on the Germans who came on this booty: he had pulled the safety pin on each of two frag-mentation grenades, and carefully stuck one grenade into one end of the bedding roll, the second in the other end. Indeed, it must have worked.

The Germans followed our retreat more cautiously than expected. Had they pushed us hard we should have had a rough time given the difficulties attending any retreat, our previous losses, the limited road net, and our almost total lack of air cover; as it was, we suffered no further heavy damage. German aggressiveness was no greater, one may guess, because of general difficulties as respects supply and a fear of becoming overextended. We and the British on our left ultimately occupied, this time, tactically sound defensive positions, hard to crack; moreover, Rommel (who personally reconnoitered the situation) had gained the elbow room he needed to withdraw his forces coming out of Libya into northern Tunisia.

As the division operations officer I had worked out the plan (for the use of CCB and an associated British armored brigade on its left) for the defense against and then pursuit of the German units in our valley. Actually there was no battle, but when the German forces began to withdraw, we followed.

In my jeep I trailed British tank units that were moving down their side of the valley against German delaying detachments and multiple German antitank mines. We (my driver, another officer, and I) were not far behind the leading British tanks when we came onto a British MP at a crossroad. He had on a cap with a bright red top and immaculate long white cuffs drawn on over his sleeves. He stood in the middle of the road, and his signals were as crisp and formal as though he were standing in the middle of Trafalgar Square.

He stopped us, and said we could go no further, for the road was mined. How did he know it was mined? "Well," he said, "if you look you'll see a little pile of dead Arabs and camels in the road. That shows it's mined!" But how about the area to the right of the road? "Look to the right," he said politely, "and you'll see more dead Arabs and camels. More mines." Well, how about to the left of the road?

"I'll let you know presently," said the MP. "I see another party of Arabs and camels coming up now."

Well, actually, neither we nor the British (nor the Germans, for that matter) were that heartless. There was a party of Arabs approaching, but I'm sure the MP didn't direct them into the minefield. It is true, however, that the camel, who flaps his big flat feet down hard onto the sand, was an excellent one-time antitank mine detector. He couldn't be used a second time.

In the fighting, who were the Arabs for? Of course, the Free French Army contained colonial African regiments that ultimately fought capably against the Germans, but I don't know that any American ever inquired into the matter of loyalty among the native civilian population. The Arabs were just there, either working in a field or walking or riding a burro or camel along the road or huddled in front of their miserable little shacks or tents. Arab children were consummate beggars, sidling up to any American in uniform while proclaiming, stoutly, "America okay! Soldier okay! German no okay! America win war!" and then the punchline, with hand extended: "Chocolat? Cigarat?"

I suppose the answer to my question is that the average Arab didn't give a damn who won, though it is probable that Allied soldiers were less demanding than the Germans. There were stories, none of which I could verify, of Arabs killing wounded and robbing the dead of both sides. It almost certainly happened, but I can't guess how frequently.

Tunisia, incidentally, is the site of many fascinating old Roman and Carthaginian ruins, some of them standing alone in the desert, some of them in a surprisingly good state of preservation. One of the more ironic sights was that of a tiny black goatskin tent full of ragamuffin Arabs pitched alongside what 2,000 years ago was a large, handsome basilica—and which even in ruin was still an impressive structure. The scene made one reflect on the progress of civilization in the last two millennia.

The 1st Armored Division spent the next week or so working hard at repairing the heavy damage done to our combat battalions—replacement of men and equipment. And repair to our morale. By and large we weren't proud of ourselves—but with exceptions: some units had fought hard and effectively.

After a hurried rehabilitation the division was moved back into action in the Gafsa-Macknassy area, perhaps 50 miles south from where we had been. I recall that, as per Ward's instruction, the march order I wrote required that movement of division elements, when it was done in daylight, would be at a distance of *200 yards* between vehicles—such was the extent of German dominance in the air.

Near the little desert town of Gafsa someone spotted two rough wooden crosses stuck in the desert sand: each was tenderly decorated, in honor of the fallen, with a bunch of desert flowers, apparently by inhabitants of Gafsa. It was at once sad and funny to see on one cross, roughly printed, the words "Old Garbage Pit" and on the other "Old Latrine"—testimony to a faithful obedience of regulations by some U.S. outfit previously camped there.

In the action that followed we were visited by Gen. Omar Bradley, who at that time was not much more than a footloose troubleshooter for General Eisenhower, but who eventually earned the high respect of the Army itself and that of the country as a whole. At the behest of General Ward I outlined to him the plan for our forthcoming attack, among other things telling him of the mission of another attached regiment of ex–National Guard infantry. The order to the regimental commander, which I wrote, was to take a low range of hills, about four by six miles in area and occupied lightly, according to our intelligence estimate, by Italian infantry—at the same time the regiment was not to become so thoroughly engaged in the hills that it could not be quickly assembled and withdrawn for commitment elsewhere. General Bradley, in his gentle, homey way, said that looked okay except for the last part: he suggested that a commander ought to be given a clear mission but not told how to execute it. Theoretically correct by the book, of course. But I knew this regimental commander: he was slow and sure, too slow and too sure, and so were his battalion commanders. I argued for my wording, but General Ward overruled me. Sure enough, those 3,000 doughboys captured a few hundred willing-to-quit Italians but got so wrapped up in those confounded hills that it took three days to get 'em out—much to the disadvantage of the general action, where they could have helped a lot. The moral is that sometimes one must break the rules, and one must know the strengths and weaknesses of subordinate commanders.

I retain, incidentally, the highest regard for General Bradley. This would be a good place to admit that one of my worst errors as Division G-3 was the abandonment, on some hectic occasions, of the form known to the Army as the "5 paragraph order." Each of the five paragraphs and their subparagraphs is devoted to specified subjects: the form thus constitutes a valuable checklist. In times of stress and hurry, however, an unwise commander or staff officer is tempted to abandon the form in favor of so-called letters of instruction. It is a fatal habit, if carried to more than a *very limited* extent. I counsel my successors against it.

During this time we were visited by Popski's Private Army. The PPA was strictly British. The British military loves the bizarre and adventurous, and had lots of special little detachments dedicated to special purposes. Popski's Army, perhaps twenty men strong, always lived and worked well behind the German lines. It wore the full British uniform with a red and yellow PPA patch on the shoulder. Its function was to harass—by murdering small isolated parties of German soldiers—and by blowing up things, such as trucks and bridges. Its transportation was the American jeep, of which it had several.

Popski himself was a Pole apparently brought up in Britain. His visit to us was utilitarian: he needed resupply. We gave him ammunition, food, gas, and oil, but could provide him no replacement jeeps. So he stole three from another outfit nearby and was gone.

To our great relief, General Fredendall was relieved from command of II Corps and returned to the United States, being replaced by Lt. Gen. George Patton. I had known General Patton as a major when I was still a boy, and his family and my wife's family were very close. As everyone knows, he was profane and colorful, wearing two pearl-handled pistols, not for shooting anybody but for show; and he had stars stuck all over him. More important, however, he was aggressive and bold, willing always to risk greatly to achieve greatly. He shook up II Corps Headquarters by getting it off its behind and fining everybody for poor saluting or appearing without a helmet; he shook up the divisions by telling them that he wanted to see more dead bodies, American as well as German. But, to my dismay, he brought up the erstwhile commander of the 2nd Armored Division, then back in Morocco, to replace General Ward.

Before that last action he came to our division headquarters, by that time back in the flats from which Rommel had chased us a few weeks earlier. He wanted to see our forward elements, and I was assigned to guide him. In a jeep I led his command car, the latter conspicuously decorated with a general officer's red flag and white painted stars, to (among other places) Rabaou Pass, just south of Faid Pass, both recently abandoned by the Germans. I came to a place in the road from which Army engineers, equipped with mine detectors, were removing occasional German Teller mines. "Teller" in German means "plate"; Teller mines are powerful charges, activated by pressure and designed to break the track of the heaviest tank. I stopped my jeep, dismounted, and went back to tell General Patton that we could go no further without being blown up.

But Georgie was deliberately making a show of boldness, wherever he went. "The hell with that," he said loudly. "Let's go! Ham [my nickname], lead the way!" Well, I figured this was possibly my last act. Driving past the astonished engineers I moved down the road. Patton's command car had a wider track, but his driver, who had obviously lost all his enthusiasm for the trip, kept his left wheel pair in one of my jeep tracks but risked blowing up via the other pair. Then a light tank, which had been waiting for the engineers to clear the road, joined the parade, and so help me it hadn't gone fifty feet before it hit a mine. I'm not sure what the casualties were, but the event caused the general to have a change of heart: we backed out, following our own tracks as accurately as we could.

This all sounds absurd in the telling, and it was in the act, too. But George Patton had to make an impression to instill new life and vigor into "the troops," and this was a sample of his way of doing it. Because of this and other feats of derring-do it didn't take long for every officer and soldier in his corps to know he had a new and different commander.

Our new boss in the division was Maj. Gen. Ernest Harmon, who had commanded the 2nd Armored Division in the landings in Morocco. He was a cavalryman, like Patton, and a good polo player. Like Patton he was feisty and profane, wore knee-high cavalry boots and breeches, and loved war with a passion.

He smoked constantly. When he wanted a new cigarette he first patted his breast pockets, which were usually empty, and then pointed a finger at his aide, a big Irish captain named Pat Rooney. Rooney's responsibility was to produce a cigarette, and then a lighter. Harmon would give the lighter two flicks—never more than two. If it didn't light he'd rear back and throw the lighter as far as he could, preferably into a cactus patch.

Harmon brought with him, from the 2AD, his own Chief of Staff and his own G-3—so I was fired. The Army is usually pretty tidy about things like this, but I was left floating—not sent anywhere or given anything to do. So I "sort of" attached myself to the division's reconnaissance battalion, commanded by an old friend of mine, and a place where lots of things would be going on during combat. Meanwhile the division continued the process of its own rehabilitation and retraining, and contact was made between Allied forces in Tunisia and General Montgomery's British Eighth Army coming out of Libya.

FULL COLONEL

6 After a few weeks we were moved, behind the line held by the infantry divisions, into northern Tunisia, and given a sector for our operations. The Germans were withdrawing and consolidating their forces for the defense of the Tunis-Bizerte area in northeast Tunisia, the Allies following carefully. I was with a recce (reconnaissance) company entering the town of Mateur, which was prominent on the map but almost undefended by the enemy, and in the process I encountered a newspaper reporter who wanted to know my name and what was going on. Having nothing better to do, I talked to him.

I should note that my wife, in my absence, had gravitated along with a number of other "war widows" to Falmouth, Massachusetts, where she, newly fortified by a typing course, was working as a secretary at the Woods Hole Oceanographic Institute then much engaged with war work. She awoke one day to learn by the local newspaper that FAL-MOUTH BOY IS FIRST INTO MATEUR, and I was named as the boy. Not only was this grossly inaccurate as to who first entered Mateur, but I had never laid eyes on Falmouth and couldn't have found it on a map.

Our recce elements began running into German fire a mile or so northeast of Mateur. In my jeep I motored up under the cover of a low ridge, dismounted, and walked up toward the crest to see what I could see. Short of the crest I encountered what I would describe as a very untypical American lieutenant. He looked to be in his early thirties—my age, while most lieutenants were about 22 or 23—with weathered, crinkled skin and four missing front teeth. It was easy to guess he was a ranch- or farmhand from Texas.

I introduced myself and, since he was a stranger, asked how long he had been in the division. The answer was about half a day. He had been flown from a training center in Texas to New York, put directly on another plane for Casablanca, on another for the Replacement Depot in Constantine in eastern Algeria. I think they fed him a meal before trucking him to our division, which assigned him to the 81st Reconnaissance Battalion, which assigned him to Troop A, which assigned him (about six hours before I met him) to command of the 1st Platoon of Troop A. This chap had taken about three days to get from a training camp in Texas to command of the most forward platoon of the leading division of the Allied forces in Africa. I suggested that he must have been surprised by that sequence of events. He said no, he wasn't, but he was impressed: "The Army," he said, "really gets around."

After I had absorbed all this, I asked him where the nearest German positions were. "Oh," he said, "right over on the next ridge." That sounded a bit pat to me: in modern war, one sees the enemy but rarely, and that usually when you're shooting directly at him and he at you. So I asked, how did he know the Germans were there? "Oh," he said again, "you can see them. The whole damn ridge is covered with them."

That to me was nonsense. But we crawled up to the ridge top and, by God, the whole slope of the ridge about a mile away was dotted with German soldiers. With field glasses I could see them frantically digging emplacements for antitank guns, machine guns, and riflemen. Looking at ten times the number of Germans I had seen in the previous four months in Africa. I was flabbergasted, but my new friend wasn't at all— it seemed quite normal to him: here we were on *our* side and over there were all the Germans on *their* side.

I visited the same area about noon the next day. With perhaps forty or so tanks, the 2nd Battalion of the 13th Armored Regiment of the division had attacked across the valley but had been driven back short of getting to the objective, the heavily defended ridge on the far side. Several of the battalion's tanks were burning out in the wheatfields in the valley bottom, and the battalion commander was missing.

My memory is very fuzzy about how I, footloose up to then, got involved in the fight. General Harmon in his book, *Combat Commander*, says I told him the battle wasn't laid on right (he had laid it on) and that he appointed me forthwith as the new commander of CCB—to which the battalion belonged—but I believe I was appointed simply as the battalion commander, Vice Lt. Col. Henry Gardiner, an outstanding citizen-soldier then lying wounded (fortunately not seriously) out somewhere in the wheat alongside his disabled tank. Whatever the title of my new assignment, I was ordered to attack again at 1700 hours. I was directly informed that this was to be the key attack in the division area—it had to go.

I assembled the three tank company commanders—all fine men, all ready and willing to try again. One of them, however, I had to relieve—his tank, too, had been destroyed, and his wide back was one great suppurating burn. Every officer and man in the division had been issued a tiny little morphine surrette which he pasted to the inside of his helmet, but of our little group the others had already used theirs on men wounded on previous occasions—only I had my surrette on hand. I removed it from my helmet and in my nervousness I dropped it in the tall grass. We scratched around, but never found it. A fine beginning for the new battalion commander.

But one thing I did right, I asked for and got the fire support of all three of the division's artillery battalions and, with their forward observers (notably a Capt. Sid Combs), laid on a comprehensive supporting fire plan that included a heavy smoke screen on our right flank—for according to the company commanders it was heavy antitank fire from that flank that had defeated the earlier attack. Attached to the battalion was a company of the division's reconnaissance battalion, and a company of "tank destroyers"—tank-like vehicles useful in supporting, by direct fire on enemy antitank guns, a tank attack.

We took off on the dot and got across that valley in a quarter hour, thanks considerably to the weight of our artillery and direct fire support. I was exhilarated and scared in about equal proportions—this was my first action as a battle commander. I vividly recall looking down out of my tank turret at many German infantrymen and antitank gunners huddled down in their emplacements. Once our tanks (each with two machine guns) were among them their belligerence abated. We waited in the area of the objective until the reconnaissance company, following, caught up to us: it had the means to round up the prisoners and shuttle them off to the rear.

We moved onto the next ridge in generally good order, but then we lost momentum. German 88mm antitank guns and tanks took us under fire—at considerable distance, sure enough, but we began to take some damaging hits. And to confound the problem German high-angle artillery began to fall: artillery doesn't hurt a tank much, but it encourages the tank commander to pull in his head and button up. And coincident with all this my tank radio went on the fritz. Radios don't work well for me: this was not the last time that things went haywire because I lost communication.

We were bogged down in a highly exposed position. For me there was nothing for it but to climb down out of the turret of my tank and run around to about five of the tanks nearby—then to climb laboriously up the outside of each, banging on the hatch cover until I could get the commander to uncover and listen to me. Well, this is a poor way to issue orders, but we got moving and once underway restored our order and momentum.

The further we got into enemy territory the quieter things seemed to get, so we went quite a way—five miles, perhaps—stopping only as night began to fall, in a sort of natural bowl among the bare hills. We had outrun our following recce company and were quite alone, so we went into a laager formation—or to put it another way, we circled the wagons, put out outposts, arranged for sleeping by turn, and got some rest. To its great credit, the reconnaissance company caught up to us about midnight with our trucks, allowing us to replenish ammunition and gasoline. This we did at once and as quietly as we could—we rather expected the morning to find us surrounded by Germans. In the midst of all the activity the horn of one of the half-tracks somehow shorted out and put up a shrieking wail that would do credit to a banshee. This lasted for some five harrowing minutes despite the mechanics' frantic efforts to stop it—not an easy job because the wiring of a combat vehicle is armored with tubular steel and thus very hard to get at. We thought the noise would attract every German tank in the area.

First light found us alert and ready, but nothing happened, and as the sun rose we could see no enemy anywhere, even from the ridge of the bowl. My radio was working again. I was informed that the Germans had begun to abandon their positions on the flanks of our small (but deep) breakthrough, and I was given orders to continue movement northeast, which we did.

I forget the details of our progress other than that at one point in the afternoon, after a not-seriously contested movement of about 20 miles, I had to make a choice: to take a lowland route bound to be occupied and defended by the enemy, or to chance a rough upland route over some pretty steep hills, a route that would allow our small battalion force to penetrate deeply enough into the enemy rear to really embarrass him. I chose the latter, realizing that I might well put our tanks into some impossible terrain pocket and thereby out of action at a crucial time, to my everlasting disgrace. But it worked: we got through and down to a point overlooking a valley chock full of enemy support units.

Sometime during our labors a lieutenant appeared with a large bag of paper money: francs, in all a couple of million, printed in Germany. I assumed, I'm sure correctly, that the German administration in North Africa printed the stuff to pay their troops and even Arab commercial companies in their service. One of our patrols had scooped up a German paymaster. I took the bag and pretended, for half a day, that I was rich.

The Germans, by late afternoon, could not fail to see us, but were not in very good shape to do anything about us. As night fell hundreds of enemy machine guns, mounted on vehicles of every description, were pointed into the air and fired, apparently as a gesture of surrender, in anticipation of the end of hostilities. The night sky was resplendent with streams of tracer bullets arcing across the black sky. I remember my surprise at the widely varying colors of the German tracers.

We spent the night in the hills but next morning descended, in a single file of vehicles because only the narrow mountain track was possible to navigate, into the valley. I don't know why I was foolish enough not to think that I might encounter German units or individuals that hadn't got the word about surrender; in any case I got way out in front of the tanks in my jeep, driven by Corporal Scully, and soon found that we were in the midst of many bivouacked German units, all of which were fully armed, but none of which showed any signs of hostility or indiscipline. We regarded them with some trepidation—after all, the day before they would have killed us—but were happy to note that each unit displayed a white rag tied to a stick. We were intensely curious about them, and they, equally curious, stared at us. No words passed, no sound—all was silent except for the engine of our jeep. But the sight of Germans in the thousands began to impress me: I had a problem.

Very shortly thereafter I had the great good fortune to encounter, standing alongside the road, a German party headed by a major general: I knew him to be that because he wore a cap, not a helmet, and because he carried a fancy silver-scabbard dagger with the German double-headed eagle on one side of the hilt and the swastika on the other. There stepped forward, immediately, a German captain, who turned out to be the general's adjutant. He gave me a smart military salute, not that silly stiff-armed Nazi thing, and then in perfect unaccented English introduced himself and said that his general had volunteered him to become my assistant and interpreter in order that the German troops in the area could be moved efficiently to the proper prison camps. He told me quite pointedly that I should accept his services, inasmuch as some 20,000 Germans (most of them service troops) were in the general vicinity, and because he knew where all the German units were, where the German food dumps were, and most of the German commanders: they would follow his instructions implicitly, as he in turn would follow mine.

Well, this was manna from heaven. I accepted immediately, and after relieving his general of a beautiful pair of 10-power field glasses, about five times as well-made as the best American product and which I used constantly—with great benefit—for the last two years of the war, we got underway.

I wish I remembered this captain's name. He had served for a long period on the Russian front, where he said the fighting was much more intense and brutal than in Africa, and where the weather was equally unattractive. He had been wounded twice and evacuated back to Germany, and after recovering was sent to Tunisia. His superb English came from his upbringing in an international compound in Tokyo; his father was the professor of German at a Japanese university, and his best child-hood friends were children of American and British professors at the same institution.

My initial contacts with him were stiffly formal: I had seen too many dead Americans to get chummy with this fellow. But I had to depend on him for many things, and what's more, if in time of peace he had been a guest at your dinner table or mine he would have been exceptionally interesting, highly intelligent, very agreeable company. So the inevitable happened: in the course of three days of close association, mostly in an open jeep, we developed not exactly a friendship but a pretty firm ac-quaintance.

Inevitably we came to the point at which I asked him why the Ger-mans, by reputation a highly intelligent people, had accepted Hitler. He said that Hitler brought hope. Before his rise to power the German economy was a shambles because of the burdens inflicted on Germany by the restrictions and reparations specified by the Versailles Treaty end-ing World War I; moreover, the German as an individual character was the pariah of Europe, with whom few foreigners would do business. In-flation was such that a ride on a streetcar would cost maybe 10,000 marks—a laundry-basket full of paper.

He said that many Germans had suspicions about Hitler and his methods, but the fact remained that the Fuhrer had solved some very serious problems and, more important, had restored to the German people a measure of pride. Hitler, moreover, recognized Bolshevik Rus-sia for what it was: an enormous threat to Western civilization. If, he said, it should happen that Germany should lose the war (and he wasn't at all sure at that juncture that it *would* lose the war) Great Britain and the United States should take great care not to weaken Germany too much: we should recognize that Germany had stood, ever since World War I, as the eastern guardian of Europe against the threat of international communism. "When this war is over," he said, "you and your allies will have to stave off, with military power, the advance of the Soviet Union, and you must have a strong Germany on your side!"

That was pretty prophetic, of course, but my informant ignored the ignominious pact between Germany and Russia in the overrun of Poland. When I brought that matter up, he said Hitler was guilty of that and other terrible mistakes. On the other hand, I believe that he knew little of the concentration camps and nothing of the slaughter of the Jews. The full story of the Holocaust, we may remember, came to light only after American forces overran the camps, almost at the war's end.

After three days, in which time we managed to get all the prisoners in the battalion sector into the huge barbed wire enclosures some 20-odd (as I remember) miles away, my German captain and I agreed it was time he rejoined his countrymen. He gave me a pretty beat-up Leica camera for which he would have no more use—and which, incidentally, was of no use to me either—and then, at the gate of a prisoner stockade, he hopped out of the car, gave me a snappy salute, and said, "I shall see you, sir, on the steppes of Russia!"—turned on his heel and disappeared.

I'm glad to say that that last prediction was no good, but it is noteworthy that he identified the predatory nature of the Soviet Union more than six years before it became evident to the U.S. government.

Shortly after I parted company with the captain I came onto a small abandoned German food dump. I first gathered up a lot of huge—three kilos each, maybe—German cheeses, but then came across a stack of cans with labels, printed in French, "Coeurs d'Artichokes." That sounded so good to me, tired as I was of Army C-rations, that I abandoned all the good cheeses in favor of the artichoke hearts. That night I opened a can to go with my supper, to find that it and all the other cans were filled with horrible dirty-looking boiled carrots. The Boche, I decided, had had the last word.

The division settled in the area southwest of Tunis to rest, celebrate, replenish losses in both personnel and equipment, catch up on administration, and generally straighten itself out. To my surprise (because my service in the division had not been very distinguished), I was promoted to full colonel and assigned to the command of the 13th Armored Regiment. This consisted of three tank battalions, each (at full strength) of fifty-four tanks, a reconnaissance company, a headquarters company, a maintenance company, and a band: altogether, about 3,000 officers and men and a whole flock of tanks and ancillary vehicles. I felt rewarded far beyond my desserts.

You may wonder about the band. It was a damned fine band, and its playing contributed significantly to morale. And in combat it knocked itself out handling ammunition—160-odd tanks use up a whale of a lot of shot. The whole regiment loved the band.

This was also a time for superior headquarters to look us over administratively to discover our crimes and misdemeanors as respects equipment and its maintenance. A tank company in those days had seventeen tanks assigned, plus a couple of jeeps and two 2½-ton trucks for kitchen and supply purposes. Lacking was a three-quarter-ton truck for errands of a thousand descriptions. To remedy this deficiency our people over the last several months had stolen three-quarter-ton trucks from other manifestly less deserving organizations, taking care to provide the vehicles new serial numbers and unit markings. This process is known as the moonlight requisition. Anyway, at this time of reckoning we lost many of our precious three-quarter-tons.

That was disheartening, but there was some consolation in a coup I managed to engineer in the field of personnel. In those days it was always hard to get rid of a bum—the paperwork was endless and generally unproductive. The regiment at the time was manned almost completely by fine, battle-seasoned soldiers, but we had about thirty-five bums who wouldn't fight or cooperate or otherwise pull their weight. It would have been best to shoot them, but I knew that would cause trouble. I got word that a personnel convoy from the Replacement Depot was delivering a batch of badly needed replacements to make up for our battle losses; when all our incoming soldiers got out of the trucks we, in the general confusion, piled our bums into the trucks—they were willing enough to get out of a combat outfit—slammed the tailgates shut, and waved the convoy on. We never heard of them again.

At one point in this period of relative rest but very little recreation we decided to have a regimental gymkhana, but though we (despite heavy combat boots) could have races and broad-jumping and that sort of thing we were generally hampered by lack of game equipment—a few volleyballs but no soccerballs or baseballs. In partial correction of this deficiency I invented a game I shouldn't have.

The rules were simple. We laid out a field about half the length of a football field, and each team was composed of about twenty-five soldiers representing different tank or infantry companies. In the center of the field were twenty-one sandbags filled with what we had most of in Tunisia: sand.

The length of the game was set at 15 minutes. Each team lined up about 10 yards in front of the goal line it was to defend, and when the starting whistle blew each team rushed to the pile of sandbags and sought to move the bags across the opposite goal line. The winning team was judged to be that which put the most sandbags across. No additional rules seemed necessary.

Trouble was, when you are carrying a 50-pound sandbag you are not very good at running or anything else, and you are uniquely vulnerable to a tackle: it can break your bloody back. What's more, you are tempted as soon as you get your breath back to kill the tackler. Of course, we did not break any backs or arms or legs, or really kill anybody, but what we had was closer to murder than to sport—the participants shed as much blood as sweat. We canceled the tournament at the end of one game.

Our next orders were an extraordinary surprise: we were to move some 1,300 miles west to a camp that the 2nd Armored Division was vacating near the Atlantic seacoast of Morocco—for a period of recuperation and training. I don't know how many hundred thousand tons of men and equipment there are in an armored division, but there's a lot. The long expensive move, by train and road, made no sense to me, then or now, but there must have been a reason not apparent to us: maybe it was deemed politically desirable to maintain an American force in the west of Africa.

Our tanks made the trip by rail or by tank-transporter, but I went in my jeep, and I must say it was interesting: most of it farmland and orchard wrested from the desert. Some impressive mountains were visible to our south, and the road often touched the Mediterranean on the north. We encountered Arabs by the thousands, but were not greatly impressed either by them or their crummy little villages. Some Arabs had fresh eggs for sale, always one egg at a time, and others really delicious tangerines. Some cities, like Algiers, Oran, and Sfax, had attractive and apparently very affluent suburbs, but their Arab quarters (medinas) were crowded, dirty, and in some parts incredibly smelly.

A French general who had been captured by the Germans in the first part of the war, and who had then escaped and managed to get to Africa, was the new commander of the field forces of the Free French in Africa. They were allied, of course, with us. And in every city, town, and village along our route were new signs of red printing on white cloth, each proclaiming: "UN SEUL BUT: LA VICTOIRE!—*General Geraud.*" This of course was comforting, and indeed some of the best fighting units on our side in Italy, later, were Free French and French Colonial.

It was a matter of a few weeks before the division finally closed in a cork forest a few miles inland from the Atlantic coast. Pyramidal tents, each holding eight men, were provided us—a great luxury—and each man had a cot and a mosquito net. Officers were put into small wall tents. We went to work, hard, on maintenance and training. Training facilities were limited, but we made do and in the next several months we improved our tactics and gunnery and battle drill.

There were only a few additional events worth recording.

The Army is full of rumors, and one rumor was that because the division had fought extensively in Tunisia the presently assigned personnel were all to be sent home. Our men obviously weren't altogether aware of the size and nature of the war and didn't expect it to be long. The rumor was a strong one and took some time to be laid to rest. But after it was, there was no special resentment.

Another matter pertained to the sexual urge of healthy young males. The cork forest was not far away from the city of Rabat, whose population included some French but was mostly Arab. Division headquarters declared the town off-limits except for carefully conducted tours on off-hours. This may sound heartless, but the prostitutes of Rabat were riddled with venereal disease of all varieties; moreover, Islamic Arab custom dictates that a nonprostitute that consorts with a European or American will suffer disgrace and additional serious disadvantage.

As was true in nearly all Arab cities, most of the houses occupied by the French were outside a solid, high (maybe 10 feet), white-painted adobe wall that enclosed the medina, or native area. Our division headquarters established military police patrols at each of the several gates into the medina to keep Americans out.

Moroccan women in those days wore white cotton robes and head-cloths that literally covered everything but their eyes and hands. Some of our more inventive (and smaller) soldiers bought this apparel and thus disguised got through a gate to the medina and probably got venereal disease to boot. Stopping this was not entirely easy. It is true that if an MP lifted the skirt a bit he could tell from the feet whether the occupant was an impostor, but a non-Arab doesn't lift an Arab *woman's* skirt without running the danger of having a dagger stuck in him. And a 10-foot wall is not too hard to get over, with the help of your companions, if the incentive is strong enough.

But our main nonmilitary event was the locust invasion. Our regiment was camped within the edge of the cork forest, but alongside were several Arab cornfields. One day we noticed on the ground three or four thin columns (maybe three inches wide) of tiny grasshoppers coming out of a cornfield and heading west through our camp. The grasshoppers, so help me, were walking, not hopping or flying—they were obviously very immature. Cornstalks, a few yards back along the column, were covered thickly with grasshoppers. Perhaps 50 yards further back the grasshoppers were gone from the cornstalks but so were the leaves—all of them.

Well, said I, we'll fix these grasshoppers' wagon, and ordered that a foot-deep ditch be dug along the edge of our camp, and that used engine oil (which, with all our vehicles, we generated in enormous quantities) be put in the bottom. The grasshoppers deviated not an inch: they went down into the oil, died by the hundreds and thousands, and eventually formed a bridge—more accurately a dam—of grasshopper bodies over which the surviving millions proceeded right into our tent area.

Military tents are impregnated with a heavy and (when the tent is new) rather foul-smelling preservative and waterproofing, and ours therefore were not to the taste of a grasshopper. Wool blankets were equally unaffected. But mosquito netting! That was grasshoppers' meat and gravy: swarming over the net, they ate everything but the heavy cords that held the netting together. A soldier returning after a hard day's work had only the bare string outline of a mosquito net to sleep under.

We continued to fight with shovels and oil, not without some success, but the supply of grasshoppers was infinite; and when they got larger and began hopping they became much harder to block. The columns, of course, became much wider as the insects became bigger. The dirt roads we used were sticky, in crossing areas, with thousands of squashed grasshoppers. Then close observers (and by then we were all close observers) began to notice the development of wings, and next day increasing numbers of the little bastards lifted out of the columns and into the air. And soon, believe me, they were in the air in tens of millions— great insect clouds so thick that they literally dimmed the light of the sun. Insect contingents—maybe a million or so at a time—descended on one field after the other, cornfields being preferred; and on the fields they chose the cornstalks would be stripped of every vestige of green. And mighty few fields were spared.

The great flights moved east, toward the interior, and soon disappeared from our area altogether, leaving in their wake absolute devastation on most corn and other fields. To all of us who witnessed it it was an unforgettable demonstration of what the Bible means when it speaks of the plagues of locusts which, every seventeen years, devastated large areas of ancient Egypt. We didn't know our neighboring Arab farmers, but we were terribly sorry for them.

ITALY

7 While we were in the cork forest the invasion of Sicily was launched, obviously without our participation. Shortly thereafter we were alerted to move to the vicinity of Oran, there to prepare for further shipment to the combat zone—which everybody guessed, correctly, to be Italy. We made the trip to Oran via many trains and long road convoys, and settled down in the arid country southeast of the city.

About this time a group of our young lieutenants by some magic unknown to me got hold of a case of American beer, but the beer was, like everything else in the vicinity, about 100 degrees hot. So they took it to a pal, a P-38 pilot at Tarafoui airdrome south of Oran. The pilot put the case where a radio had been in the tail of his airplane and took it on his next assigned high-level reconnaissance mission. He was careful to come home at about 30,000 feet, where the temperature was well below freezing, and then set landing flaps and coast directly down to a landing, upon which a great (cold) beer party was had by all.

We continued training in all departments of combat, but were terribly hampered by the desert heat. A special trouble arose from the fact that the interior of a tank could get as high as 140 degrees, despite the effects of a small ventilator fan, and that temperature was more than the human body could stand for more than a half hour or so. So tactical maneuver with the tanks themselves was out of the question: we made do with map exercises and terrain rides in jeeps. Manipulation and sighting exercises, and actual firing with the two machine guns and the main gun of the tank, were all so onerous in the heat that we decided to make the training day start at about four in the morning and conclude when the sun got too hot, and then resume in the late afternoon.

We selected a firing range in some low desert hills, and in the afternoon before the first tank company was to engage in firing practice set up targets of U.S.-issue coarse white "target cloth" at ranges of from 1,000 to 3,000 yards. This was simple: we just draped the cloth over selected bushes sparsely scattered over the hills. The tanks with allotted ammunition were spotted on an irregular firing line the night before, and reveille set for about three.

We got up, had breakfast, got in the tanks, and waited for dawn to break so we could start shooting. Dawn broke as scheduled, but no targets: the Arabs had got 'em all, and would soon be wearing the cloth as burnooses, or those super-baggy pants, or kaffiyehs. Well, I had a solution: we set up the targets again, but this time targeted a machine gun on each one and loosed a few bursts of fire on each during the following night—a device sure to keep away the Arabs. The tank company as before got up at three ready to begin shooting and as the light improved started searching for targets—but there weren't any. In one or two places there was a little blood, but that's all.

We were reluctant to post guards way out there all night, for it would have resulted, probably, in some dead Arabs and perhaps some dead soldiers. So we settled for the less efficient scheme of putting out the targets just before daybreak.

U.S. forces inevitably killed Arabs accidentally from time to time in motor or firing accidents, and a standard reparation was set up. I've forgotten the precise figures, but they were something in this order: a dead woman cost us about $100, a donkey about $150, and a man about $200—all based on productivity.

According to higher headquarters we were still "over" in certain items of equipment. Among such items were .50-caliber machine guns. As pointed out in chapter 5, the German forces enjoyed a pronounced superiority in the air over the battlefield in Tunisia, in consequence of which our supply people scrounged from the ordnance supply depots a considerable quantity of these guns. Our mechanics devised a T-mount, made of three-inch iron pipe, which could be bolted to the bed of a half-track and which would hold two guns and a rough circular iron sight—not a very sophisticated arrangement but one that at least put a lot of bullets in the air against the Stukas and Messerschmidts.

But now, according to our masters, they were excess baggage and had to go. Fortunately, one of our people discovered that a destroyer squadron based in Oran harbor was having trouble with Stukas when they ventured near the coast of Sicily. We consulted with the right people and a deal was set up whereby we sold the Navy one pair of .50s and a pipe mount for 100 gallons of ice cream. This swap lasted until we ran out of guns, or the Navy out of ice cream, and was manifestly to the advantage of all concerned. Indeed, it probably shortened the war.

Sicily was eventually overrun, without our help, and a major landing was made at Salerno, south of Naples, with practically no participation by our division. Soon after that Naples fell to the Allied forces, and we were ordered to embark for Naples and to make a landing there over the docks. Pretty tame stuff.

The division made the trip in a great many ships over a period of a couple of weeks. I with a part of the regiment sailed on the *Orontes,* a passenger liner built for the Great Britain–Australia trade, and since I as a colonel was the senior American aboard I was made U.S. commander of troops. This was okay except for the fact that included among the troops were 504 nurses, divided among six or seven nurse units, and all of these women had trained at Camp Howze, Texas. Camp Howze was named for my father, by then long deceased, but Camp Howze was by reason of isolation, heat, and general lack of charm and recreational opportunities extremely unpopular with draftees and, certainly, the young nurses who were trained there. That someone named Howze would now have temporary command over them was regarded with manifest distaste by every young lady aboard.

I am a great admirer of the Army nurse as an individual, but I believe that females en masse can become difficult. When only an hour at sea, all 504 were crowded into the grand salon for instruction, by a British ship's officer, on how to use the inflatable life-preserver. He managed, by careful instruction, to get every nurse inside a preserver, and then in a moment of inadvertence cautioned them: "Remember, *don't* pull the cord, because . . . " My God, half the nurses jerked the cord instantly— the room was filled with a hissing noise and they were all jammed together in one solid pack by the increased circumference of their preservers.

On the day before we were due in Naples the ship's radio received the news, relayed to all aboard, that Italy—not Germany, of course—had quit the war. Despite anything that could be said to the contrary, some of the troops and apparently all of the nurses took this news to mean that there would be no further fighting in Italy. Loud were the cheers and great was the joy on the SS *Orontes*.

The 504 nurses had been crowded into the first-class accommodations on the ship and had their meals at the first sitting in the dining room. The officers aboard were at the second sitting. About seven that evening a steward appeared in the captain's cabin, where I was having a final drink with the ship captain and a British Army lieutenant colonel of World War I vintage permanently assigned to the ship. The word was that there would be no after-dinner coffee at the second sitting: the nurses, thinking that the war was done, practically speaking, had scarfed up all the little Spode after-dinner coffee cups and saucers as souvenirs.

After dinner I assembled the seven nurse unit commanders, each of whom held the rank of captain, told them that the war wasn't exactly over, provided each with an empty C-ration carton and bade them collect the Spode in their charges' possession. They got most of it back, but only at the price of further deterioration of my standing with the Army Nurse Corps.

It took some weeks for the division to be brought over from Africa and assembled in the farm and orchard land northeast of Naples. Of my service in Italy I'll omit much. There were many weeks on that peninsula during which the fighting occurred in such tightly forested mountain terrain that there was no possibility for the proper employment of large armored forces. Often we were consigned to the role of general reserve.

It will occur to the reader, quite correctly, that tank forces, as compared to the infantry, had it easy. The close terrain of Italy kept us often unemployed while the infantry divisions spent long, uninterrupted, and often punishing months in the line.

Frequent exposure to severe weather, especially in the mountains, and the constant danger of death or mutilation had a telling effect on infantry health and morale: it became a common saying that the only way out for the individual doughboy was to become a casualty. Infantry divisions were indeed rotated in and out of the line, but Allied overall strength level dictated about five months in for every one month out. Ultimately the North European theater—the invasion of France and the eventual attack on Germany itself—became the public focus of interest, but I venture to say that the fighting in Italy, for the infantry, was the toughest and most disheartening of the European part of the war. B. H. Liddell-Hart, the eminent British military analyst and historian, in his *History of the Second World War,* says that by January of 1944 U.S. Fifth Army losses in Italy had risen to nearly 40,000—a total far exceeding the enemy's, and had suffered a loss of 50,000 sick during the three months' duration of the bitter winter struggle in the mountains.

My regiment was initially camped on a two-level farm not far from Naples. Wheat was growing on the ground, and overhead on trellises about 15 feet high were hop vines. About three or four times a week, generally in the early night, German bombers visited Naples Harbor: we had a great view of the tracers of the antiaircraft guns on ship and shore as they rose into the sky—a strangely beautiful effect—and we could hear the crump of distant bombs.

The targets were the ships themselves and the dock area. Most of the American merchant ships were manned by merchant marine seamen, who were regularly given 125 bucks every time their ships were in an area under hostile aerial attack. The sailors on Navy ships in the same area, and Army soldiers on the docks, naturally got nothing in the way of extra pay—as of course they should not have. But neither should the merchant mariners—this war was everybody's business. Merchant seamen were not our favorite people, because they sometimes robbed new tanks being transported by ship of their tools—and that, under some circumstances, could result in an unnecessarily disabled tank and dead American soldiers. Not funny.

Mount Vesuvius, near Naples, was plainly visible to us, and one day it erupted, mostly with ash. An enormous grey plume stretched westward across the old city of Pompeii (itself destroyed by an ancient eruption of the same volcano) and out over the Bay of Naples. The coastal highway was so heavily covered with ash that traffic could not move on it, and several inches were deposited on the island of Capri, some 20-odd miles out in the bay. So sudden and heavy was the deposit of ash that several American combat aircraft, temporarily unable to fly because of maintenance difficulties, were destroyed at their base at Campo de Chino Airport not far away. The eruption lasted for weeks.

Because of the terrain, the war in Italy was largely one of position: German forces, established in one of a succession of natural defensive positions (usually a combination of mountain and river), would hold on until infantry, artillery, engineers, and assault boats could be laboriously assembled in sufficient force to chase them out, always at the expense of heavy casualties. Meanwhile, other German forces, with the aid of Italian forced labor, had selected and prepared another strong defensive position further north, and the scenario would repeat. Never was it possible for our tank battalions to be fully deployed on a wide front against major enemy forces because the Germans chose never to fight a major engagement in open terrain.

This diminished the extent of employment of the armored divisions (one U.S., one British, one South African, and two Canadian) in Italy, and that in turn reduced the number of our casualties. Perhaps this should have been satisfactory to us in our division, but it wasn't at all: we had enormous firepower and considerable mobility, were in the theater and ready to go. It dismayed us to realize that we weren't always useful.

Soon the U.S. Fifth Army, the senior U.S. command in Italy, together with our British, Canadian, New Zealand, Indian, Polish, Free French, and French Colonial allies—and I may have forgotten one or two—

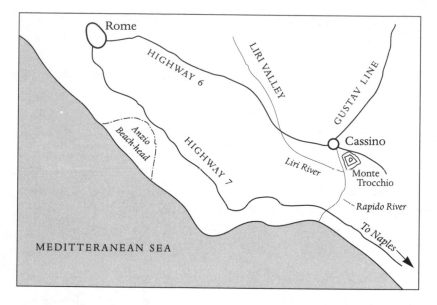

Map 2.

found itself thoroughly stymied by the enormously strong German defensive positions in the mountains stretching northeast and southwest from Monte Cassino, not far above Naples. This was the notorious Gustav Line.

The Allied command decided that the best way to break the stalemate was to coordinate an attack on the Gustav Line with an end-run over the sea, which U.S. and British naval and air forces in the Mediterranean now dominated almost completely. The amphibious operation was mounted principally in and around Naples Harbor, where an enormous quantity of shipping, including hundreds of over-the-beach assault boats, were gathered. The assault forces were to be put ashore on beaches not very far south of Rome, where no German forces were judged to be: if our people could get far enough inland to block two essential highways (No. 7 and No. 6—see Map 2), the western third of the German defensive position could not be properly supplied and would thus be very susceptible to an Allied attack. It was thought that the Germans might be thus persuaded to abandon the whole of the formidable Gustav Line.

Considering the size and complexity of the amphibious operation, it is remarkable that German intelligence did not anticipate it. Landings were made on 22 January 1944, in the vicinity of the small towns of Anzio and Nettuno, almost entirely without resistance, only one German combat battalion being (in rest status) nearby. Initially, four U.S. and British combat divisions and large quantities of supporting artillery and supplies were landed. Without effective opposition these forces, under the command of the U.S. VI Corps Headquarters (Lieutenant General Lucas) quickly established a bridgehead about 18 miles wide and 12 deep—and stopped of their own volition.

The German Fourteenth Army headquarters (General Mackensen) reacted with remarkable speed, and so did eight German divisions, up to then in general reserve, now dispatched to the beachhead area. There ensued four months of bloody attack, counterattack, and stalemate: the Allied forces (gradually increasing in strength) occupying a flat cultivated area by the sea, the Germans the low hills surrounding the flat area. The higher ground afforded the Germans the stronger positions and, to the discomfort of the Allied forces in the beachhead, excellent observation for their artillery forward observers.

A stalemate at the beachhead was not at all in the plans of the Allied High Command, under British Field-Marshal Viscount Alexander. Since the landings were largely unopposed for the first few days there was general astonishment when the forces in the beachhead bogged down short of accomplishing their objectives, the cutting of the two primary highways.

There has been much speculation about this, but although I was not involved either in the planning or the execution of the Anzio operation I arrived at a conclusion that I still hold: there had been an amazing miscalculation among the staff planners. The troop strength provided for the operation was ample to effect a landing even if it was opposed (which it wasn't) but not enough to hold against German counterattack a beachhead *big* enough to reach the objective: the highways.

So the VI Corps just ran out of soldiers. Instead of breaking the deadlock between the Allies and the Germans on the Gustav Line the Anzio end-run simply perpetuated it—at least for a time. It may be argued that the second front ultimately stretched German defensive resources so badly that a general attack by Allied forces (at this time in a slow process of strengthening) succeeded.

Now let me back up a bit. In my regiment we had been disappointed when we found that as part of the division's CCB we were to be excluded from the new adventure at Anzio. The bulk of our division was included, not in the initial assault but as a powerful reserve and counterattack force. It had a considerable amount of fighting after German forces first managed to encapsulate the beachhead and then tried, unsuccessfully, to break it up altogether.

On an ad hoc basis CCB's headquarters and mine, both still in the south, were combined. CCB was commanded by a brigadier general, so I was second-in-command, a not-too-satisfactory arrangement to me because my regiment constituted most of his strength: in addition to the 13th Armored Regiment he had only a battalion of armored infantry and an armored field artillery battalion. We were behind the infantry lines facing the naturally strong, heavily defended Monte Cassino, the top of which was crowned by a Catholic monastery. It was the strong base of the western half of the Gustav Line.

After at least one unsuccessful effort on the part of the infantry to take Monte Cassino, Gen. Mark Clark, commanding Fifth Army, the senior U.S. headquarters in the Mediterranean area (General Eisenhower and his headquarters having removed from Algiers to London), made the decision to use the 36th Infantry Division, erstwhile of the Texas National Guard, to force a crossing over the Rapido River and establish a bridgehead on the far side. Through this bridgehead our CCB, spearheaded by the 13th Armored Regiment, was to exploit the breakthrough by pushing as rapidly as possible up the valley (see Map 2) of the Liri River—*comparatively* open ground—while following troops of the infantry divisions shored up our flanks. It was judged that the salient thus established would, in connection with the landings at Anzio (to be made shortly after the attack across the Rapido), unhinge the western sector of the German position.

Of course we made careful plans, did map rehearsals, and polished up our techniques, especially in gunnery. But our part of the show never came off—because of the lack of success at the Rapido. That stream was typical of a number of what the Italians called "torrientes," mountain streams carrying off torrents of snow water in the spring. Like many of its brethren, the bed of the Rapido was higher than the surrounding cultivated area, so the river (which was only about 40 feet wide, but about three feet deep and very rapid) had to be contained between dikes about five feet high.

The strange configuration of the Rapido had developed over many centuries. Before humans intensified cultivation of the Italian valleys, a typical mountain stream, emerging into a flat valley, changed course repeatedly as its successive beds filled with the rocks and gravel it brought out of the mountains. An uncontrolled stream would thus distribute tons of gravel over a wide area, but as the Romans or their successors in Italy developed a greater need for farmland the streams were confined between dikes. The continuing buildup of the stream bed, however, required a gradual increase in the height of the dikes to confine the water. The result was an unusual obstacle—a stream whose bed was sometimes higher than surrounding terrain. Such a stream was often hard to bridge without flooding large areas, which in turn might serve to enlarge the obstacle.

The area short of the rapids was flat and somewhat heavily wooded, and on the far side had only scattered trees on a gentle slope leading up to a number of very low hills, where the German infantry had its positions. An initial setback occurred because the 36th Division's reconnaissance patrols and its engineers didn't check sufficiently for mines short of the river, wherefore some of the bridge pontoons were blown up as they were delivered to the bridge sites. As the bridges (the easternmost christened Harvard, the other one Yale) were being assembled and later when the infantry ran across them, German artillery and machine guns took the areas under fire with terrible result: my people on reconnaissance to the areas dubbed Harvard bridge "Chocolate Alley" for the number of bloodied corpses in its vicinity. Many other bodies washed down the river.

By early afternoon the attack had proven a failure. I went down to the wooded area just short of where the bridges had been, and which the

Germans were still shelling, to talk to two of the 36th Division's infantry battalion commanders. I was very unpleasantly surprised by what I heard.

Here I should interject that the comments that follow will affront many veterans of the 36th Division—and I live in Texas. I should therefore say first that the comments are based only on conversation with the two lieutenant colonels and therefore not on thorough investigation, second, that my comments really reflect not on the rank and file of the division but on division headquarters, and third, that I have earlier in this work acknowledged bad performance on the part of my own division, to which I was sentimentally very closely attached.

It is true, moreover, that the Texas Division had had its initial action in the assault landings at Salerno, further south in Italy, where it had been severely mauled. It is extremely unfortunate for an outfit to be too badly hurt in its first battle—far luckier are units initiated more gradually into the terrible trauma of combat.

Of all the 36th Division's actions I judged to be mistaken, I think the worst was the handling of the division's organic tank battalion—more then fifty tanks strong, each tank carrying a powerful 75mm or 76mm cannon, ample high-explosive ammunition, and a high-powered sight. That battalion was assembled in the woods short (south) of the Rapido, a few hundred yards from the river, prepared to exploit the breakthrough as soon as the infantry battalions had established a firm bridgehead on the far side. Well—I had *three* battalions of tanks prepared to do that mission. The infantry division, including its tank battalion, essentially had the job simply of getting us across the river, not of exploitation.

It didn't accomplish the first part. The two infantry battalion commanders I talked to told me that the number of riflemen in each of their three rifle companies, which had started that morning at about 110, had been reduced to about 18 to 20 men each; the rest were killed, wounded, or captured—mostly the last. I asked the battalion COs what the artillery fire plan was: each said, in effect, "Well, the artillery fell in front of us for awhile, but then it lifted." That, so far as I could tell, was all they knew about it, when each should have had definite knowledge of each planned artillery fire concentration and an ability, through accompanying artillery forward observers, to manipulate the fire to suit their special needs.

The tanks of the 36th Division's tank battalion, instead of squatting idly in the woods, should have been lined up behind the dike on the near side of the Rapido River, the dike providing them unusually good protection against enemy antitank fire. Each tank should have had the mission of "overwatching fire," which in this case meant spotting German machine-gun and rifle positions on the low hills about 300 yards north of the river: whenever an enemy machine gun or even a rifleman fired, one or more tanks should have blown it or him away—instantly.

In a word, so far as I was able to determine, six infantry battalions of the division attacked without the artillery and tank fire support they needed to succeed; with that support I'm confident they would have succeeded. In the years after the war many members of the Texas Division blamed Gen. Mark Clark, the Fifth Army Commander, contending that it was inexcusable to commit the division to an attack across a river and into a valley dominated, on its east, by a series of peaks affording the enemy excellent observation for the direction of artillery on the hapless Americans. It was necessary, they said, to take the high ground first.

That last is, of course, the conventional wisdom, but in this case I disagree. Clark (who in the course of the long campaign did indeed make several mistakes, in my opinion) in this instance was right: the attack could have succeeded if it were better executed. The contention that our forces could not have bypassed the high ground on their right should be considered in light of our ability to keep that high ground, with our immense superiority in artillery and combat aviation, harassed by high-explosive fire and blinded, for much of the time, by smoke. If our 1st Armored Division tanks and armored infantry had been able to run the length of the Liri Valley (not a certainty, of course—it would have been a hard fight), it would have broken the stalemate that lasted in fact for about three additional months. The Gustav Line could have been penetrated by the 36th Division, thus changing the history of the Italian campaign.

After the abortive attack by the 36th, the combined CCB/13th Armored Regimental headquarters remained on the reverse slope of Monte Trocchio, as I remember, a couple of miles from Monte Cassino, the latter with the abbey, an enormous structure, at its very top, and the village of Cassino at its base. The flat valley of the same Rapido River separated Trocchio from Cassino. Lots of troops were sheltering behind Monte Trocchio, so it became an occasional target of high-angle fire by German artillery, causing our headquarters a few casualties.

The top of Trocchio afforded an excellent view of Monte Cassino, the monastery (which because of the bitter fighting in its vicinity became very famous) and the town—all the defensive responsibility, it turned out, of the German 1st Parachute Division. Our point of observation permitted me and others to witness the frequent heavy shelling of the town and mountain slopes—but not of the monastery, which Allied intelligence at the time thought was probably not occupied by the Germans in deference to the Geneva Convention. We were also able to watch, through field glasses, the heartbreakingly unsuccessful attacks, a week or so apart, by a succession of infantry divisions, American, New Zealand, and Indian, on the terribly steep, bare slopes of the mountain.

Eventually the suspicion grew that the monastery, still (then and now) occupied by an order of Catholic monks, was also being occupied by German defensive forces in defiance of the international laws of war prohibiting the occupation, for military purposes, of religious structures.

To this day I am not sure whether the suspicion was a correct one—Liddell-Hart, the English military analyst, says it wasn't, and so do the Germans. But we were informed of an impending massive air attack, including date (15 February) and time; the information was provided in order that ground troops would stay clear of the target area. I climbed Monte Trocchio, with my 10-power field glasses along, to see the show.

It was an *amazing* show. I (and many others) witnessed what must have been the heaviest concentration of conventional firepower, in terms of tons of explosive per acre, ever laid down. On that small area the U.S. Air Forces dropped more than 400 two-engine bomber loads, and more than 300 four-engine bomber loads, of high explosive and napalm, all in the course of a few hours.

Each formation of bombers came on almost the same line of approach, often directly over my head, at a height (above me) I would estimate at no more than 1,000 feet. Using my glasses as I lay on my back

I inspected each flight of perhaps ten or twelve ships as it approached, and through the open doors of the bomb bays could see the bombs while they were still stacked in their racks. It was an awesome sight.

Much of the Cassino mountain, town, and monastery disappeared in the fire and smoke of the countless heavy explosions and napalm: it looked impossible for any form of life to survive. But some did: soldiers of the German 1st Parachute Division. Of course they were badly shaken up, had lost a substantial number of killed and wounded, and I suppose lost some to simple shellshock, but Allied infantry patrols investigating the situation after the bombers went home found the area still defended. It was only several weeks later that Gen. Wladislaw Anders's Polish Corps, at the cost of many casualties, took Monte Cassino.

Unfortunately—inevitably, I guess—some bombs fell short, killing some Allied soldiers. One British unit near the Rapido River erected a sign beside a huge fresh bomb-crater in their area: SAMPLE OF AMERICAN DAYLIGHT PRECISION BOMBING—"daylight precision bombing" then being the system advocated, practiced, and advertised by the U.S. Eighth Air Force in Britain in its role of bombing Germany. The British Royal Air Force, on the other hand, preferred strategic bombing by night.

In a foregoing paragraph I mentioned the Polish II Corps. Inasmuch as Poland was totally overrun by the joint—and criminal—efforts of Germany and the Soviet Union in 1939, I better explain how a Polish Army Corps came to be fighting in Italy in 1944.

After the 1939 victory of the Russo-German forces in Poland, many thousand Polish soldiers were imprisoned in the Soviet Union. One of the prison camps was occupied almost completely by Polish officers. For reason still obscure to this day, the Russians moved some 8,000 or 9,000 of these officers to the Katyn Forest, in Russia, and killed the whole lot, burying the bodies in mass graves.

A Polish general, Wladislaw Anders was a prisoner, but not one of those executed. He was, however, brutally mistreated and starved for nearly two years by his Soviet captors, and his three wounds went unattended. But one day his treatment dramatically improved and a bit later he was asked by the Russians if he would be willing to command a Polish army corps under overall Russian command, against the German Army—which Hitler by that time had used to invade his erstwhile ally. Believing that this would greatly improve the lot of the prisoners, and because he loathed the Germans as much as he did the Russians, Anders agreed. The Russians immediately provided him treatment for his wounds, comfortable quarters, and plenty of food.

But he found first that he was very short of officers, and inquired of the Russians where they were. He never got a satisfactory reply, and certainly not the information that the officers had been executed as they knelt, hands tied behind their backs, in front of mass graves.

Eventually the Russians told Anders that they would not be able to equip his corps, which we may assume consisted of more than 25,000 men. Quite amazingly, he asked for and was granted permission to move his corps out of Russia, and was provided trucks for the purpose. He moved all those men many hundreds of miles down to Iran and thence to Iraq, where they were fed, reconditioned physically, issued equipment (mostly British), and then transported to Italy, where they joined the Allied forces and fought gallantly and very effectively against the Germans.

This to my mind is a great story as well as a tragic one—tragic because a substantial majority of the Poles captured by the Soviets never got out of the USSR alive. And it also had a tragic ending: at the meeting at Yalta, in the latter part of the war, Roosevelt and Churchill granted Stalin outright ownership of a great deal of what had been Polish territory, and (presumably by implication) the authority which the USSR held, until 1983, over the rest of that country. When the war ended, then a large percentage of the men of the magnificent Polish II Corps were essentially stateless, separated from home and whatever family remained. Many of those who did go home, according to some Polish ex-officers whom I met in 1984 in Rome, were executed by the Russian occupiers, and many disappeared. And many, like the two I spoke to in Rome, remain still in Western Europe as permanent expatriates.

May God love the noble Soviet Union!

ANZIO

8 Eventually we received orders to rejoin our division in the Anzio beachhead. We obediently trundled back to Naples, loaded onto a variety of landing craft, and made the short trip up the coast without incident. The regiment was assigned an area in the approximate center of the beachhead and dug itself in—that last being a highly inappropriate thing to do for an armored unit whose strength theoretically lies in firepower and movement. But life in Anzio meant life under recurrent enemy artillery fire, and since we were informed that some weeks would intervene before we would leave the area we did the digging—even for our tanks, to keep the tracks from being blown off. We were encouraged in our digging by the sight of the Allied cemetery we passed, near the village of Nettuno, as we came ashore—it already contained over 6,000 crosses. More were to come.

When we had reintegrated into the division, worked out our counterattack plans and were otherwise settled, we set up our volleyball courts. Volleyball was the great military sport of World War II: one required no more than a net and a ball and a flat bit of ground. It was good fun and good exercise. We had our own court at regimental headquarters.

We at headquarters also had our own private battery of German artillery. Apparently only one battery had us on its firing chart, but that was enough to keep us entertained. Fortunately, one can generally tell from the sound of the guns (assuming they are close enough to be heard, not always the case) whether the fire is coming very near you. In this case we came to know instantly when we were the target, and since Willie the Hun frequently seemed bent on breaking up our volleyball game we dug extra foxholes near the court. When we got the magic signal we scattered like a shot-up covey of quail, each player for his own hole. It was not unusual for the ball to be still bouncing around when the first rounds came in.

In chapter 5 I spoke of the superiority of German tank and antitank weapons as compared to ours. Inasmuch as I am about to describe my own small adventures in connection with the breakout of the Anzio beachhead I think it desirable to bring the weapons situation up to date.

By this time the greatest disparity in weapons lay in quantity. Our superiority here was staggering: we plastered the Germans with so much more artillery than they could afford that the prisoners we captured referred to the "belt-fed" (ammunition is belt-fed to a machine gun) 105mm howitzer, our primary indirect-fire weapon.

It is curious to observe, sometimes, how English words can be perverted. When an artillery projectile bursts, the steel casing breaks up into jagged bits that fly out in all directions. It is these bits that cause casualties—wounds, often very severe, and death. In World War II we came to call these bits "shrapnel"—a total misnomer. Shrapnel was a device of World War I, in which one of the most common types of artillery projectiles was of a cylindrical tube filled with a hard resin-like matrix holding dozens of iron balls about three-eighths of an inch in diameter. The round carried a time fuse designed to explode the round in the air, ideally about 10 yards before ground impact: a charge in the base of the cylinder blew the matrix, which disintegrated instantly, and the balls forward out of the cylinder. The iron balls, forming a lethal cone as they came out of the cylinder, were called shrapnel.

Our rounds in World War II were more efficient, and cheaper to make. The bits of steel into which the casing disintegrates are properly called "fragments," not "shrapnel," but the word "shrapnel" somehow caught on, and fragments will be "shrapnel" forever onward. Ask any veteran of World War II.

On our side we had a generous number of light artillery spotter planes, which were extremely effective in spotting enemy targets and bringing artillery fire on them. The Germans had the equivalent, the Fieseler Stork, but in quantity only a very small percentage of our total.

We had more tanks, more infantry carriers, more trucks, and especially many more combat aircraft than they did. And the Allied navies ruled the waves and kept us well supplied.

Quality was a different matter. Our artillery was better then theirs, but not much. The German tanks were better than ours, though ours had improved through the introduction of the faster and therefore more effective 76mm gun to replace the 75mm. The Germans still outdid us with the Mark V Panther and the Mark VI Tiger tanks. Their antitank guns, which they employed in quantity, continued to be superior to ours, and the very low profile of the 75mm AT guns made them uncommonly easy to conceal. Inasmuch as we were on the offensive and they on the defensive a single well-placed, well-hidden antitank gun could under some circumstances kill several of our tanks before succumbing itself.

Both sides, of course, employed what we in our Army called "bazookas"—a recoil-less rifle light enough for a single man to fire as it lay across his shoulder. A 2.76-inch (in diameter) rocket came out the front of the weapon and pursued a somewhat wobbly course toward its target (habitually an armored vehicle) and in some cases hit it. A "shaped charge" in the rocket head was effective in penetrating the armor of a tank if that armor was not too thick.

The Germans took this device a step further in developing the Panzerfaust, which means "armored fist." Instead of a 2.76-inch warhead it had one about 6 inches across and therefore very much more powerful than our bazookas. Yet the launching tube was much smaller because the warhead was mounted on a stick: only the stick, then, fit into the launching tube. The result was an infantry weapon of very short range but of very great killing power, even against our tanks' heaviest armor. We held the Panzerfaust in great respect.

Enemy machine guns, also in plentiful supply, I would rate superior to ours because they and their ammunition were lighter than our

Brownings (which had not been improved upon for the past 15 years) and, I would guess, more reliable. They also had a vastly greater rate of fire. One could tell the nationality of a machine gun when it spoke. Each of our shots were distinct, "rat-tat-tat-tat," while their guns fired so rapidly that their sound was "bur-r-r-r-rp!" The sound originated an expression among our soldiers: the "burp gun," though the term itself actually referred not to the German rapid-fire machine gun but to their submachine gun, carried like a rifle. It had the same rapid-fire rate but a comparatively short range; though no more than a scattergun, it was deadly in very close combat.

Among the most annoying of German weapons were the mines. Mines are very effective defensive weapons, but they are next to worthless to the attacker, and we were the attacker. The Germans never changed from the antitank Teller (plate) mine; they didn't have to, because the Teller mine would cut the track (at least) of any tank we had, and sometimes kill or wound one or two members of the crew. It did dreadful things to lesser vehicles such as a truck or jeep—and to their passengers.

The Germans became really artful in the design of their antipersonnel mines, which were often used separately in areas the Germans thought would be walked over by Allied personnel, but which were almost always present in antitank minefields—in order to make the removal of the Teller mines by our engineers more difficult and dangerous.

A very prominent design was nicknamed the "Bouncing Betty." It was the size and shape of a lard can and was buried with its top just below ground level. Protruding above ground was only a very-hard-to-see little metal trigger. When this was kicked or stepped on, a powder propellant at the bottom of the can was ignited, throwing a slightly smaller can of explosive and metal balls—buckshot—about six feet into the air, and when *it* exploded a lot of people could get hurt.

Another design was the "shoe mine." This was a very small, flat, hard-to-see wooden box full of explosive; when one added a cap and left the box top half open a man's foot would detonate it—and in the process be blown off. The commander of the 4th Indian Division lost his foot to a shoe mine on Monte Trocchio. Perhaps our special hate for these things lay in the fact that they probably cost the German government no more than two bits each to manufacture, while you could lose your whole bloody foot if you trod on it and, if you were alone, bleed to death.

The Germans also had a miniature radio-controlled tank called the Goliath. Filled with high explosive, it was theoretically capable of being maneuvered into our lines and there detonated. Almost alone among German weapons, it was not a success.

Finally, I would mention the Nebelwerfer, which the British referred to as "Willie's Worst Werfer." *Nebel* means "fog," *werfer* means "thrower": "Fog thrower." As its name implies, it was originated by the Germans as a weapon to "throw" fat, round smoke canisters for perhaps three miles. On landing, the canisters were detonated by a weak explosive and thus released the chemical smoke—often useful for blocking enemy observation. To produce lots of smoke quickly the launcher had multiple barrels—maybe twelve or more. The barrels were fired in ripples: one at a time, but each following the other at a very short interval.

The Germans, unfortunately, converted some of the big rocket-propelled canisters from smoke to high explosive. So now each one, on landing, detonated with a most frightful crash, and the concussion alone could destroy a truck or kill a man at some distance. But the weapon had disadvantages: it had a very distinctive sound—"werp! werp! werp!"—as successive rockets left the launcher, and the projectiles came in so slowly that it was usually possible for a man who thought he might be on the target to walk to a nearby foxhole before their arrival. Of course, if he was on the target, he had to be sure to get to the foxhole.

VALMONTONE

9 At the time (late May 1944) of the breakout from the Anzio beachhead I would characterize the 13th Armored Regiment as being in very good order: we had had time to replace our battle losses, to get our equipment in shape, and to train. As an example of our good status I cite the fact that every battalion executive was qualified to serve as a battalion commander, and each tank company had about two or three officers to whom I would have entrusted the command of the company. That is real wealth, indeed.

The 1st Armored Division, the 3rd Infantry Division, and the 1st Special Service Force (SSF)—a special Ranger-trained U.S.-Canadian outfit of three small regiments—constituted the main effort in the breakout. Within our division the two combat commands, each with two tank battalions and one armored infantry battalion, attacked abreast. I was put in command of a reserve consisting of the remaining tank and infantry battalions and some odds and ends. The reserve was not intended for commitment as a unit: mine was to be a dispatcher's job, sending reinforcements up to the combat commands as directed.

Our attack echelons ran immediately onto quantities of antitank mines, despite the efforts of the engineers of the infantry divisions to clear them: one report was that more than 100 tanks had their tracks cut. The division commander told the reserve to fix 'em: we gathered up all available recovery vehicles, worked all afternoon, all night, and all the next day and got most of the crippled tanks back in action.

Aside from the mines there were few difficulties and all objectives were taken, partly no doubt because of the artillery battering that preceded the attack, partly because of elaborate deception measures that led the enemy to think we would attack in another area. There were not many fresh bodies where I was working on mine-damaged tanks; most were old German dead, black and so shriveled that in some cases they were no longer of interest even to the flies.

The next day things went even better. In the afternoon I got instructions to send my light tank battalion, which was in reserve, through our forward lines to take the day's final objective. I issued the hot dope to the battalion and company commanders huddled up alongside a tank while the enemy shelled the area with what seemed like special enthusiasm. This little tableau seemed to repeat itself throughout my participation in the Italian campaign.

About nine that evening I was directed by the division commander to take command of all of my regiment, less one company, and with it the next day attack to take the 4th Objective in CCB's sector, remaining under command of that headquarters. The accompanying map indicates that we were headed toward the mouth of a valley that led to Valmontone and the hitherto unreachable Route 6 leading to Rome (see Map 3).

Just as we started, a heavy high-explosive round blew up one of our light tanks and slaughtered its crew: the other lights scattered like flies and pushed on. They somehow encircled a Ferdinand self-propelled 88mm gun and forced its crew to abandon it despite the heavy armor it carried. I looked at it closely a bit later: our little 37mm guns had hardly dented its armor. I don't know why its crew bailed out—maybe the engine quit.

Both battalions were well handled and made good progress. The medium tank battalion (Lt. Col. "Bugs" Cairns) on the right came in sight of the road running northwest from Cisterna on which was a big German column of trucks and tanks; it had been wounded and stopped by our aircraft. Cairns completed the job, at the same time contending with other German tanks firing into him from his right rear. When I got up to the head of his force, which by then was all mixed up with the destroyed German column, there was carnage indeed: bodies and pieces

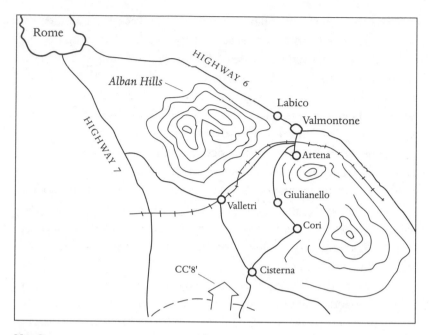

Map 3.

of bodies strewn among the scores of wrecked and burning vehicles. Our Air Forces added further excitement by strafing the entire area, including our part of it.

I should take a moment to explain that though I complain often about attacks on us by our own Air Forces, fighter aircraft inflicted a major part of the damage suffered by the German Army: if our Army could get the enemy out of his fortifications and onto the road during daylight the Air Forces could and did punish him terribly, and when *we* were its target we threw out copious quantities of yellow smoke grenades to identify ourselves, and the fighters would (usually) lay off. So the net results of Air Forces attacks were of great benefit to us: light damage on ourselves, heavy on the Germans. But that doesn't mean we didn't squawk about being shot at by our countrymen.

Our 1st Battalion (light tanks, Lt. Col. "Popsy" Carr) was making only slightly slower progress than the 3rd Battalion, but our regimental Reconnaissance Company (Capt. John Crittenden), which I had established on Carr's left flank to protect it and maintain contact with CCA, was having trouble. CCA itself was meeting all kinds of opposition—it had been stopped practically on the line of departure. In consequence, as Carr progressed, Crittenden was badly stretched, and finally reported that his contact mission was being carried out. This was all right, except that the contact was mostly with the Germans behind CCA.

Carr, too, was getting sporadic fire from his left; therefore, he gathered his tanks on the right part of his sector and pushed along against his private enemy, a little group of German tanks, thus stretching poor Crittenden more and more. In the late morning, several enemy tanks came into Crittenden from his left front: he engaged them and they retired. It was a puzzling situation: it seemed that the German was meticulously observing *our* boundary between CCA and CCB—he loaded the front of CCA, and as we progressed through our sector he merely turned his flank and shot at us.

Cairns, meanwhile, had progressed beyond the Cisterna-Valletri road, this being the German line of retreat from Cisterna. A staff officer of CCB reconnoitering Cisterna in the afternoon found it still partly occupied; about 1,000 Germans, thus cut off, surrendered shortly thereafter to the advancing troops of the 3rd Infantry Division.

In the late afternoon someone in a higher headquarters ordered me to reinforce Carr with one of the medium companies of the 2nd Battalion, which I had held in reserve all day. I felt that this was an improper thing to do, for Carr already had a tank-destroyer company attached, everything was going smoothly, and opposition was light. F Company was so dispatched, however, and with it went the 2nd Battalion Executive Officer. Shortly after his arrival, after he dismounted from his tank and went to see Carr, an incoming mortar round killed him. This was George Johnson, erstwhile commander of Company D and as gallant a tanker as I ever knew.

During the day my little command post (CP), consisting of nothing but tanks and jeeps, was shelled repeatedly but not very accurately—we had no casualties. Our regiment ended the day at the head of a salient reaching deep—about five miles—into the enemy lines.

That evening I went back to see Brig. Gen. Henry Allen, the commander of CCB, to tell him that we were obviously in a soft spot; I begged that the whole 1AD be diverted to our area to exploit what we thought was a definite breakthrough. Allen agreed, and relayed the opinion to Division, commanded by General Harmon. I was (a week or so later) given to understand that Harmon enthusiastically approved—and the book he wrote (*Combat Commander*) confirms this. I don't know for sure the reaction of VI Corps, but knowing General Truscott for the get-up-and-go soldier he was I'd bet my hat he forwarded it with strong approval to General Clark, who commanded Fifth Army. And Clark, if he got the recommendation, quite inexplicably turned it down, deciding that his main thrust, including almost the whole of the armored division, was to go the "short way" to Rome—west of the Colli Lazialli (see Map 3), a pretty rugged area otherwise known as the Alban Hills.

It was a dreadfully bad decision. It is a cardinal battle principle that in attack one should reinforce success, and we had success—admittedly because the Germans were somehow unable to get reinforcements into the Velletri Valley, as will be seen in the next few pages. Had the main force of the Fifth Army been sent the "long" way via Valmontone, Rome would almost certainly have fallen many days sooner, and the major part of the German forces in western Italy would have been trapped and presumably, though the battle would have been a bloody one, largely destroyed.

When I got back from CCB I tried to get some sleep in a ditch, but after an hour was called to the Division CP. I made the long dusty trip back, tired as I could be, arriving at about 2:00 A.M. I was told that with my 3rd Battalion and the division's 1st Battalion, 6th Armored Infantry, the 91st Field Artillery Battalion, and a company each of reconnaissance, engineers, and tank destroyers (TDs), I was attached to the 3rd Infantry Division under the name Task Force Howze (TFH). My 1st and 2nd Battalions and my recce company were to revert to the main part of the division.

I was sick about all this, being very anxious to continue the deal of the day before. However, I alerted my new outfit as best I could and set off to find the CP of the 3rd Division. I got there shortly after daybreak on the next day. I was reinforced by another TD company and the British 24th Field Regiment, Royal Artillery, and told that our mission was to lead the advance of the 3rd Division to Artena, permitting the division to reach that town (of about 5,000) without fighting. We were not to take the town.

We managed to get underway before the set time—1100 hours. But though this regrouping business may confuse the enemy I guarantee that it also confuses us: the key people in the outfit get no sleep the night before the next day's battle, and there are many difficulties in getting organized, the orders out, and the radio nets set up. In my case I had no sleep for two nights running.

Although many German vehicles, some still burning, littered the road, we met no initial resistance. But many German prisoners came into us out of the woods to our right, making it look as though we were doing a whale of a job. At one point when I in my armored car was just behind a tank I saw it depress its gun and fire three rounds into the wheat just in front of it. I thought this was imbecilic, but went ahead to see an emplaced 50mm German antitank gun with its crew strewn bloodily around. What was it waiting for? It could have destroyed two or three of our tanks. The crew must have been exhausted—and asleep.

At another point one of my experienced tank companies engaged in a pretty heavy firefight with an enemy that, so far as I could see, didn't fire back. The company was not supposed to go that way anyway so, now in a tank, I went ahead of the company and ran down the low ground in front of the "enemy" ridge without drawing fire. The company sheepishly went on about its business. There is no good excuse for this—one can only say that battle is sometime infinitely confusing.

We didn't take the time to sweep the valley, but investigated places we didn't go with fire from our main guns. One tank fired at a pile of stuff on the road near Velletri, to our left; it proved to be a stack of nebelwerfer ammunition, which was set afire. The rockets commenced discharging, undirected by launching tubes and therefore flopping about with a sort of fluttering scream all over the sky. They didn't explode when they hit, but I confess we paused a bit to see what would happen next. Also, my tank was engaged at one point by an antitank gun I've yet to see, but other tanks blew it up.

Shortly thereafter the company I was with (Company I, 13th Armored Regiment, under Captain Dempsey—I will mention this company several times again) was held up in its effort to get up the road running (via several bridges over shallow but precipitous valleys) north from Velletri, by heavy barrages of what we identified as 155mm fire from what we thought was American artillery. Tanks can survive light artillery, but a 155mm round can destroy one if it hits the top of the turret or back deck. I tried through my own 91st Field Artillery Battalion to get the fire lifted, but they could find no one who would admit firing it. In any case, I left that area to see what was going on elsewhere.

I had gotten only part way across the valley when my armored car, following the tank in order to make sure I had radio communication, smashed its radiator in a wadi and fell out of the column. Some bit beyond that, my tank's engine coughed and went dead, and my radio died with it. Because the engine would occasionally restart, and chuff along for a few yards, I wasted a lot of time with the tank—all of which time I was out of communication. Perhaps I should have abandoned the tank and walked to the road to my northeast in the hope I could commandeer another vehicle. But I might not have found one—the road was largely bare of traffic at the time. In any case I let false hope for the engine get the better of me, and the results were simply awful.

When the tank finally started we limped over to the road and found our armored infantry making the final clean-up of Germans in the woods, and received word that the tanks had gotten to Artena after a fight and where the infantry was mopping up: somebody told me later that there were 600 German casualties in the woods, but I was and am much inclined to doubt that. The Germans were still in Artena, up on the mountain slope; but its clearing was not in our mission. I was waiting with the infantry for my radio to be repaired. I thought the word had gotten indirectly to Cairns, the tank battalion commander, to get on across the main northwest-southeast valley with his tanks and attached armored infantry to cut Highway 6 in the vicinity of Valmontone. Eventually I got into an alternate tank (with its radio, however, also unworkable) and went up toward Valmontone to consult with Cairns.

About a mile short of Valmontone I found him, pretty heavily engaged—three of his tanks were burning within my view, and he was receiving artillery and flat trajectory tank and antitank gunfire. His tanks were withdrawing; I asked him why. He replied that he had repeatedly tried to get in touch with me (but, of course, could not) and then finally got a call from his artillery forward observer who said that he was told to relay to him (Cairns) my orders to withdraw to the railroad track several hundred yards to his rear. I have not the foggiest idea as to the origin of that message: Cairns and I agreed to investigate the matter later, but within 48 hours the forward observer was dead, so the mystery remains.

In any event, the area was pretty hot and Cairns said that he had engaged a large quantity of infantry (he gave the figure in many hundreds) coming into him from the east, as well as a number of tanks to the north. It was, moreover, late in the afternoon, and tanks in those days had not the equipment necessary to operate effectively in darkness. I therefore authorized him to retire south of the railroad, helped him get his tanks in and organized, and outposted with elements of the 1st Battalion, 6th Armored Infantry.

He had been within 600 yards of Highway 6 before he turned back. Were it not for my ineptness in respect to that confounded radio we could almost certainly have cut the road, the main artery of supply for the western end of the German forces in the south. Whether we could have held positions astride the road all night is another question; the Germans would have used all means available to destroy our block—and us.

I went back to the rear echelon of Cairns's command post, where I was told I had just missed seeing Maj. Gen. "Iron Mike" O'Daniel, commanding the 3rd Division—I was to await him there. So I did, staying all night, with not much sleep, in the smelly half-track. He never showed up.

After-action reports for this day, 26 May, show that the rest of the 1st Armored Division, along with the 34th, the 45th, part of the 36th Division, and, I believe, parts of the 88th Division, jumped off on the main front (the "short way") at 1100 hours and fought all day and ended up not far from the line of departure, and that the Operations Report (I think of Fifth Army) contains the statement, "It was a definite mistake not to continue to press along the Cisterna-Valmontone Axis"—on which axis my small outfit, despite my fat-headed performance as respects the dead radio, had progressed seven miles against very light opposition. The VI Corps log of incoming messages also contains this:

"Friendly planes have strafed our troops three times in the last two hours. Tell the Air Corps to get the hell out of the air, as we can get along better without the SOBs." There was more, but that language is enough to make me pretty sure that the author was our division commander, General Harmon.

The German Tenth Army operational log, an English translation of which I have read, includes the following for 26 May:

1. It reports the breaching of the German line near Cori and our advance to Artena (actually we got well past Artena).
2. It reports that the Panzer Division Hermann Goering (which had been brought up from Army reserve) attacked from a line west of Labico with the division objective being a line 2.5 kilometers north of Giulianello. This is undoubtedly what our tanks ran into south of Valmontone, but it was hardly a full division attack.
3. It says, "In order to master the situation in the area south of Valmontone" Commander-in-Chief-Southwest (Kesselring), ordered Tenth Army to transfer the following units to LXXVI Panzer Corps during the night of 26 to 27 May: a regimental group comprising two battalions . . . the 5th Projector Brigade with one regiment (of Nebelwerfers, no doubt); and two heavy antiaircraft battalions. These were 88mm antiaircraft/antitank guns.
4. It says, "At the earliest possible hour on 27 May [that being the next day] Panzer Division Hermann Goering [presumably reinforced with the above mentioned units] will attack enemy forces which have penetrated as far as Artena. They will drive the enemy back to the line: 4 km south of Velletri—2 km south of Giulianello—Rocca Massima."

That news frightens me even now. At this time the 3rd Division was just coming up the road—a long thin truck and foot column of tired infantrymen, with only our small force screening the front. If I'd known of the German orders I don't know what I would have done; in our ignorance of them, we just stayed where we were.

Early next morning Cairns called in to say that a considerable number of infantrymen were coming across the rolling wheatfields toward his tanks: could they be our own? I said no—to stop them, and jumped in my own tank, again operational, and went out to join him. The enemy was very visible, running and crawling through the wheat about 300 yards away. We slaughtered them—I imagine I killed half a dozen or more with my own tank gun. Why over the ridges in daylight? Needless to say, the attack, if that is what it was, collapsed.

The 3rd Division took all day to take Artena. The German poured considerable artillery into my people, with the tempo of the fire increasing gradually all day. I pointed out to the 3rd Division that its left flank and its line of communication coincided, for it had no infantry out with or even behind our I Co near the road. Later on, elements of the 15th and 30th Infantry Regiments were pushed out a little way, but I Co still stuck out like a sore thumb and was very vulnerable. I also requested that the division get infantry out abreast of our line in front, and establish contact with our right flank.

We picked up several members of the Hermann Goering Division that simply drove into us on motorcycles and in automobiles. They—one artilleryman, a battalion reconnaissance officer—were on a mission to select battery positions near Lariano, well to our rear. They were quite astonished to find us in this area.

In the late afternoon, when I was attending a division meeting at the CP of the 7th Infantry Regiment in preparation for the next day's attack on Valmontone, I got word that an enemy attack was developing. I rushed back to my CP, where I was told that a considerable quantity of German infantry was coming in on I Co, and our 91st Armored Artillery and the attached British artillery were cutting it up—but simultaneously enemy self-propelled guns had worked through the woods on Dempsey's left and set two of his tanks burning. About that time a terrific amount of enemy artillery came into the area of the 1st Bn 6th Infantry, which area immediately adjoined my CP—this was heavy-caliber fire. While this was still coming down, we got more trouble—again what we suspected was Allied 155 artillery laid down a terrific pounding on us; I am sure that it must have been a battalion concentration. I yelled to our 91st FA to use artillery communications to have this fire cut off; again no artillery headquarters would admit firing it, and it continued. The shells came over our heads only a few yards of our CP—I know it came from the south or southeast, and though it is remotely conceivable that it could have been German guns firing from the hills southwest of Artena, that seems highly improbable. At any rate, as a result of this double pounding the 1st Bn of the 6th Armored Infantry was badly cut up. The battalion commander, Jack Deffenbaugh, was killed, and killed also, at their radios, were all three of the artillery forward observers in the area—including the one that had given Cairns, the day before, the "relayed" message alleged to be from me. At the CP, now a combined one of TFH and the 3rd Battalion, all telephone wires were shot out and tree limbs and shell fragments showered into the sunken road.

An enemy infantry attack now came into our position, but it was thrown back, partly by our artillery and partly because of the gallant fighting of the wounded 1st of the 6th—and partly because of the mysterious artillery barrage, from somewhere, still coming in. In the midst of this I decided to move my CP back—we could maintain no wire, and not even liaison officers could get to us where we were. So we moved back about 1,000 yards, very slowly. I issued orders to I Co, which had already been chased back a short ways, to retire about 1,500 yards, to refuse the vulnerable left flank. Gradually the activity died down, with our main position intact, and I was told that at least part of one battalion of the 7th Infantry had come up abreast of us on our right.

The German report for 27 May boasts that the Hermann Goering Division reached the railroad line and highway west of Artena. So it did; that was our line of resistance, and we held it. More significant are these statements, quoted verbatim:

The Army considers the following to be the intentions of the enemy: First, to make a breakthrough in the area between Aprilia and the Albanese Mountains . . . , second, to make a breakthrough towards Valmontone with the bulk of its forces, in order to surround the southern flank of the Tenth Army, and to cut off their communications to the rear. . . . It is the main mission of the LXXVI Panzer Corps to drive the enemy back to the Velletri-Rocca Massima Line, which he has penetrated in the vicinity of Valmontone. This is essential.

On the other front, the armored division did maintenance work in preparation for further action, while the five infantry divisions continued a fight that made little or no progress.

At daybreak of the twenty-eighth I moved the CP forward again to a spot where we were shelled intermittently all day long. I sent I Co back to occupy its original position, as a matter of principle; it accomplished this without opposition. General Truscott visited me during the day and told me to pull out the 1st Bn of the 6th, which had had heavy losses; this battalion and the 91st Field Artillery both reverted to the Armored Division. I saw three 6 × 6 trucks coming back heaped with the dead.

The enemy attack had convinced the 3rd Division that our attack to take Valmontone was to be no pushover, so plans for it to be made this day were canceled. Accordingly, the 3rd Division took over our positions and dug in, and with the exception of two platoons my outfit was permitted to withdraw to a rear area to do needed maintenance.

The German report for the twenty-eighth says, among other exhortations for extreme effort, "The Commander-in-Chief, Southwest, will hold central Italy and defend Rome under all circumstances. . . . All available reserves will be concentrated in the area of Valmontone, in order to stop the advancing enemy and repel him towards the south."

We spent the twenty-ninth in the area around Giulianello, where the Hun was still successful in reaching us, sporadically, with a 170mm gun.

On the other front there was still no significant change. The bulk of the armored division was recommitted on this day, and the operations report makes this comment, "The day's attack was costly and fruitless. Poor coordination between . . . elements of the 1st Armored Division and 45th Infantry Division permitted enemy infantry and tanks to infiltrate behind the tanks and attack friendly infantry in the flanks and rear. Our losses [in tanks and personnel] relatively high."

From the 1AD operations report for 30 May: "Gains . . . were negligible, vehicular losses heavy. . . . We had . . . inflicted only very light losses on the enemy." And for 31 May, "Opposition was determined, as on previous days. After advancing 500 yards all along the line, elements failed to move further. . . . 45th Infantry Division took command of the division sector. . . . Relieved tank and Infantry elements withdrew to assembly areas to perform necessary maintenance and reorganization." I give these unhappy reports only to indicate the ferocity and great strength of German resistance in the Western area.

On the night of 31 May TFH again took position in the line, on the left flank of the 3rd Division, and at 0500, 1 June, the combined attack jumped off for Highway 6 and Valmontone, the TFH objective being Labico. On the previous day, the 85th Division had moved across the rear of the 3rd and had entered the Colli Lazialli and advanced north over the hills.

Our attack went quite slowly, and, on the whole, poorly. Replacing the 1st Bn of the 6th Armored Infantry was the 1st Bn of the 7th, of the 3rd Division—and although I think these doughs did very well, I don't believe our tanks cooperated as skillfully as they should have. Artillery support was adequate, the 59th FA replacing the withdrawn 91st, and the British field regiment was still with us. Our tanks were overcautious, I think, although I must say they took considerable casualties from enemy snipers on the steep hillsides, who shot several tank commanders through the head.

I had the personal pleasure of doing a considerable amount of shooting from my own tank, in support of elements in front that were tackling the successive ridges. We had trouble and casualties from enemy mines; we knocked out a few antitank guns, killed a number of infantry, captured a fair bag of prisoners, and received a lot of enemy artillery fire, which did damage to the infantry but not to the tanks. Three of our tanks were hit and burned by solid shot. By nightfall we had come abreast of the 3rd Division infantry, and that's all. I was disappointed, for I had hoped we might make a deep penetration.

However slow we were, the 3rd Division with our help must have ruptured the position of the Hermann Goering Division, for next day things were much easier and we got to Labico. While the tanks reorganized near the railroad, I sent the Rcn Co to find a route over to the highway northwest of the town; an enemy tank killed one of the reconnaissance tanks plus an assault gun before we chased him out. The 3rd Infantry Division had Valmontone.

During the night of 2 June, my TFH was relieved from attachment to the 3rd Division and placed directly under II Corps, which had by this time taken over command of our front from the VI Corps. We were further reinforced by the 756th Tank Bn, commanded by an old cavalry friend of mine, Glenn Rogers, and by the 1st Bn of the 349th Infantry, and by a TD company. I got orders to take this outfit to Rome as quickly as possible, but about midnight a lieutenant colonel from the 88th Division arrived to give orders to Roger's 756th, which he said was attached to his division on an order of a later time date than had my orders. I forget the details, but somehow I was convinced that these new orders were right, and gave in. Naturally the 88th Division told Rogers to go straight to Rome, and the 756th tanks and mine were accordingly interlocked, bright and early next day, in a tight embrace on Highway 6. General Keyes, the commander of II Corps, flew over in a Cub and dropped a message: "Howze—get these tanks moving!" I located Rogers, and we conspired; he agreed to put himself under my command. So I shunted his battalion, with the 1st Bn 7th Infantry attached, onto roads south of the highway and we started moving, Cairns and Rogers abreast, and the attached infantry following behind.

The 756th had more difficult country, and both battalions had considerable opposition from German delaying forces that fought us, sporadically, all the way. An air observer told me later that forty German tanks were pulling back in front of us, a fact that would have scared me silly had I known. From time to time I became dissatisfied with our speed, and the caution with which the tanks would size up each bit of terrain before going over it—so I would issue orders to put a platoon on the road and barrel down it at 10 miles an hour. I would watch this platoon—in a few minutes the lead tank would stop and burst into flames. Here again was a dilemma —it was difficult and unpleasant to dispatch an element on what amounted in part to a suicide mission, but on the other hand such a maneuver frequently resulted in our gaining 2,000 or 3,000 yards in 30 minutes, at the cost of a single tank. I hated to see the dead men, but I think nevertheless that the system, though not always in use, paid off.

On the whole we made great progress, and outran our following infantry. Because we didn't bother to clean up bypassed territory, the troops in rear had some pretty hot times—my own CP, which I did not see all day, was pretty badly beaten up by enemy tanks that fired into it from its rear—and it was a couple of miles behind us. I remember also getting very irritated about some footloose brigadier general who lopped off one of my attached infantry companies and sent it out to clean up a German pocket that was firing on the road from the north. I realized that our flank was wide open, but I felt that the Germans were too disorganized to attack in the short time that my columns took in getting past, and I felt that following infantry divisions could take care of themselves, which of course they could.

At one point Rogers was pretty much pinched out, so I passed him behind Cairns and put him on the north; since both my flank and rear were now exposed I emplaced a wandering TD company, not attached but lost and enthusiastic, at our right rear to protect us, and when infantry came up later I attached a company to the TDs.

Cairns, meanwhile, had come up hard against German resistance in a large group of factory buildings, and with his accompanying infantry was busily engaged. Rogers's tanks had moved rapidly in the north to secure all the objectives that I had assigned him: these were the crossroads of the extensive road net, and bridges across the Aniene River: most of the bridges were destroyed, but we got one intact, and outposted it on the far side with tanks. Rogers's tanks got into the gravy two or three times, cutting up and capturing German columns—the bloodiest mess was caused when he encountered a column of horse-drawn artillery. We also had ineffectual long-range flat trajectory duels with enemy on our north. Our own aircraft strafed us three times, although we were very meticulous about reporting our positions. They strafed my little group of CP vehicles once: I remember with great clarity shifting rapidly from one intersecting roadside ditch to the other as the five P-40s came in from one direction and then the other, in spite of the yellow smoke candles that we set off.

Sometime during this day I remember being with Glenn Rogers, waiting for tanks to come up—or some such thing. At any rate, over our heads all sorts of bullets and fragments were flying, and as we cowered there in a ditch Rogers, a student of literature, said, "You know, I wonder what would Walter Mitty do in a case like this?"

In another incident my jeep driver, Corporal Scully, went off the road, with only his pistol with him, into a bunch of scrub trees to relieve himself; he came out with about twenty German soldiers, their hands up. The noise of our nearby tanks made them peaceable.

In the late evening the SSF came up according to Corps orders and took over our sector, and we came under its command. We were delighted, for the problem now was to get through the built-up environs of Rome, and that was an infantry job. Gen. Bob Frederick's three infantry regiments formed a line beyond our tanks, and we felt safe and comfortable indeed. General Frederick made his CP with mine, in a brick house near a crossroad, and no sooner had he come in than the German Luftwaffe took over the missions of the U.S. Army Air Forces and commenced a long harassing bombing and strafing attack on us, setting some vehicles afire. After this Frederick remained busy getting his outfits into position, but I decided to get a little sleep; I was just settling down, however, when Glenn Rogers brought me, as a personal present, a German colonel picked up by his people. I was too sleepy to object, and Rogers departed. Shortly thereafter the Luftwaffe reappeared, and really worked over our crossroads, and the German colonel and I were chased around and around the building as the aircraft changed directions time after time. The German spoke no English and I no German, but we worked very well together in figuring out where to go next.

Meanwhile the western front was still in the south—the armored division attacked during this day, but progressed only a few kilometers. The enemy had begun to weaken, however, for on the night of 3–4 June all sorts of plans were set up for a race to Rome.

Next morning, General Frederick took my 3rd Bn of tanks, and with his 1st SSF Regiment took off down Highway 6 for Rome. Very shortly he got into a pretty heavy fight, and the tanks were at a great disadvantage because of the enormous number of houses. I stayed at his CP, awaiting orders. Generals Clark (Fifth Army) and Geoffrey Keyes (II Corps) came by, and were present when Rogers on the north flank called in over the radio that he was again being attacked by friendly aircraft, and had had some infantry shot off his tanks. I, of course, had yelled about this matter before, on several occasions, but this time I was able to point out to both the Corps and the Army commanders the diving aircraft—and this time we got real action, and no further attacks. I believe it was at this time, too, that I suggested that I be given orders to cross the Aniene to cut off part of the German retreat out of Rome, but the suggestion was disapproved because it was out of the sector of II Corps.

I fiddled around all morning, but finally decided to jump the gun a bit. I had twice sent up to Frederick for permission to organize a force to go into Rome astride the railroad on his north, and even went so far as to send word to the troops to get ready. I finally asked one of Frederick's own staff officers to suggest this attack, and this time got the go-ahead. I had already alerted the commanders, and so when I arrived at Tor Sapienza Rogers of the 756th Tank Bn, Akehurst and Walker, commanders of the 2nd and 3rd SSF Regiments, and Isenhour, commander of the 1st Bn 7th Infantry, and the proper artillerymen, were assembled and awaiting orders. There was no time to get too elaborate, and we finally jumped off (at 1530) with the 2nd SSF Regiment in the lead, followed immediately by the medium tanks; each infantry platoon had an assigned tank section. Immediately resistance was encountered and, no matter what its character, the infantry whistled up a tank that blasted it out. This attack made fine progress against considerable resistance; we lost two tanks, but knocked out five plus some guns, and killed and captured a good bag of prisoners. One battalion of Walker's 3rd SSF Regiment I had broken up into little patrols of about platoon strength; each one was armed with a map and typewritten instructions in Italian, which I got a local Italian civilian to write; these instructions ordered any Italian that might be picked up by the patrol in Rome to lead it down to a specified bridge over the Tiber. As soon as the attack reached the heavily built-up sections of Rome (where I thought the enemy could not hold a continuous line) this battalion was turned loose; getting into the city, most of the patrols were led accurately and directly to the bridges, some moving by taxis and wagons—the scheme worked fine.

Cairns and Frederick had, I believe, encountered the strongest opposition, and had fairly heavy losses in tanks and personnel. For one, the commander of one of the SSF Regiments, Marshall, was killed by a 20mm projectile through the forehead. Another incident worthy of mention is that of a lieutenant of the 13th Armored Regiment who finally led his platoon to a small knoll only after losing two of his tanks in the attempt; just as he reached the knoll he saw eight enemy tanks pulling out on a sunken road not 50 yards from him—and he couldn't depress his guns low enough to engage them. I didn't hear him, but I was told that his screams over the radio were a classic of dismay and frustration. Fortunately, three of the enemy, two Mark IVs and a Tiger, made a wrong turn a little later and were set ablaze.

As soon as I could I gathered a company of Rogers's tanks and took off, in the rapidly deepening twilight, for the center of town, with the intention of reinforcing the infantry on the bridges. The streets were completely empty, doors and windows shuttered tight. Finally, because I was going too fast in my jeep, the column became separated, and I with two vehicles waited while Rogers went back to pick up the lost tanks. Presently a darkened window opened, and apparently someone heard us talking—there was a scream "Americano!" and a goodly portion of the population of Rome rushed out and threw themselves upon us with shrieks of joy and altogether too many kisses. We fought this attack off for the rest of the night—I shall not go into boring detail, but I can say it was both gratifying and annoying. We finally got to the bridges where we found our infantry patrols and, making all secure, went to sleep in the center of Rome.

With excellent timing, the Germans gave up their positions against the American main effort south of Rome. Elements of the 1st Armored Division got to the bridges about midnight.

After the fall of Rome, there ensued considerable discussion as to who got into the city first—who won the race. I do not believe the argument was a good one to foster. I remember that a corps staff officer called me up, some days later, to ask when we got in—I replied, about 6:30. He said, "Well, that makes you first. The 88th Division got in at 0830." I had to say then that I meant 6:30 in the evening, 1830 hours. Of course, my hour was given as the time we had free entry into the city, and I suspect that the other hour was the time at which some patrol reached the city limits, which our forward elements actually got to on the evening of the day before. Certainly we had a first-class fight running into the late afternoon of 4 June—mostly within the city limits, true, but denying us entry into the center of Rome. After our people were on the Tiber bridges, elements of the 88th arrived and began shooting at us; they shot my S-3 Air through the knee with a machine gun and ended the war for him; they shot General Frederick twice (minor wounds) in the arm; and they shot through the shoulder an unattached engineer colonel who had been giving me unsought-for advice all day, thus saving me the trouble.

A second point has to do with the Air Forces. I have mentioned, as matters of actual, unadorned fact, the number of attacks delivered on our own troops. There were systems worked out later which lessened the number of these occurrences. And here I must say again that the Air Forces by and large did a great job in tearing up German columns after they got moving, and had no small part in the success of the battle.

Next I must reiterate my belief that had the whole armored division been committed via Valmontone we should have been in Rome many days earlier, and the bag of prisoners cut off in the south may have been enormous. I must also acknowledge that I make considerable claim for the accomplishment of my troops. Perhaps I can alleviate an unfortunate impression on the reader by saying that this was one of the more successful jobs that we did—we accomplished a lot, despite several errors, on this occasion, but I have given you other instances in which we did poorly and got our ears pinned back.

COMBAT COMMANDER

10 After the fall of Rome and the rapid German withdrawal across the unforested, unmountainous area just north of Rome, the division was assembled, behind infantry lines, in the vicinity of Lake Bracciano to reorganize. I'll spare the reader the details: it is enough to know that the three regiments—two of them tank regiments, the other armored infantry—were disbanded in favor of the formation of separate battalions: three tank battalions (each of three medium tank companies and one light tank company) and three armored infantry battalions. The division artillery did not change more than superficially. Three headquarters served directly under the division: Combat Commands A, B, and R ("Reserve").

The compositions of the combat commands were variable. That, in fact, was the idea behind the reorganization—in all battles thus far experienced it had been necessary to break up the regiments, assigning their battalions to the control of the combat commands or to ad hoc task forces. The new organization made the process easier. But it broke up, as a tactical unit, the 13th Armored Regiment, of which I and all its members were so proud. It was a great personal disappointment to me.

As a colonel I was to spend the rest of the war commanding a Combat Command (there being only two brigadier generals authorized) or as a task force commander.

During the process of reorganization I thought it a good idea for the

13th Armored, before it disappeared as a combat unit, to have one last farewell formation—a salute to our officers and men thus far killed in action. We found a small, rocky, flat-topped promontory jutting out into the Tyrrhenian Sea, and on its top the regiment was drawn up, colors and guidons flying, in dismounted formation. Our sturdy band, its members' hands cut and bruised by the handling of incalculable amounts of ammunition, played appropriate music, including the regimental march, and the chaplain conducted a memorial service. To all this I added what I considered to be an appropriate tribute to fine fighting men.

Then we had Taps and the gun salute—not by a squad of riflemen but by a platoon of five tanks firing their main guns. Each of the three traditional volleys went off with a highly satisfactory bang. The high-explosive projectiles, each with a time fuse cut precisely to three seconds, arced out over the sea, where they burst simultaneously in a perfect row, again with an impressive crash. I think we all felt this to be a highly appropriate farewell to gallant tankers lost in the defense of freedom.

Although I just wrote "lost in the defense of freedom," I really challenge that familiar, routine phrase, at least in part. I came to believe during the war that soldiers don't fight and die primarily for country or freedom or other lofty purpose—they enlist for those reasons, perhaps, but after training and a little experience in combat they fight for their buddies, their squad or tank or gun crew, mostly, and then their platoon, their company, and maybe their battalion—in descending order of importance. Even the regiment is too remote, and the division much more so. As "team spirit" drives a successful football team, so does intense loyalty—a mutual dependence in circumstances of extreme danger—make combat soldiers fight with valor and great energy. They don't tell themselves to be valorous—they just clobber those SOBs (the enemy) that interfere with getting the job done.

This, in my opinion, is the real explanation why some American units fought so much better than others. It is quite true that first-class officer and NCO leadership is essential to the creation of an effective combat unit. But if that leadership is good it not only trains the unit well in the tactics and techniques of combat, it also fosters small-unit cohesiveness and continuity.

It is interesting to note that while the American Army sought to keep units at strength by frequently replacing losses, the Germans, whether by necessity or intent, allowed their units to fall well below strength. One can't be altogether sure, but that may be why the German Army fought so well—while squads or platoons grew numerically weaker, they maintained a very close personal association. When divisions got *too* weak they were withdrawn from the line and given a full schedule of replacements and time to retrain.

I shall not address the events of the summer and fall of 1944 in any detail. When the enemy moved, we in our division fought his rear guards until he again went to ground in a strong mountain defense position. As usual in rough terrain, the infantry divisions did practically all the work in breaching major German positions. When we were employed, it was in "pursuit" through the hilly, forested terrain of Italy in circumstances that sometimes allowed a small German delaying force to bring more guns to bear on us than we could on it: two or three German tanks in position awaiting the appearance of our lead tank as it came around a bend—while perhaps twenty of our tanks stood helplessly unengaged behind it. We were, of course, superior to the German in artillery; but he could usually position his delaying detachments—on a reverse slope, or in a deep draw—where our howitzers could not reach them. And artillery is largely ineffective against tanks anyway.

The enemy delaying force habitually reinforced its position with antitank and antipersonnel mines—not many, usually, but enough to complicate matters and slow us down. And kill some of us.

German demolitions were almost a standard feature. The least difficult for us were large trees—sometimes many of them—laid expertly across the road by explosive cutting charges. If the terrain was right the biggest delay was inflicted by a blown bridge or a crater that simply removed the road as it ran laterally across a steep hillside.

In the general circumstances of our "pursuit" (given our glacial rate of progress I can't help but put the word in quotes), we often lost the lead tank, which usually carried a platoon leader, in each of our several columns. In each tank hit by an armor-piercing round our human casualties were two or three, of which one or two would be killed. All movement would come to a halt while impatient commanders in ascending order of rank gravitated to the head of the halted column to investigate the cause of delay. In many cases we had to wait for our infantry, and often our engineers, to help resolve the situation—upon which everything would surge forward for a mile or so to another manned road block.

About a dozen years later our Army began to utilize helicopters in its tactical procedures. How even a handful of those machines would have altered the history of the Italian campaign! With a few of them at our disposal we could have avoided being surprised by enemy ambush, and whenever we encountered a roadblock we could have, at once, emplaced riflemen with antitank weapons and mines *behind* the German delaying detachment, thus either forcing its very prompt withdrawal or, more commonly, its destruction or capture—this sequence to replace the historical one in which enemy delaying detachments could usually be extracted from each position and thereafter used again and again. Moreover, our comparatively rapid forward movement would have afforded the Germans much less time to strengthen their blocks by those damnable demolitions—further increasing our speed.

And finally, that speed between major German defensive positions would have cut drastically the time available to German infantry divisions to fortify those positions, making them far easier for our infantry to breach. It is no exaggeration to say that the presence of a modest number of helicopters, on our side but not on the German side, would have cut the length of the Italian campaign by half, and greatly reduced the toll of dead and wounded.

As before, in southern Italy, the summer and fall of 1944 afforded no opportunity for a substantial number of our tanks to be deployed in line of battle against an equally deployed enemy. In our forward-inching progress, already described in general terms, we profited (when profit was to be had) by occasional German error. Once, for example, the largest part of the sizable German delaying force on one road made a wrong turn as it withdrew: most of an infantry company and a couple of tanks went up a steep road leading to a deserted Italian resort at the mountaintop. We followed them up, and after a short exchange of fire they surrendered—a nice haul. Sometimes, also, we found ourselves on a road paralleling, across a deep narrow valley, one on which was a retreating German column: with our great advantage in tank guns we could pound such a target unmercifully, breaking up the column and sometimes compelling the surrender of many men and vehicles.

Sometimes our reaction was, however, a bit less than optimum. Late one afternoon one of our tank companies, to which was attached a platoon of four tank-destroyers, climbed (without opposition) a finger ridge leading to a long, higher, wooded ridge along which ran a winding dirt road. The tank and TD crews were dead-tired after a long grueling day.

The company commander reckoned he would have to spend the night on the ridge top in laager—circling the wagons, so to speak, against the Germans. There is always some confusion in these circumstances as the company commander makes up his mind as to how to use the terrain, what sectors of defense to assign to each platoon, where to put the outposts, and so on. In the midst of this hiatus a battery of German horse-drawn artillery, according to what the battalion commander later told me, trotted up the road through the middle of the milling tanks and TDs—and no one did anything to stop it. Indeed, one of the TDs was seen to traverse its turret so the gun would not impede the German movement.

There is, of course, an important moral to this story. *Every* military combat unit must be carefully conditioned to react to the unexpected, no matter how bizarre. If it is not so conditioned it will, sooner or later, end up with egg on its face.

On one occasion I came onto one of my columns halted by a German delaying detachment, in thoroughly typical fashion, at the bend of a mountain road. The infantry platoon on hand in this case was not one of our own—it came, under circumstances long forgotten, from an infantry division, and was further distinguished by having an American-born Chinese as the platoon commander. His "point," or leading pair of scouts, had poked their noses carefully around the road bend to see two German Tiger tanks (the big ones, with 88mm guns) lying in wait for us. Something was obviously wrong with the German dispositions—

there was no outpost to warn the tanks of our approach. And then someone told me that just before my arrival our people had captured a small German infantry detachment caught napping back down the road. Obviously the outpost.

Considering that too many persons contributed to it, we worked out a pretty good plan. With the lieutenant and his two-man bazooka team I crawled to the top of a heavily wooded ridge from which we could look down, at a range of no more than 50 yards, at the two Tigers. Our weapon was only a 2.75-inch bazooka (a recoil-less rifle) whose projectile could not possibly penetrate the 6-inch frontal armor of a Tiger, but the explosion of its warhead would, we hoped, disconcert the Germans and serve as a splendid signal for our two leading tanks to come around the corner and engage the Tigers.

The four of us on the little ridgetop had to wait for a specified time to elapse before we could engage. With my extra-powerful German field glasses I observed, at very close range, the two German tank crew commanders, sometimes conferring on the ground, sometimes in their tank turrets. They were obviously (and understandably) much upset at the lack of any word from their infantry outpost. We also watched a crewman dismount to relieve himself against the tank track—the tank commander permitted that, but then hustled him back in. I rather expected that some of these men had not long to live; I remember my strange sensation at observing, at such close range, healthy young human beings of whom some were experiencing their last moments on earth. This somewhat sentimental reverie went into reverse when the leading Tiger's commander, head and shoulders out of his turret, fixed his field glasses directly on where we were hidden behind some scraggly low bushes. We dared not move so much as an eyebrow, expecting momentarily to see the huge gun swing onto us and blow us away. This ghastly period seemed to last forever, but apparently the lieutenant could detect nothing to back up his suspicion: to our vast relief, he eventually shifted his gaze elsewhere.

The moment came: the bazooka man let fly, and the projectile arced high in the air and descended precisely—a magnificent shot—on the glacis of the leading Tiger. The shaped charge made no more than a scar on the thick steel plate, but it did scare hell out of the Germans and caused our two leading tanks to come around the bend and then pound the side armor of the leading German tank with armor-piercing projectiles, disabling it. I saw the surviving crewmen abandoning ship, so I raced down the hill and, according to plan, jumped on the back deck of one of our tanks. From this doubtful vantage point I directed the tank across the bridge spanning a deepish stream bottom into what was some kind of a mining installation—a small office building, a couple of work buildings, and a warehouse, all constructed of galvanized iron sheeting, surprisingly new and shiny. The warehouse had a ground-level concrete floor and was almost empty, and whoever had emptied it left the wide swinging double doors, at each end, open and free of restraint. As we approached the near end of the warehouse I could see, right through the long axis of the building, the main road, now on the far side of the creek from us. And up that road, to our right, I could see the second German tank, thus far unengaged, begin to move right to left across our front.

I had the gunner of my tank lay at a point about three feet off the road surface about 20 yards in front of the Tiger; he then fired a succession of armor-piercing rounds at that spot as fast as the loader could get rounds up the spout. Actually, after the first round he couldn't see the spot or indeed anything else—because of obscuration, the dust raised by the strike, and the fact that the garage doors, activated by the concussion of the gunfire, were swinging wildly open and shut. Several of his shots went through them. But his blindness was no problem—he had only to reset the gun on the previous lay as indicated by marks we had put on all tank-gun traverse and elevation wheels.

Well, I couldn't tell any more than the gunner whether we had hit the second tank. But we had. We found it later, abandoned with a collapsed road wheel and other evidence of our fire, a few miles down the road.

Two Tigers, one crew, at no cost to Uncle Sam. While we were congratulating ourselves on this small victory the Corps commander, in a jeep, appeared—way up front where he had no business to be. I knew him only moderately well, and he me. After applauding our modest success he showed me the 1:50,000 map in his lap and asked me to indicate our position. Then he moved his finger, on the map, to the next town, about five miles away, and asked its name. "Sir," I said, "that's Montieri."

"Howze," he said, "I want Montieri by nightfall!"—whereupon he drove off. I remember feeling grateful that I hadn't said Berlin. He was a very good commander, too, in most respects, but we didn't get Montieri for three days and then only through the efforts of two battalions.

Most Italian cities were not terribly damaged by the war—not, certainly, like the cities of Germany, ravaged as they were by American and British airpower. But the Italian countrymen, most of whom lived in small towns on hilltops, had a rough go. For one thing there was very little to eat, and what there was to eat could often not be cooked for lack of fuel. In our company messes, therefore, it was common to see Italian peasantry begging for food, so the mess sergeants put out extra, carefully washed garbage cans into which our men dumped the uneaten contents of their mess kits—meat and bread in this one, vegetables in the next, for the benefit of local citizenry waiting patiently in line nearby.

I don't think it was because of the war, but a very common sight was that of Italian peasant women doing laundry at the side of a running stream or ditch. In many instances the place they worked had not been improved over what nature provided by so much as putting one stone on top of another. One was moved to believe that the lot of peasant women was still that of the time of the first Caesar.

We didn't see much of what we called, I'm not sure how accurately, the "Partigianis," the men of the Italian resistance, a movement that sprang up after the Italian surrender. But the Italians traditionally hated and feared the Germans, and we learned later that the German forces in Italy had had to divert a portion of their combat strength to the protection of certain of their vulnerable supply and communication installations and their supply truck convoys. To the extent that this was true, it was a substantial help to us. But throughout my 20 months in Italy I never had a partisan leader volunteer the help of his men in our operations.

It seemed to me, however, that individual Italians were pretty courageous. They stuck to their villages, or their houses, as the war rolled over them; they seemed to have no other place to go. It was not uncommon for an Italian farmer to send his son to get his few remaining cattle out of the pasture because German artillery was falling there, or for a woman, tears streaming down her face, to sweep the front porch while incoming shells exploded nearby. Nor was it unusual to see Italian civilian dead in a newly captured village, whether by our fire, German fire, or German execution because of partisan activity.

Despite the war Catholic priests, in their flat black hats and black gowns, were everywhere, in city and countryside. I once asked one who spoke English a question, in substance as follows: So many of your people are hungry, ragged and filthy, while many of your churches (even those in small villages) are handsomely decorated in genuine gold. Why cannot the riches of the church be diverted to help the thousands of the very poor—at least to provide them soap, which would help ward off disease? I remember every word of his answer, which at least was unambiguous: "Better that ten thousand persons die of sickness," he said, "than one soul be lost to Heaven."

The Piper Cub, a very light aircraft flown by Artillery pilots and used extensively and effectively for the direction of artillery fire and for liaison, was able to operate off tiny unimproved fields in mountain valleys and sometimes on mountainsides. One of these short strips was known as the Ski Jump, for obvious reasons. A Cub on a southerly takeoff would tear down a steep slope for four-fifths of the runway, then up an equally steep slope and practically jump into the air. Landing south was a bit different—the slope of the hill more than offset the effect of a light wind, so the aircraft wanted to run on down the field and take off again, but if the pilot was quick and strong enough on his brakes things were still okay. Landing north was fine because the slope would brake you. Taking off north was sometimes a magnificent gamble, requiring neat calculation of opposing factors—sometimes a combination of steep uphill slope and variable wind glued the airplane to the ground, so it and the pilot would end up out in the bushes.

I once had occasion to visit, in a Cub, a fairly large, flat treeless area recently given up by the Germans. The Luftwaffe had apparently used it as an auxiliary airfield. A smooth grassy area looked like a runway, so we landed on it. Thereupon a number of British soldiers with sticks came out of the surrounding woods to mark the tracks of our tires through the grass.

I inquired of a British officer, a Sapper (equals U.S. Combat Engineer) standing nearby. "Well," he said, "we're here to clear this field of mines so the RAF can use it. All the crates nearby show that the Boche must have thoroughly mined the place. But your tracks through the grass give us a leg up—that part of the strip, anyway, appears not to be mined." He did not appear as grateful as I thought he might.

After I did my business we gingerly pivoted the Cub around its front wheels by lifting the tail; we climbed in and made a max-power takeoff, following our own tire tracks. It was nice to get airborne without blowing up.

During a day in which everything had gone wrong, one of our soldiers brought in a German whose uniform was covered with an Italian peasant's civilian clothes. He arrived while I was having a conversation, by radio, with my division commander, General Harmon. After my business with the general was finished I said, in my current dumb state of frustration caused by all that had gone haywire, "By the way, General, a German soldier has just been brought in wearing civilian clothes. I think he's a spy. After he's been interrogated at the Division prisoner cage I recommend he be shot."

Harmon's reply was typical: "The hell with that. You shoot him!"— and he hung up. But, of course, I didn't shoot him, and neither did anyone else. The man was simply a deserter.

One day I took the opportunity to motor across the peninsula to visit the Canadian Armored Corps, of two divisions, on the Adriatic coast. First-class fighting formations, they were no better off than we: they faced a series of precipitous canyons carrying streams out of the mountains to the sea. But it was good to swap experiences with their officers, and to learn one another's tricks of the trade.

On the way back I spent a night at a British billet and was startled to hear several young officers, at mess, attacking Churchill. They'd heard that he had opposed, in Parliament, a bill to increase the salaries of

British schoolteachers somewhere—or maybe everywhere, I don't remember. In the course of debate, they said, Churchill had resorted to asking for a vote of confidence for his government. In effect, he had made the Parliament choose between overthrowing his government, which, of course, Britain could not afford to do in the middle of a war, and giving him his way in the comparatively inconsequential matter of teacher's pay. My hosts strongly resented his tactics. I recalled this incident when, shortly after the war's end, the British people turned Churchill out of office, provoking his virulent (but ever elegant) denunciation.

Throughout the war I carried with me, in the back of my jeep, a red, very thin, bound book: *The Principles of War*, by Count von Clausewitz. I had read it through perhaps a dozen times, and through that repeated reading had memorized many of the most trenchant passages. Because of its great clarity, its classic literary style, and the military genius of the author, I found the book eminently sustaining in times of stress—it was something to cling to, to refer to when an operational plan went awry, when units went kiting off on the wrong road, when subordinates seemed to lose their minds, or when your luck was bad. In other words, on a normal battle day. The book was reassurance, a friendly voice reminding me of the inescapable, grinding friction that characterizes even well-conceived battle operations, and that if one has planned reasonably well, has made allowances for difficulties and delays, and has taken every possible measure to make success a certainty, things just might come out pretty well.

French-African Colonial regiments were a colorful lot, and although they fought well they did sometimes cause confusion because each had its own uniform—and sometimes its own standard of behavior. The French Goums, enlisted from an Arab mountain tribe, wore baggy brown-and-white striped cotton bloomers—that's right—and matching pullover blouses. No helmets. They were reputed to be badly frightened by enemy artillery fire, and when a Goum infantry company passed, on foot, through an Italian village the men considered it proper to loot the houses. This convention resulted in their continuing their march down

the road, after a slight delay, with individual men laden with such ameni-
ties as overstuffed chairs, mattresses, and wall mirrors—all to be discarded after a few miles.

Their specialty, however, was work at night—with knives. Unen-
cumbered by helmets or anything else that rattled they were expert at
the long, patient, silent crawl, which took them as necessary under
barbed wire and past minefields. When a Goum arrived at a foxhole he
felt carefully into it, and if his hand encountered a body he cut its throat.
I don't know the source of the information, but we heard that the Germans didn't like the Goums.

CAMP DOGPATCH

11 As fall became winter, with snow and cold, military operations slowed perceptibly. Both sides went pretty much to ground. The infantrymen on the higher mountains, of course, were the most miserable.

There were other armored divisions in Italy, as frustrated as we. One was the South African Armored Division, which, during the early winter, we relieved from its static position along a mountain ridge. The South Africans looked good. All combat elements were white, but most officers had orderlies that were "colored"—not black, but East Indian. On each of my overnight stays at the South African divisional headquarters, while planning for the relief, I was awakened in the morning by a kneeling servant who whispered in my ear, very softly, "Tea! Tea! Tea!" until I awoke and took the cup.

The South Africans had a rough dirt road that ran along the forward side of the ridgetop constituting the front line for about a mile. This was the "Mad Minute," so named because a German antitank gun crew on the next ridge, about a half-mile distant, habitually did its level best to clobber any vehicle that ventured to use the road in daylight. The alternative to the Mad Minute, however, was a rough, interminable drive back down the ridge, through the division rear, and then back up to the top.

One day I told Corporal Scully, my jeep driver, that to get my job done in time we'd have to do the Mad Minute. He said nothing, but then proceeded to drive us over the stretch with elaborate care, avoid-

131

ing all the bumps and slowing at each turn. I wanted to kill him, but elected to tough it out with him. The German, it so happened, didn't shoot at us, perhaps because of a very light fog, perhaps because he'd run out of ammunition.

About this time word descended through Division Headquarters that I'd been overseas well over two years and was eligible therefore for a month's leave during which I could return to my wife in the United States. I decided, however, that a second parting would be too hard on both of us—the first was bad enough—and asked if I might instead have a month's leave in France. Nobody had ever asked for that before, but it was granted, so I got the Air Forces to give me a ride on a transport aircraft already bound for Marseilles.

On the airfield at that city, as I was sitting with a cup of coffee in a crowded wooden refreshment shack run either by the British NAAFI or our Red Cross, I forget which, there was a sudden loud "Pouf!" in the kitchen as a gasoline stove blew up. Almost instantly the three feet of airspace below the low ceiling filled with heavy black smoke, intensely hot. The customers, all of them military, fell to their knees and crawled out, most of us carrying our coffee. From the outside we watched the place burn flat in no more than 10 minutes.

SHAEF (Supreme Headquarters, Allied Expeditionary Force), with General Eisenhower in command, was then at Versailles, not far outside Paris. I checked in there, had a horrible meal of Brussels sprouts in what had been a luxurious Paris hotel, and was provided a jeep and a driver and permission to go anywhere I chose. It didn't occur to me that my driver had not yet heard a shot fired in anger—in Italy I hadn't known anybody who hadn't. As we went east and ultimately in among our artillery positions he became, naturally enough, increasingly apprehensive. At one point, as I snoozed in the seat beside him, we passed directly in front of the muzzles of a carefully camouflaged battery of 90mm antiaircraft guns which by that time had been pressed into service as long-range ground-to-ground artillery.

At precisely the right moment the whole damned battery let fly, simultaneously. I was nearly blown out of my seat, but instantly thereafter became frantically engaged in trying to keep that flying jeep under some kind of control. The driver had turned everything loose—we went into and out of the ditches on both sides of the road and ultimately ended up in a beet field, fortunately not one bordered by a barbed wire fence.

Early one afternoon, we got to Nantes, a city in Loraine, and I went to see General Patton. The full weight of his Third Army that morning had been launched in attack across the Moselle River. According to his macho image, Patton (christened, I think by newsmen, as "Old Blood and Guts") should have been at the front, brandishing his pearl-handled revolvers, swearing at his soldiers, and urging them on. But where was he? In his large, comfortable office in a hotel in downtown Nantes. There was—is—nothing wrong in that. He had already visited his commanders and troops and issued the necessary orders—he needed now to be near his communications, at which point he could monitor progress, consult with his staff, and react to problems.

He told me that there would be many interruptions as his staff brought in reports and news, but to have a seat and talk to him. It was hardly an uninterrupted conversation, but it was interesting (between reports) to hear him lecture me about the arts of war and leadership and to tell him of events in Italy and how my mother was and how Mary was getting along in Falmouth. Sometimes we talked simply about life in the old Army and why we were not better prepared for this gigantic world war. But I remember him saying that we were doing pretty well considering that a very few years previously we relied primarily on the horse for battlefield mobility and had, all told, only 130,000 men—including the Air Corps, later the Air Force, in that number.

That was a great experience for a 35-year-old colonel. That evening I spent about three hours on an enormous hotel bed with three other officers—old friends on Patton's staff—and Marlene Dietrich, all of us fully clothed, of course. She was on a trip to entertain the troops. She was fun to talk to, and very familiar with France. She described the city of Nantes as "hopelessly bourgeois"—just a provincial town.

I spent the next three weeks chasing around eastern France, Belgium, and Holland, visiting friends and seeing what was going on by way of fighting. I had no function whatever: when what was "going on" got too hot, I simply told my friends that it had been nice seeing them, tipped my hat, and departed for more congenial and less dangerous places.

I remember on one occasion talking to Col. Jack Hines, a close friend, a fine soldier and horseman, and a son of an ex–Chief of Staff of the Army. Within a week or so of my seeing him he received the cruelest wound of any of my friends: a high-explosive shell burst on the side of his tank as his head and shoulders were out of the turret. It carried away both his eyes, his nose, part of his forehead, much of his jaw and most of one hand. He lived the rest of his years in darkness and pain.

It was a great pleasure to see my older brother, also a colonel and in command of the 36th Armored Infantry of the 3rd Armored Division. His predecessor in command had been killed in action. My brother was later reported to have fought magnificently in the Battle of the Bulge, Hitler's last great thrust in Western Europe.

Much refreshed, at the end of my month's leave I went back to Italy.

The winter was long and, for Italy, cold. In anticipation of eventual breakout into the valley of the Po River I was relieved from other duty and charged with doing what could be done to prepare the division for crossing the hundreds of streams, irrigation ditches, and drainage canals that laced that broad, flat, fertile valley. I found an Italian government tree farm near Florence with thousands of poplar saplings about four inches in diameter—ideally suited to my new task. I established Camp Dogpatch there.

I suppose it was a bit unseemly to create something called Dogpatch near the famous city of Florence, one of the world's cultural centers. The northern Italians—a good-looking people, many of them blond— rather disdain the south of Italy: the expression is that Italy goes down only to Florence, below that is Africa. Florence is also the site of the Ponte Vecchio ("Old Bridge") across the Arno River. It is noteworthy that the German Army, for all the bad things we used to say about the Germans during the war, didn't blow the Ponte Vecchio, only because it was, and is, one of the great art treasures of the world. They de-stroyed all the other bridges in town, and sparing the Ponte Vecchio was a sacrifice to them. They did blow down some six- or eight-story brick buildings, over the street approaching the bridge, and the one leading from the bridge: the streets were 20 feet deep in rubble. But in only a matter of hours our bulldozers had opened the way to traffic.

One Saturday night in Florence I attended the first (after the German departure) performance of the city's symphony orchestra, which had been, and is again, world famous. I enjoyed the first half of the concert and, after the intermission, returned to my seat for the second half. To my astonishment the conductor escorted onto the stage a U.S. soldier, dressed in battle fatigues. It was Corporal Friedman, of the 13th Armored Regimental Band—who once or twice, to the delight of our headquarters, had played for us a concerto on his violin. The violin was of a famous make—not a Stradivarius, but one of comparable quality—which he had bought, no doubt at a low price, somewhere in the Italian countryside. And Friedman himself was a distinguished graduate of the Eastman School of Music. Well, anyway, our boy played beautifully and was given a great ovation by the mostly Italian civilian audience. It was a thrill for me to hear and see it all.

At Camp Dogpatch we devised two gadgets. One was the fascine: in our case a bundle of the small tree trunks, each cut to a length of 10 feet, around a center of three gasoline drums which, after their ends were cut away, were welded end to end to form a large-diameter pipe. Three light steel cables drawn tight around each bundle gave us a fascine about 7 feet in diameter and 10 feet long: one, two, or three of these gizmos dropped into a canal or drainage ditch a little too big for a tank to cross unaided would form an instant tank crossing and at the same time allow the water to flow—thus preventing a possibly strong current from washing the fascines away.

To carry the fascines we removed the turrets from perhaps twenty-five battle-damaged tanks, and where the turret had been we welded on a large slanting steel rack to hold the log bundle—the fascine—and devised a triggering device that would allow the vehicle commander, without exposing himself to enemy fire, to dump the bundle precisely where he wanted it. We made lots of extra fascine so the fascine carriers could go back and reload.

The idea for our other gadget we got from the British. Again we removed the turrets from about thirty old tanks, and on the top of each welded, in parallel, two regular heavy steel treadways—treadways originally designed to stretch between the pontoons of the standard engineer floating bridge. At each end of each treadway thus mounted on the tank we hinged another treadway, and to hold up the free ends of the front pair and the rear pair we mounted, fore and aft on the hull, a heavy steel I-beam from which supporting cables ran to the free end of each treadway. By means of other lifting cables and a power takeoff from the tank engine we were able to lift the free ends of the treadways, fore and aft, about 16 feet off the ground and lock them—that was the traveling position. The whole contraption looked approximately like a gigantic, prehistoric two-ended black lobster, stalking about with its four huge claws lifted in an attitude of attack—in either direction.

Point was, however, that it worked like a charm. An "Ark," as we called it, again copying the British, could waddle itself into a narrow canal or stream up to five feet deep; once in the bottom it could allow its fore and aft treadways to flop down, and presto, there was a tank bridge, ready for immediate use by any number of tanks. Even a wide stream often has no more than one or two channels as deep as five feet—one or two Arks could span the channel, letting the battle tanks ford the shallower parts of the crossing. Also, several Arks could be placed in tandem to provide a bridge across a wide channel.

And like the Elephant Child (of Kipling's *Jungle Book,* after the Crocodile stretched his originally stubby trunk) we found additional advantages: the Ark could get tanks up low vertical cliffs (up to about 10 feet) and across railroad tracks running along an artificial embankment too steep for an ordinary tank to climb. The Ark just dropped its fore claws on the cliff or banktop, and its aft claws behind, affording the battle tanks an easy grade to climb up and over the obstacle.

At Camp Dogpatch we not only built all these wonderful gadgets, we also trained crews to operate them and the battle tank battalions to use them operationally. And when in April of 1945 the U.S. Fifth Army broke out of the mountains into the Po Valley, there we were, all dressed up and ready to go—and what happened? The Germans took off across the Po Valley like a scalded cat, rarely destroying so much as a road culvert. This was a great relief to the division as a whole, of course—but for all of us who had worked so hard at Dogpatch it was a tad disappointing, too. But it was very correct for the division to have anticipated the worst and to have prepared for it.

In late April an attack all along the line of contact gained the Allied forces general access to the Po Valley. But though the German forces were in disarray the fighting continued: on the first night one of the finest infantry battalion commanders in our division was practically cut in two by a German machine gun.

The mission of my task force was to exploit north in the general direction of Lake Como, cutting off retreating German forces whenever possible. For reasons forgotten, things went badly at first due to my fault and others'—I remember being in a frustrated rage. About 12 hours thereafter, the new division commander (Maj. Gen. Vernon Pritchard— he had been a famous quarterback at West Point) and I, I'm sure for very insufficient reasons, were both in a light tank tearing down a flat valley road—in the dark and, of course, without lights. I'm sure we were doing almost 20 MPH when we hit an immense crater, I'd guess 10 feet deep and 25 across, courtesy of a German demolition team. The tank leapt into the left side of this great hole, turned on its right side, and slid down the bank, coming to rest almost upside down at the crater bottom. My head and shoulders had been up through the turret hatch— I remember, as we slid downward, putting my right arm up against the rough dry gravel to keep the tank from going vertically onto its turret top—not a compliment to my judgment under pressure. In any case, we all had very much in mind the picture of gasoline dripping on a hot engine, and were glad to have an escape route.

In the next few days practically all action was confined to the roads themselves—multiple vehicle columns hurrying along a vast network of intersecting roads in a well-populated valley. We inflicted lots of damage on the retreating German columns because their communications systems had been badly disrupted by the displacement of all their headquarters, whereas ours were still in good shape. Since we knew where we were, where our friends were, and where the Germans were likely to be—and they had no idea that we were so far into their rear area— we often had the advantage of surprise. Our probing columns were highly alert to the possibility of encountering Germans at any road junction or crossroad, whereas their people were often astonished by our sudden appearance and immediate attack, which usually left several German vehicles afire and bodies on the road.

This frequently resulted in surrender. Our column commander in such case had an immediate problem, but he could take no time to disarm all the new prisoners, and so usually did no more than make them get off the road and display, as prominently as possible, makeshift white flags. We also reported their locations to following armored infantry units, which were usually able to arrive in pretty short order.

When we got all the way across the valley one of our tank battalions reported the end of Il Duce, the once imperial, strutting, jut-jawed Benito Mussolini. The reader may know that when Italy surrendered in October of 1944 Mussolini was rescued from the custody of the new provisional Italian government by German commando forces. In the north of Italy, which the Germans still occupied, Mussolini tried to enlist the support of Italians to continue fighting alongside the Germans. He was partly successful: some thousands of Italians obeyed him.

At the town of Duomo on the southeast shore of Lake Como, Mussolini and his mistress were found by a sizable force of Italian Partigiani in the hands of a small German *Schutzstaffel* (SS) escort headed for Austria and then Germany. The escort offered little or no resistance. The Partigiani leader on the spot elected to shoot both Mussolini and his lady companion through the back of their heads, thus removing the necessity for a trial. The bodies were taken to Milan, and there hung upside-down, by their heels. Their bodies were displayed for some days on the city's main square.

During the last days of the fighting there occurred, for me, the crowning absurdity of a long war. After 42 hours of almost constant moving and frequent (though brief) engagements, a very small party of vehicles belonging to one of my columns took a wrong turn one midnight and blundered into an isolated German-held area. There was no shooting, but the Germans had the drop on our people and declared them captive. Almost immediately thereafter, however, the heavy tracked vehicles of an also-confused battery of American armored artillery (mine again) were heard thundering down the road. Our group "captured" by the Germans pointed out that with our tanks (they hoped) approaching, it was much more appropriate that the Germans surrender to them. The Germans agreed, though it soon developed that there were no tanks and everyone in the artillery vehicles, save the drivers and gun chiefs, were sound asleep, and the guns had breech and muzzle covers firmly in place.

If the story sounds as though the war in Italy was a bogus one, let me remind you there were 749,000 men killed, wounded, or missing on the two sides. The fighting, complicated by extremely difficult terrain, had been bitter, terribly costly, and seemingly endless. The surrender in Italy came on 2 May 1945.

The Allied forces relished the new state of peace, of course, but all were engaged in what the British termed "tidying up the battlefield" and tending to many other things that needed doing. I began to think about the possibility of going home but was instead ordered to proceed with one tank battalion (forty-odd tanks) to Aosta, an Italian town of about 5,000 in the Val d'Aosta, a deep 100-mile-long valley between the Italian Gran Paradiso on the south and, on the north, the spectacular range bordering Switzerland—the highest of the Alps. The valley terminates at the Petit St. Bernard Pass, just southeast of Mont Blanc.

There were no Germans remaining in the Val d'Aosta, but there was a small French headquarters and a full regiment of Chasseurs Alpin— tough Free-French mountain troops who on parade marched in a very distinctive fast shuffle. Already in the valley also was the 81st Reconnaissance Battalion of our division; the tank battalion was an additional show of force. I was to command both U.S. units.

What was a strange French force doing in the U.S. Fifth Army sector of Italy? The Chasseurs had apparently detached themselves without U.S. authority from the U.S. Sixth Army Group, which included a variety of Free-French forces, and had come through the Petit St. Bernard Pass— by digging through 20 feet of snow. We figured the whole business had been instigated secretly by General de Gaulle, a gentleman often characterized both by Churchill and Roosevelt as generally insufferable.

Well, I'll skip the details. The French paraded around among the villages and so did we, we flexed our muscles and so did they, and we had multiple discussions about who had the right to be there and who had not. It developed that the primary reason for their presence was that Mussolini in 1940, when the Germans had already overrun the Low Countries and most of France, sent his army through the Val d'Aosta and the Petit St. Bernard Pass to attack in flank and rear the French forces retreating before the Germans—this being Mussolini's notorious "stab in the back." Who occupied the valley had become in some minds, therefore, a matter of principle, of national honor.

Soon after my arrival I met a professor of the University of Turin who was the head of the Italian Partigiani in the valley. Despite his French title and name, Count d'Entreves identified himself as a staunch Italian patriot, and enthusiastically offered me the services of his 3,000 armed irregulars against the French, if it came to serious difficulty. I managed to persuade him that the world right then, at the end of a terrible world war, couldn't and wouldn't abide the spectacle of American forces allied with Italians (very lately our declared enemies) fighting the French (our traditional allies) over the ownership of an Italian valley: such an event would react seriously against Italian interests. What really had to be accomplished now was the disarming of his force. He eventually agreed, and thereafter built a small mountain of widely assorted pistols, rifles, and ammunition near our headquarters in the town of Aosta.

Although relations had become amicable, the matter of valley ownership was still unsettled when I said goodbye to everybody, including the Count d'Entreves—a very sensible, worthwhile patriot—and left Italy, my beloved 1st Armored Division, and Corporal Scully for home. I cannot confirm the story, but I was later informed that Pres. Harry Truman sent de Gaulle a message to the effect that an American food convoy (one of several being sent to a very hungry France) was halted, dead in the water, in the mid-Atlantic. It and following convoys would return to America if the French were not out of the Val d'Aosta in 48 hours. So out they got.

Within a few years the French built a tunnel through the base of Mont Blanc, the highest of the Alps, to the head of the valley, but the Italian flag still flies over the Val d'Aosta. I'm not sure that justice is well served by that, considering the evil nature of the "stab in the back," but the area is properly Italian by reason of population and geography.

I flew home in an Air Force C-54, the military version of the old DC-6. The floor of the passenger cabin was of nice-looking bare hardwood without furniture of any sort. In one corner of the cabin was a pile of unfolded Army blankets extending to the ceiling, and a large supply of not-very-far-out-of-date American magazines. It turned out to be a nice sort of trans-Atlantic crossing; each passenger just took a bunch of blankets, went to bed and stayed there, mostly asleep. It might have been a bit different had the weather been rough—we would have slid, as a pretty solid mass, from one end of the plane to the other.

As I walked down the gangway in Miami I threw an unfinished pack of cigarettes in the trash can at the bottom, and have not smoked one since. And then I went home—a home I'd not seen before, in Falmouth, Massachusetts. But Mary was in it. Believe me, she looked good.

FORT RILEY

12 We had a happy month's leave in Falmouth, where Mary had many friends—among them the garbage man, who had been very solicitous about how I was faring during the war.

I had stopped in Washington to see my beloved and delightful mother. My sister—whose husband (a colonel) was still in Europe—was also in Falmouth, as were a number of other Regular Army wives. And so was Barney, my wife's amiable, beautiful Irish setter, and Bayou, our highly independent cocker. I had orders to report to what was still called the Cavalry School, at Fort Riley, Kansas. When leave ended, we drove out there in our car: it was nice to see more of my country again, after more than three years overseas. Particularly gratifying was the fact that its people were not hungry and cold, its cities and towns not devastated, its farms not lying fallow and scarred by tank tracks and shell holes, and a large portion of its young men not dead or forever crippled.

Riley especially was a sight for sore eyes, particularly because we found so many of our very close friends there. It was a sort of refuge for horse soldiers back from the war, and commanded by one, Maj. Gen. I. D. White. Although the horse cavalry regiment was gone, of course, there were still about 300 horses that the Army had not as yet sold. I picked for my use a big, rawboned half-breed bay named Royal Flush—though we called him "Pie Plate" because his knees were so big and flat. For the three years I was at Riley I rode Pie Plate from

8 to 10 A.M. every working day, almost without fail. I believe I was the only officer to do this, but my superiors never questioned it, for I was the appointed Director of Instruction at the school and we had a good deal of outdoor training to give the students. Everyone knows that there is no better way to look at any outdoor activity than from the back of a horse. And, of course, it was good fun and good exercise.

On one occasion I rode Pie Plate in a steeplechase, but over solid timber jumps, not brush. We came in third—but in a small field, I admit. After I got my modest prize for being third I was approached, out in front of everybody, by some friends of mine with a large wreath, the sort which is habitually hung around the neck of a horse when he is formally retired, by reason of old age, from further competition. In this case they hung the wreath around *my* neck, the implication being that I was a bit old for the sport of racing over timber.

One morning, someone called Mary to say that I was overdue at a lecture I was scheduled to present. She got in the car and found me, on the horse, and made me swap vehicles. I took the car to the lecture hall. She rode Pie Plate back to the stables, her skirt leaving her pretty exposed, pantyhose not having been invented yet. Fortunately, she had nice-looking legs.

In the first few months I spent at Riley, the school was devoted to re-treading cavalry officers who had had a relatively short time in Europe, or hadn't been overseas at all, for service in the continuing war against the Japanese—which we, in ignorance of the atomic bomb, thought would last another year or more. A new class of perhaps twenty started every Monday morning and, after two weeks of concentrated instruction, was graduated on Friday afternoon. This produced a confusing leapfrog effect: a class entering every Monday, a class graduating every Friday.

My immediate boss, the school's Assistant Commandant, made a point of addressing each entering and graduating class. On one occasion he gave the graduating class his entering class speech: told them what the rules were, where the library was, what was expected of them, and at the end brought the house down when he said, very forcefully, "I may not know you now, but *I'll know each one of you intimately before you leave this post!*" A month or so later he gave the entering class the graduating speech. Actually, though, he was a good man; the leapfrog effect just got to him.

When the two bombs fell on Hiroshima and Nagasaki my immediate thought was that armies had suddenly become obsolete—I figured I had just run out of a profession. This was not very good thinking, of course, because it ignored the fact that the new weapon was too big, too broadly destructive, to be used except in extreme circumstances and against a major target. The bombs did end the war, however, and changed the character of our school: it was renamed the Ground General School—a frightfully uninspiring title—and put to doing all sorts of instruction the Army was reluctant to locate anywhere else. Our most important task was to further educate, in the specifics of leadership and tactics, each freshly graduated class from West Point. This was not too good an idea—the new officers had just completed four years of concentrated academic instruction and were ready for something else.

I did invent for these classes something I christened the "Military Stakes," an event wherein the students individually ran a cross-country course requiring each one, at each of a series of stations, to execute a military task—something like twenty-five of them, ranging from riding a horse bareback (which some had never done before), to breaking a balloon with a rifle, adjusting the fire of an artillery battery, getting a truck out of a ditch, estimating the range to a target, assembling a machine gun, repairing a faulty radio—etcetera, etcetera. All were practical tasks requiring some knowledge and ability and in some cases lots of initiative, and all were done against time. The Military Stakes were soon adopted by the Military Academy itself and named, to my disappointment, the Buckner Stakes, after Gen. Simon Bolivar Buckner. I would have liked them to be called the Howze Stakes, not after me but in honor of my father, once Commandant of Cadets at West Point.

Another task I enjoyed was establishing a proper organization of the armored cavalry reconnaissance platoon. With the aid of some damned good NCOs I did the job in about four weeks, experimenting in the field every other day with a varying combination of riflemen, jeeps, radios, tanks, and weapons. Each day on the terrain we did perhaps five separate little exercises of my devising, some of them two or three times, and on each intervening day we reorganized slightly, adding and subtracting men and equipment according to what we found worked best the day before. At the end of a month we submitted an organizational structure that was adopted throughout the Army and lasted for some 30-odd years—and I'm not sure it's very different even now. I venture to say that ours was the best system of arriving as a good structure for a tactical unit—better far than working up, in an office, a paper solution that is then exhaustively tested but not altered from day to day to adjust to the requirement.

One of the pleasures of service at Riley was the Sunday Hunt, which Mary and I attended about every other week. There are very few foxes in Kansas so we hunted coyotes; but more often, it must be said, we pursued a "drag"—a bundle of rags and burlap impregnated with the scent of a coyote and then dragged across hill and dale by a Huntsman on a horse. That sounds unimpressive, but the facts are that a drag leaves a plainer trail than a live animal, wherefore the hounds and horses run much faster, and the Huntsman (in our case a mounted soldier) laying the drag could take us over a variety of courses and where there were lots of fences to jump.

Our hunt staff in their pink coats prided themselves on their strict attention to hunt protocol. At each check (a short period at which the staff and the "field"—the rest of us—dismounted and took a breather) they would gather the hounds into a tight, controlled pack before they themselves dismounted. On one such occasion a young officer riding with the field, apparently not greatly impressed with the way things were going that morning, had separated from the rest of us and on his own hook gotten up a jackrabbit, which he pursued at full gallop. Yelling to the rest of us, "Look! I got a *real* quarry!" he chased that rabbit right past the pack of hounds gathered at the check. Although surrounded by the pink coats of the dismounted hunt staff the hounds, baying loudly in their excitement and delight, took off after the rabbit, and were not recovered for another 30 minutes by the hard-riding, hard-swearing hunt staff. The offending rider had slid off his horse and commenced grazing it, but his disgrace was palpable.

After the hunt the staff and field always gathered at the hunt club building, or a nearby farmhouse, for hot buttered rum or whiskey. It was a delightful way to spend a brisk Sunday morning. Mary and I have always been habitual churchgoers, but we sometimes forfeited that in favor of the hunt.

Our very pleasant three years at Riley were interrupted by a tempo-rary-duty tour at the traditional site of the Command and General Staff College, Fort Leavenworth, Kansas, where I was a member of what was called the First Command Class—the first of only two. The Army for some reason had thought that it might be good to supplant the Army War College with a new high-level, five-month course at Leavenworth. The idea didn't float for long, but I was flattered at being selected for the first class. The Air Force at the time still belonged to the Army, and was amply represented. The students, almost all colonels, had extensive war experience and were high-quality people—full of beans and glad to be still alive. None was inclined to take the course very seriously, but every-one had a happy (and instructive) time because of the company. Perhaps the bull sessions were the most valuable part of the five months—there was lots of battle-induced know-how among us.

In the three years at Riley our family expanded by two baby boys, Bill and Guy Howze. They were lovingly tended by Joey May, a large black woman with a speech impediment: when you spoke to her a large si-lence ensued during which she would struggle to form the words she wanted, and when she finally succeeded they arrived with explosive force. Our friends telephoning the house had to get used to this: they would hear the phone being removed from the hook but then had to wait patiently until Joey May got vocal.

Joey May also had syphilis, but it was under treatment and examin-ing doctors assured us that she was, under the circumstances of active treatment, totally safe. Sometimes as I took a guest on my arm into the dining room I informed her, if she were an old friend, that the cook had syphilis—never did one, all good Army wives, blink an eye. Our two lit-tle boys adored Joey May, and when we ultimately left the post for Washington Mary threw her arms around Joey May and bawled like a baby.

Good old Fort Riley. In one five-month span the official temperature at Manhattan, Kansas, only 30 miles away, went from 31 degrees below to 117 above—a variation of 148 degrees. Riley after the war was much changed from what it had been before—but partly because of its horses, partly because communism was not yet recognized as a worldwide threat, partly because only we had the atomic bomb—it retained some of the relaxed, pleasant atmosphere of the old Army. That atmosphere was dissipating rapidly, however, everywhere, and would disappear altogether at the outbreak of the Korean War.

THE PENTAGON

13 In 1948 I was ordered to Washington as a student at the National War College, the senior U.S. military school, and on graduation from that school had to spend three years in the Pentagon.

Although Mary, I'm sorry to say, suffered all sorts of inconvenience and frustration in trying to bring up two frequently sick little boys in a small house in a big city, my tour at the War College was otherwise pleasant and very instructive. It seemed very unfair that I should receive so much inspiration and pleasure, on a very relaxed schedule, while my wife underwent so much difficulty.

Students of the National War College were selected officers, mostly at the colonel level or its equivalent, from all the military services and the State Department, plus one or two from other government departments; also present in those days was a representative of each of the military services—Army, Navy and Air—of Canada and Great Britain.

In my time the NWC was essentially a lecture course; we had a lecture at 8 each morning, and usually a second one at 10. I'd guess it was the world's *best* lecture course: our speakers included the president and one ex-president, Herbert Hoover; the primary cabinet members including the secretary of state, several college presidents, prominent members of Congress, the ambassadors to the United States from all the Allied powers, all the major U.S. military overseas commanders, each of the military chiefs of staff, senior military figures from our major European allies, and our ambassadors to those countries. We were always free to question the lecturer at length.

The rest of our work time was devoted to committee study and discussion of various national and international geopolitical and military subjects, and the writing and presenting of committee reports and recommendations thereon. In late spring the work culminated in committee solutions as to how World War III was to be fought under the conditions existing at the time. I was one of the committee chairmen on this occasion, and our committee was pleased at being chosen as the one to present its solution to the rest of the class—plus some representation, in this special event, from the staffs of all services and the Joint Chiefs in the Pentagon. The presence of these persons was flattering and our solution was a good one. It might have had some influence on national military policy.

I remember with great fondness noon hour at the National War College, mostly because it was two hours long. I often played squash, great fun and a magnificent game for the otherwise sedentary. A squash ball, however, has thick black rubber skin and is pretty heavy and quite firm: when it hits you, it hurts. At one moment during a game with a fellow student, a Navy Aviator, he was in front of me, well bent over in readiness to return my ball. The ball coming to me at exactly the right spot for my forehand, I r'ared back and swatted it with all the strength I could muster. The ball caught him square in the center of his right buttock and then, every ounce of its energy expended, dropped to the floor like a dead sparrow.

As might be expected, my opponent let out a loud bellow of agony, but though the initial pain of such a hit is indescribable it doesn't last long, and after a little not-too-damned-friendly conversation we finished the game. His right rear end, however, remained a sight for curiosity, admiration, and discussion among students and faculty for the next two months. The bruise consisted, as I remember, of six perfectly concentric rings of purple, green, red, blue, black and yellow, though probably not in that order. I never got a chance to ask his wife if she enjoyed it, too.

Others in the class and faculty played baseball or tennis during the noon break, and for one period in the spring I joined the yachting crowd. There was a crummy little boat-for-hire place on the Potomac River just outside the War College fence. The sailing "yachts" we rented there were 17-foot catboats and would carry two. We had not one but two races each noon hour. The Army, Air Force, and Marine colonels and the civilians had no trouble sailing these small craft, but the Navy captains often had to swim in. The rest of us understood perfectly: when a Navy captain gets on a boat—any boat—his instinct is always to stride about as if on the bridge of a man-of-war. And over they'd go.

Memorable also was the time a military policeman appeared at the lectern as we all sat awaiting the beginning of the 8 o'clock lecture. He asked who was driving a Chevrolet with such-and-such license number. One of us raised his hand. "Sir!" said the MP. "You are parked by a fire-plug, your lights are on, the motor is running, all four doors are locked and the keys are in the ignition."

The National War College was an outstandingly instructive experience. To my great dismay, however, I was doomed for the next three years to serve as a member of G-2, then the designation for the Army's Intelligence Branch, in the Pentagon. Mary with two small boys continued to be pretty confined and miserable in Washington and I disliked the atmosphere and environs of the Pentagon. I was initially assigned as Chief of the Collection Division of G-2, and was so unimpressed with its activities that after a few months I recommended its abolition—and the recommendation was approved! Of course, it shouldn't have been: a proper intelligence organization has to have something devoted to collection, and the division was later reactivated.

Meanwhile, I had fallen out of the frying pan and into the fire: I was made executive officer (who had very little executive authority) of the Intelligence Division—the one that actually derives the intelligence from the mass of collected raw data. I quickly discovered what the working hours were: one was expected to arrive at seven in the morning, and to stay until the hour hand of the clock made full circle, or something very close thereto. This was a far cry from the delights of Riley and the War College, and I thought very unnecessary—a sort of competition to show how conscientious one was. But I did it for a year, squawking all the time, until I was put into the front office as a sort of coordinator of certain functions among the several divisions of G-2.

Meanwhile, of course, the Korean War was underway, and in the first few months thereof it was not altogether certain that our forces would not be driven into the sea. It was an infantry and artillery war, and I missed it; no one asked for my services as a tanker, and besides, assignment as a member of the General Staff was, by rule, very rarely interrupted by other assignment.

I sought respite from life in the Pentagon by asking for airborne training and was accordingly dispatched to Fort Benning, Georgia, for the three-week course. I was 42 at the time and had congenitally bad knees, but with perhaps a very small bit of sympathy on the part of the airborne school NCO instructors I made it successfully, despite the endless running, sit-ups, and push-ups. Taking that course had pronounced effect on the remaining part of my military service. I wanted the training not simply to get out of the Pentagon for a bit, but because I liked the kind of fellow who "went airborne." There is some adventure in jumping out of an airplane, and it's good for the soul and sometimes even for the digestion.

Only one event at Benning warrants recording here. After a few days of arduous conditioning, the trainee is introduced to the 34-foot tower, that being a sturdy wooden tower with steps ascending to the top. Trainees file up the steps with parachute harness on, but no parachute: when each one gets to the top he arrives at a wide open door where an NCO snaps his harness to a pulley on a cable running, outside the tower, diagonally down to a low post set in the ground about 75 yards away. This rig simulates the jump from an airplane door. When the trainee gets to the door and takes the prescribed exit position a sergeant belts him across the fanny and yells *"Go!"*—the trainee jumps into space, falls about 10 feet, and then slides, via the pulley, down the wire to the ground.

Thirty-four feet doesn't sound high, but from that jump door in the tower it looks very high indeed—like standing on the roof-edge of a three-story house. Some aspirants cannot make themselves go out that door. To reduce their number the senior jump instructor has a little drill, and in this case I was Exhibit A. I had never made the tower jump, but I was instructed to climb the tower, alone, and appear in jump position at the door. As I stood there with the rest of my jump class (about 400 strong, mostly 19- and 20-year-olds) looking up at me from where they had been assembled in rigid formation, the senior instructor, using a megaphone, spoke to them approximately as follows: "Now!" he said. "This is the 34-foot jump tower you've all heard about! Some say it's dangerous. It is absolutely not at all dangerous! Colonel Howze, up there in the door, is a member of your class. He has never jumped out of the 34-foot tower. He is 43 years old, old enough to be your father. He's going to jump out of the tower. If he can do it, *anybody* can do it! OK, Colonel! Go!" I didn't relish it, but out I went.

In my third year in Washington I was made Chief of the all-important Intelligence Division of G-2 by "Direction of the President," those words officially justifying my assignment to the post, even though there were about eight colonels already in the division who ranked me and would for the next year serve under me. Several high-priced civilians, also there, regularly had lunch in a Pentagon executive dining room from which I was barred for lack of rank.

I would boast by saying that almost my first act as Chief of some 400 military and civilian intelligence analysts, staffers, and secretaries was to rule that (with the exception of duty officers and such folk as the in-coming-cable readers who started work about 4 A.M. and quit at 12) no one should reach his desk before 7:40 A.M. , and no one should leave his desk (in the absence of serious work that needed immediate doing) after 5:20 in the afternoon—except in emergency—when everyone might be expected to work 24 hours a day if necessary. This made me a popular chief with all except the work-nuts, of course, but I can truthfully say that our intelligence production—the studies, analyses, summaries, and conclusions that we produced in such profusion—suffered not one iota.

The tedium of life in the Pentagon was ameliorated a bit by my membership in an excellent poker game. Very congenial players—most of them Army—table stakes and a $3 takeout. This limited loss to about $25—enough to make you pay attention, not enough to hurt seriously. On one occasion, one of our players was absent seven weeks on an official trip to Europe. He got off the airplane in time to get to his house at 6:30 in the evening, kissed his wife, said howdy to his children, had supper, and made the 8 o'clock game, which lasted, as usual, to 11. We voted him the game's Most Faithful Player, but worried about how long his marriage might last.

One of my duties as front-office coordinator and then as division Chief was to accompany the G-2 himself, a major general, to the meetings of the National Intelligence Committee, always headed ex-officio by the director of the CIA. The function of these meetings was to produce National Intelligence Estimates, or NIEs, on various world hot spots for the edification—and on occasion, warning—of those who sat at the very high levels of government. I found the process of NIE development interesting and instructive, even if not always amicable, and I learned a lot about the world and what made it tick.

The director of the CIA in my time was Army Gen. Beetle Smith, whom I had met on some occasions during the war in Africa. One day as he entered the meeting, late, he announced that he had just left the Oval Office. He said the president (Truman) asked him why the Army was rejecting so many recruits for lack of physical fitness for military duty. "Why," said the president, "when I entered the Army one doctor would look up your rear while another looked down your throat. If they couldn't see each other, they'd sign you up."

As the representative of G-2 I made two delightful and highly instructive trips to Europe and the Middle East, once with Gen. Joe Collins, the Army's Chief of Staff, and one with Frank Pace, then secretary of the Army. General Collins brought along for each of our senior hosts a present: a U.S. Army general officer's Smith & Wesson .38-caliber revolver, not fancied up but nevertheless a very handsome weapon in its wooden red-velvet-lined case. It became apparent that the best way to get an eastern potentate all giggly was to give him a good-looking shooting iron. Each delighted recipient responded with a present to General Collins—maybe a sterling silver tea service or a dagger with rubies and diamonds in the handle.

The shah of Iran met General Collins and the rest of us in the Hall of Mirrors of his Teheran palace (one of five he maintained) and was very cordial. Although the Shah-in-Shah (his full title, meaning "Super-Shah") gave one the impression, by his demeanor and dress, that he was the current member of a long dynasty, his father, from whom he inherited the throne, had started as an ordinary member of the palace guard.

Shah Pahlavi was dictatorial and self-indulgent and in the ways he used his secret police reputedly brutal, but (from this Westerner's point of view) he did much to improve Iran's standard of living and bring it—or I should say part of it—into the twentieth century. With the help of a large U.S. military supply and training mission he also did much to improve the Iranian Army, Navy, and Air Force.

Our conversation with the shah was on military issues, but he took time to boast of his program to remove great tracts of land from the ownership of the aristocracy, distributing it among the peasants who lived on it. He acknowledged the use of oil money to compensate the original owners, but the net effect of the program, as he described it, seemed to be very beneficial. Moreover, he had, in the opinion of our embassy and our military advisory groups, instituted many other programs designed to modernize procedures, liberate women, improve education and living standards, introduce better agricultural methods, and otherwise make life in Iran worth living.

It couldn't have been easy. One member of the U.S. Department of Agriculture stationed in Teheran told us of the introduction of a highly productive hybrid variety of corn seed, sold at cost to Iranian farmers but of course with the caution that kernels from the crop would not germinate properly and therefore could not be used as seed for the second year's crop; new seed would have to be purchased. The farmers produced a bumper crop that first year—great profit and lots to eat for everyone. But nothing could induce most of the farmers to buy new seed for the next year: they replanted with kernels from the first crop, with disastrous results.

The shah was unquestionably autocratic and sometimes unjust and cruel, but his injustice, such as it was, was insignificant as compared to the cruelty of the Ayatollah who eventually ousted him from office. The Iran-Iraq War, which lasted eight years and cost Iran casualties numbering close to a million, would not have occurred had Pahlavi still been shah: Iraq, which started the war, would not have dared to attack a much stronger Iran.

In 1952, as now, Teheran's washing and drinking water came out of the massive Elburz Mountains just north of the city. The water (in 1950) was carried by man-dug tunnels, called ganats, through the clay under the desert floor. On reaching the city the water was released according to a complicated but fixed schedule into the gutters running alongside most of the streets that sloped away from the mountains. The ordinary citizen used this water for all common purposes, including cooking and drinking. Those who could afford it, however, drank the "Shah's Water," delivered via tanks of about 200-gallon capacity mounted on horse-drawn, two-wheeled carts. Undoubtedly, the gutter water caused sickness, but it did run clear, partly because it ran quickly and in volume, partly because the man in the street was (usually) careful not to befoul it. This system, of course, was later displaced, though very gradually, by plumbing.

The shah was a pilot, and had for his recreation a World War II U.S.-made B-17 bomber. One day, with the shah and Joe Collins in the crew compartment and Col. Charlie Dodge (my West Point classmate and also a member of our party) and the crew chief (a USAF sergeant) back in the bomb bay, the ship took off for a survey of the Iranian-Soviet border west of the Caspian Sea. I greatly regretted not being invited to go along.

Charlie said he could hear the general and the shah up front laughing and talking in the most congenial manner, causing him to wonder a bit who was minding the course. The Iran-Soviet border in the area is very mountainous and ill-defined, and the Soviets were always willing and anxious to take under antiaircraft fire any plane that strayed too close to the line. Moreover, Joe Collins, however expert at land navigation, had no experience with air navigation charts. But nothing happened.

The shah made his luxurious four-car private train available to us for a trip (about 16 hours) south to Ahwaz, the great oil center not far from the headwaters of the Persian Gulf. We enjoyed the comfort, food, drink, and service but most impressive, as we crossed that barren rocky land, was the railroad track—the track we were on, which extends north beyond Teheran through the Caucasus Mountains and into the USSR. This is the track that carried (to use Winston Churchill's figures) 5 million tons of Lend-Lease supplies, almost all American, to the Soviet

Union during World War II. We were given to understand that, on just our part of that track, we crossed or went through a total of 125 bridges and tunnels—the military implication of this being that the line is extremely vulnerable to destruction by air attack or hostile demolition teams. But also pertinent is the fact that the rail line leads from the USSR to a warm-water port (Bandar Shapur, at the head of the Persian Gulf) and a warm-water port has long been an ambition of the Russian Bear.

The Air Force airplane that had carried us to Teheran had gone on to Dhahran on the gulf coast of Saudi Arabia. To take us to the same place from the little dirt strip (with no lights) at Ahwaz was a USAF C-47, also known to the military as the Gooney Bird, or DC-3. We took off at night by the lights of a couple of small trucks.

From Dhahran we went by the large plane to the Saudi capital, Riyadh, in the middle of the Arabian peninsula, an enormous, awesome desert. Our traveling party numbered eight, but only four were allowed by our hosts to stay in Riyadh. The rest remained in the airplane, returning at once to Dhahran.

Riyadh in those days was little more than a remote oasis—a collection of adobe huts, a few palms, a few parched, ratty-looking grain fields—but served by a new, long, well-paved airstrip. Roads leading east and west from Riyadh to the coasts were still no more than dirt tracks, but paved roads were under construction. The population of Riyadh, with small but spectacular exception (the royal family), appeared to be destitute: at the market, at which most goods were simply laid out on the sand or clay, one "stall" was devoted to the sale of used pop bottles, used bottle caps, a few rusty spoons, and an unbelievably decrepit pair of shoes. The people showed much evidence of disease, especially of ophthalmia. Many eyeballs were simply opaque white blobs.

But there were a few automobiles in Riyadh, all of them either long shiny new Cadillac sedans or Ford or Chevrolet work trucks belonging to American utility companies—the latter indicating that Riyadh was in the beginning stage of going modern. And also in Riyadh was the richest family on earth, destined to become ever richer.

Of the huge royal family we saw only two persons in our 48-hour visit: the king and the crown prince. Each lived with heaven knows how many other family members in his own "palace," each a perfectly square two-story adobe mud edifice built around a courtyard. Each building occupied an area about the size of half an American city block. We were quartered in a guest house—a third building of the same size and shape as the palaces. All three buildings had small glass windows on the second floor, but in many instances one could throw a dead cat between the window frame and the adjacent mud wall. Such were the abodes of families that, even in those days, counted their wealth in billions of dollars.

A pair of Cadillacs was dispatched each time to carry us to the king's palace, two blocks from where we were billeted. On this and other (all very short) trips in Riyadh each driver, after everyone was aboard, first blew his horn three times—thus warning everybody in the vicinity that something important and dangerous was about to happen. Only then would he start the engine; and then he delivered three more blasts before moving forward. Quite apparently this was required procedure: a breach of it that resulted in some sort of accident would probably bring a terrible penalty onto the driver. The penalty for theft, when we were there, was the removal of one hand.

We saw the king, the magnificent Ibn Saud, four times. It was four times, not one, because he wished it so. This was the same king who went to Casablanca during World War II to meet (at the president's invitation) with Roosevelt and Churchill. He did that trip on an American destroyer, which carried not only Himself but a retinue of maybe sixty or so, including select members of his harem, and a large flock of sheep—live sheep, because refrigeration at the time was unknown in Saudi Arabia.

To get to the king's throne room we were first guided through a very long rectangular room at ground level, the floor being of compacted mud and almost covered by the prostrate bodies of countless Arabs in kaffiyehs and flowing white robes, each man cradling in his arms an extremely long ancient rifle and carrying across his shoulder a loaded bandoleer. The men all smelled strongly of camel and of themselves, the two odors being highly competitive.

The throne room on the next floor was also long, maybe 150 feet, and about 40 feet wide, with windows on both sides. Not one but two layers of Persian carpet covered the floor from wall to wall. The plastered walls were quite bare, and the only furniture was countless, identical, heavy wooden chairs with upholstered seats and backs, all undoubtedly of foreign manufacture. These were placed side by side, touching one another, along the very long walls.

As we entered, King Ibn Saud was already seated in a "throne chair" in the outside corner of the room. He was the biggest Arab I ever saw—about 6'2", heavily built. A very prominent scar from a saber cut started on his forehead, came down across an eye and his cheek, almost to his chin. We had been informed that he had, with the benefit of several wives and a large harem, a couple of hundred children.

According to specified protocol, we approached him and bowed, and then shook hands. He had a paw like a bear, but was quite cordial in a solemn sort of way. After being seated along the side of the room, we had to lean forward a bit and look directly to our right to see him. We had been cautioned, moreover, to keep our two feet flat on the floor—no crossing of the knees lest the king be subjected to the horrifying sight of the soles of our shoes.

Our four sessions with the king, over two days, were long, and our conversation (through Mohammed Effendi, the interpreter) pretty halting. General Collins had to carry the load for our side, and he often ran out of subjects. At one juncture he asked the king, "Do you have communists in Saudi Arabia?" Translated back and forth, the answer came back, "No, we don't." Joe Collins hoped that he had found a subject that would take up some time, so he asked, eagerly, "Well, how is it that you can control communism here in Saudi Arabia?" Translation. The king then simply pointed at himself with a large horny thumb. "When we find a Communist," he said, "*I* kill him." It was our strong impression that the king did the execution himself, with a single mighty swipe of a heavy saber.

At the end of each audience with the king, trays with hot tea and some sort of sticky meat tidbits—goat, I think—were passed around by Arabs in long white burnooses and turbans and wearing long sheathed daggers at the belt. A bit later, another servant, also suitably armed, appeared with a thick clear liquid in a sort of decanter; this was poured pretty lavishly over our hands. Thereafter came another man with a bowl of smoldering wood roots, allowing us to dry our hands by rubbing them together in the aromatic smoke. It turned out that the liquid was attar of roses, thick, surprisingly unattractive, and of incredible staying power. The odor remained with us for days—through Egypt, London, and the flight home.

In leaving the throne room, each day, we backed out, as specified. One doesn't turn his back on a king.

We made one visit to the crown prince, who later became a very unsatisfactory king, being deposed after a few years by his brother Faisal. The throne room of the crown prince was identical to that of the king, with one exception. The long high walls were decorated with about twenty wall clocks, all but one of them stopped dead. The one exception, however, was electric, and had power to it. It had a lighted green glass face, on which was lettered, in gold, the words "PHILLIPS, FAMOUS FOR QUALITY THE WORLD OVER." Extending down from the face, on either side, was a long vertical illuminated glass tube of light yellow liquid through which ascended a column of bubbles. There were no hands to indicate hours or minutes, but six or seven hands were somehow attached to the spindle for seconds, all of the hands rotating in unison around the face of the clock.

The king gave us a big formal dinner on our last night in town. Whole roasted lambs, heads and all, were lined up on the center of an enormous rectangular table; other food, mostly unidentifiable, was set out in large bowls, from which our several Arab hosts helped themselves—and us—without benefit of fork or spoon. The waiters had not much to do, but each was dressed in a copy of the elaborate red-and-white livery of Sheppard's Hotel in Cairo, the opulent effect of which was diluted by the black grease that lay thick on their white cotton gloves. Our several Arab hosts ate with their hands, mostly, and with their hands lifted tidbits off their plates onto ours.

On departure we each received a goodbye present: a long saber with much gold leaf plastered to the scabbard. This didn't compare favorably with what King Ibn Saud gave a recently departed boss of one of the Gulf Emirates: *he* got three Cadillacs and a Buick.

As before indicated, Riyadh is now a modern city and its inhabitants sophisticated, comparatively speaking. But that wasn't so in 1952.

Our next stop was in Jidda, a very ugly agglomeration of cement buildings, some several stories high, on the Red Sea. Jidda at the time was the site of all the foreign embassies, Riyadh being restricted as the King's City. By now, of course, the embassies are in Riyadh where they belong.

From Jidda, we tried to get into Khartoum, on the Nile, but were unsuccessful—the *khamseen,* the famous hot desert wind off the Sahara, was blowing, smothering the whole area in dust. There being no instrument landing facilities at Khartoum, we went back north to Cairo.

A wide boulevard leads from the Cairo airport to the city. In our car, going in, was the air attaché of our embassy in Cairo, an Air Force colonel. He pointed out, in the median, a large number of laborers in the process of removing a long line of high light towers. The reason for the demolition, he said, was the Egyptian king, Farouk, had a few nights previously driven (probably while drunk) his Cadillac into the base of one of them. So out they came.

General Collins's visit to Egypt was strictly unofficial. We talked not to the Egyptians, who already had sovereignty but still not much control, but to the British military, who were getting out. The British were not at all hopeful for the future for Egypt.

From Cairo we went to Wheelus Field in Tripoli. A fine, modern installation, Wheelus was built by the U.S. Air Force and for several years served as a very desirable stop and transfer point en route to and from the Middle East and southern Africa. We lost it to Khaddafi.

My European trip as the G-2 staff member accompanying Secretary of the Army Frank Pace was also pleasant, instructive, and intensely interesting. Our stop in Athens coincided with the Greek celebration of its twenty-fifth anniversary as a complete and free nation—the Turks had finally withdrawn from Thrace a quarter-century previously.

The day was marked first by a parade through the streets of Athens by the Greek Army. Our party was given privileged seats in the reviewing stand. The parade included perhaps sixty freshly painted tanks, coming up the wide avenue perfectly aligned in ranks of three. I was particularly impressed by the Greek tank commanders, each a fierce looking noncom sporting an enormous black mustache of military cut.

Taking the parade was King Paul, a tall man of perhaps 40, and his young queen, Frederika. They made a handsome pair.

The next event was a church service in the Athens Cathedral; once again our party was afforded seats with an excellent view. After all attendees reached their appointed places the king and queen came slowly down the aisle to appropriate music, he in uniform, she quite beautiful in a white lace dress with a very long train. As they reached the head of the wide aisle, they turned completely about to make a formal bow back down the aisle to the dignitaries who filled the pews, and thereafter repeated the bow, first right and then left, to all the people in each arm of the transept. Frederika was lovely in her movements, sweeping that beautiful, enormous train about with the most extraordinary grace and precision.

We learned that the Greeks applaud in church. They filled that one with loud cheering and hand clapping.

Our last stop on the trip with the secretary was London, where Mr. Pace's host was Field Marshal William Slim, then Chief of the Imperial General Staff. A big, powerful man, he had during World War II commanded the British campaign that, in conjunction with U.S. forces under General Stillwell, succeeded brilliantly in defeating the large Japanese military forces in Burma and southern China.

Slim had our whole party for a formal dinner, at which he spoke for perhaps 40 minutes. Perhaps because I read too much Kipling in my youth I have always been inclined to consider the British as the world's most cultured people—but maybe it's the accent that gets me. In any case General Slim's talk, a 1952 summation of the geopolitical-military state of the world, was the most informative and at the same time the most amusing lecture I ever heard. No lesser word would do: he was magnificent.

BRIGADIER GENERAL

14 In the late spring of 1952 I was promoted to brigadier general and assigned as assistant division commander of the 2nd Armored Division in Germany. This was great news for both of us. Mary hadn't liked Washington, in our circumstances, and for the most part I hadn't liked my enforced service in Intelligence, although the two long trips abroad had been delightful and my function the last year as head of the Intelligence Division of G-2, part of the Army's General Staff, had in some respects been rewarding. So far as I knew, we in that very large staff division had not been guilty of any major gaffes despite our much more relaxed approach as respects working hours.

My new assignment was the first of six duty tours, over a period of 13 years, that would complete my military service. Each of the six was absolutely tops—I could not ask for better as respects interest, variety, association, and (to use an overused word) challenge. Now 25 years after retirement I would testify that there's no more satisfying line of endeavor in America than that of service in the combat echelons of our military forces, assuming only that the individual so engaged gives his job a reasonably good try.

The Army in 1952 was still in process of recovering from the teardown of all U.S. military forces immediately after World War II. The USSR was guilty of no such idiocy, reinforcing, instead, its grip on Eastern

Europe, developing and deploying the atomic warhead and the inter-continental ballistic missile, and otherwise modernizing all elements of its military strength. The outbreak of the Korean War woke us up: the world, to our apparent surprise, was not yet entirely peace-loving.

Before 1950, the starting year of the Korean War, our military strength in Europe consisted only of what we called the Constabulary—essentially no more than light armored cavalry units patrolling the German countryside, plus our garrison in Berlin. These were occupation forces in a defeated enemy country. But by 1952 we, the British, and the Canadians had moved several combat divisions and air wings onto mainland Europe, forces not aimed at the control of Germany but to serve with other European forces under NATO, a new alliance formed to discourage the armed conquest of Western Europe by communist Russia and its allies.

The 2nd U.S. Armored Division beat me to Germany by about four months. Division Headquarters was at Bad Kreuznach in the area known as the Rhineland Pfalz, just west of the river. "Bad" means "bath"—Bad Kreuznach ("Baat Kroitz-nock") being a spa featuring baths of hot mineral water. The town itself was very clean—typical of southern German towns—quaint and attractive, nestled in a lovely valley down which ran the clear waters of the Nahe River. The most prominent building was the Kurhaus, a large hostelry designed for visiting bathers but now accommodating the headquarters of the 2nd Armored Division. Our military families were put in civilian housing, mostly very attractive, rented by our government from German citizens.

For reasons I can't remember, Mary and our two boys couldn't come with me. They arrived at the Frankfurt Airport three months later after a rough flight across the Atlantic—the boys were sick and Mary exhausted. And I, quite inexcusably, was late getting to the airport to pick them up. This was not one of the best moments of our now 59 years of marriage, but things got better when we arrived at our comfortable, roomy, spotless, delightfully appointed house in Bad K, where an excellent cook and what turned out to be an absolutely super housemaid—who loved children—awaited us.

The cook's husband had not returned from the Russian front after the war; nothing was known of what had happened to him. But on certain appointed days each year she still put a lighted candle in the window. Mary wept when she saw her do it, for she was a dear, kindly woman. The Germans were altogether to blame for World War II, but the suffering of the German people in that war was frightful—impossible for Americans to imagine.

I had found on my arrival, earlier, that the then–Maj. Gen. William Palmer—known throughout the Army as "P. Willie Palmer" and as a very stern taskmaster, and who I was told had asked for my assignment—had been promoted and had departed for another job. My new boss and the division commander was Maj. Gen. George Read, an ex-Cavalryman and once a fine polo player. He gave me the best assignment ever afforded, I believe, to an assistant division commander: I was given the sole, unsupervised function of training all of the combat elements of the division, and no other responsibility. It was almost too good to be true; each day spent in that function was a delight. I was out-of-doors all but a small fraction of my working time.

Read, to our surprise, was transferred after only about a year and a half with the division. He was replaced by Maj. Gen. L. L. Doan, known to his contemporaries as "Chubby" perhaps because he was 6'2" and lean as a rail. He was another ex-Cavalryman and a fine officer.

All of the combat elements of the division were quartered in three large ex–German Army garrisons, one near Mainz, one near Mannheim, both on the Rhine River, and one at Baumholder, an excellent military training area in the hills west of Bad Kreuznach. To get to these distant areas I did lots of jeep riding and lots of flying in an L-19 Cessna liaison aircraft, and I spent a fair number of nights in a pup tent. On one Fourth of July, at Baumholder, the water in the canvas bucket outside my tent froze over. This reinforced my earlier impression that Germany was pretty far north.

I'll spare the reader much detail, but take space to boast of some of my training innovations.

One of these was the periodic (two or three times weekly) publication of Training Notes, which by order were made required reading and study by every officer in every combat unit of the division, and there-

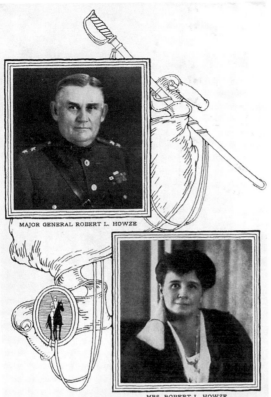

MAJOR GENERAL ROBERT L. HOWZE

MRS. ROBERT L. HOWZE

My parents, Robert Lee Howze (a major general and the fifth ranking officer in the Army upon his death) and Anne Chifelle Hawkins Howze (daughter of Brig. Gen. Hamilton Smith Hawkins of the Army).

My graduation photograph from West Point, 1930. From there I would go to serve in the 7th Cavalry at Fort Bliss, Texas.

TOP: My first private mount, Quien Sabe, 7th Cavalry, 1932.

LEFT: Mary and I on our wedding day, March 28, 1936.

TOP: Mary and I at a post fox hunt at Fort Bliss, 1941.

BOTTOM: "I would have resisted going anywhere there was no polo"—26th Cavalry polo team at Fort Stotsenberg in the Philippine Islands, 1938. *From left to right*, Lts. Ralph Haines, Jim Alger, Ham Howze, and Capt. Hall Trapnell.

In Italy I served with my beloved 1st Armored Division.

1945–46, I was a member of what was called the First Command Class, a new high-level, five-month course at the traditional site of the Command and General Staff College, Fort Leavenworth, Kansas.

TOP: This was the last steeplechase of "Pie Plate" and rider.

BOTTOM: Gen. Matthew Ridgeway (*center*), then Chief of Staff, visited the 2nd Armored Division in Germany in 1952. On the left is Maj. Gen. George Reed.

TOP: The first successful inflight refueling of a helicopter from a fixed-wing aircraft took place when "Ambling Annie," a CH-21, was refueled by a U-1a Otter on a nonstop flight from Miramar Naval Air Station, San Diego, at 0600 hours, August 23, 1956, to touch the East Coast at Savannah, Georgia, and then on to the Pentagon. (U.S. Army Aviation.)

BOTTOM: On completion of Ambling Annie's over 31-hour flight at 1330 hours, August 24, 1956, the secretary of the Army and I, as director of Army Aviation, greeted the crew, Capt. Jim Bowman, Maj. Hugh Gaddis, and Lt. Col. Joe Givens. (Army Aviation Museum.)

TOP: Mary and I made an unofficial visit at a Korean orphanage in Seoul in 1960.

BOTTOM: Mary and I (*third and fourth from left*) are with Syngmun Rhee, the Army Chief of Staff during the Korean War, and the first president of South Korea. This picture was taken following our embarrassing tardiness at church.

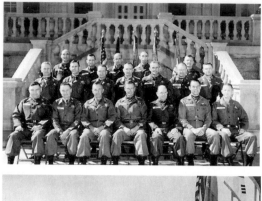

LEFT TOP: The general staff of XVIII Airborne Corps, Fort Bragg, North Carolina. I am fourth from left, front row.

LEFT BOTTOM: The military official farewell to the U.S. ambassador to Korea, Sam Berger, in 1964. White coats identify British yeomanry, by then no more than a token force in Korea. The remainder of the Honor Guard is Korean and U.S. Army units. (U.S. Army photograph.)

RIGHT TOP: Mrs. Eleanor Roosevelt and I stop for coffee at the 82nd Airborne Division troop mess during her visit to Fort Bragg in 1958.

RIGHT BOTTOM: The XVIII Airborne Corps, which I commanded, was to be part of the invasion of Cuba. I visited President Kennedy with Gen. Buz Wheeler (*center*), Chief of Staff of the Army, and Gen. Ted Parker in anticipation of the invasion.

TOP: Korean President Pak Chung Hui visits my headquarters in 1964.

BOTTOM: Mary and I stand with our two sons, William G. Howze and Guy R. Howze, in 1963.

TOP: Mary was a Gray Lady and worked one day a week at the military hospital. As senior Gray Lady here she caps a new volunteer. She and her women's club members gave assistance to Korean orphanages, hospitals for veterans, and in local disaster areas.

BOTTOM: Mary was a guest at a KMAG social event in the late 1950s.

TOP: Chiang Kai-shek and his wife entertained Mary and me formally at tea in the early 1960s. He seemed to be a highly intelligent man, very friendly toward America and, with Madame Chiang, a gracious host and a most interesting person to talk to.

LEFT: War games and field tests during the summer of 1962 were a necessary prelude to formulating the recommendations of the Howze Board. This de Havilland Caribou crashed during a demonstration in front of the Secretaries of Defense, Army and Air Force, the chairman of the Joint Chiefs of Staff, and other dignitaries. (Courtesy of de Havilland Aircraft Company of Canada.)

TOP: Senior Army Commander's meeting with Pres. Lyndon Johnson, January 1965.

BOTTOM: Office staff of CINCUNC, Korea, 1964.

a.

b.

c.

d.

e.

f.

Many experimented with arming helicopters in the 1950s and early 1960s, but the helicopter gunship was not accepted as a gun platform until the Howze Board and the application of the airmobile concept in Vietnam. Pictured are (a) the Bell OH-13, armed with rockets and machine guns to test the feasibility of firing weapons from helicopters; (b) the Bell UH-1B "Huey," armed with machine guns and 2.75-inch rockets, the first helicopter gunship employed in Vietnam; (c) the Sioux Scout, an OH-13 modified to a tandem-seating configuration and carrying turret-mounted machine guns; (d) the Bell AH-1 Cobra, the first operational real helicopter gunship; (e) the Lockheed AH-56 Cheyenne, the Army's first attempt to develop a sophisticated, high-performance gunship; and (f) the McDonnell-Douglas AH-64 Apache, made famous in Desert Storm. (a, c, d: courtesy of Bell Helicopter Textron; b, Army Aviation Museum.)

a.

b.

c.

d.

e.

I saw the evolution of the Army's Utility Tactical Transport Aircraft System (known as the UTTAS) start with (a) the H-19 used briefly in Korea, to (b) the H-21, and (c) the H-34 employed in the early stages in Vietnam to be replaced by the most famous aircraft in the Vietnam War, (d) the UH-1 Huey, and culminating with (e) the UH-60 Black Hawk, a star performer in Desert Storm.

a.

As a consultant to Bell Helicopter Textron in 1982, I saw the payoff for the Army's experimentation in the application of new technology on VTOL aircraft in the early 1950s with (a) the XV-3, continued in the early 1970s with (b) the XV-15, and culminating in (c) the V-22 Osprey, the first operational tilt-rotor aircraft. The Osprey is being built for the Marines and the Air Force. (Bell Helicopter Textron.)

b.

c.

TOP: To my obvious surprise and pleasure, Gen. Omar Bradley turned up at my retirement reception at Fort Myer, Virginia, 1965. (U.S. Army.)

BOTTOM: My retirement ceremony at Fort Myer, Virginia, included the Secretary of the Army Stephen Ailes and Gen. Harold K. Johnson, Chief of Staff of the Army.

after put in permanent file in every company and battalion headquarters for additional reference.

The notes consisted simply of comments on the good and bad points observed in daily inspection of training—and some direct tactical instruction, for I'd had more actual tank and armored infantry fighting experience than any of my subordinates. Sometimes also I quoted from the writings of von Clausewitz and Edwin Rommel, and sometimes injected a bit of humor.

The system worked exceeding well, as no other system could, in broadening the effect of whatever good I was doing in visits to the training areas. It also established training standards. If, for example, I detected in an officer's performance, or in his outfit's, a flaw I'd earlier inveighed against in the Training Notes, I had a pretty good basis for giving him a rough time, assuming he'd read the Training Notes. If he hadn't read them I could give both him and his next senior some pretty direct advice. I hope I may be excused for boasting that in later years several officers told me they still retained the complete three-quarter-inch-thick file of the Training Notes.

We instituted in all tank battalions and companies a system for frequent tank platoon training using jeeps (equipped with tank radios) instead of tanks. Only the tank commander, gunner, and driver could get in the jeep, but the loader wasn't necessary anyway. Only by using jeeps, not tanks, were we able to get German farmers' permission to use their pasture land, only by using jeeps were we able to do maybe three times the tactical platoon training we otherwise could have done. And we inflicted, in an average month of training, much less than average wear and tear on the tanks, and used less fuel.

I also laid out a 30-mile course for the reconnaissance platoons of the division, again substituting jeeps for tanks, along the German country roads leading up to Baumholder. The platoon moved in tactical formation, but no supervision was involved and no enemy was physically represented. When he reached each of perhaps a dozen marked spots on his 25-mile route the platoon leader turned to a paper and sketch map outlining the new situation facing him. After consulting with his squad leaders he issued his order and the platoon executed it, and then a little self-critique was conducted. About 12 hours of work was involved, after which the platoon camped out (tactically, but alone) for the night on the Baumholder training area. In addition to other training, recce platoons were required to run through this exercise, modified from time to time, twice annually.

We had other set, unsupervised exercises for all the tank and armored infantry platoons of the division. Incidentally, these exercises fit into another requirement: each line company commander in the division was required to send each of his platoons, once each calendar month, into the field for 24 hours of tactical training under the sole supervision of the platoon leader, whether a commissioned officer or NCO. No senior was authorized to visit the platoon within the 24 hours. This simple device did all manner of good.

Perhaps our best training device was the tactical inspection of tank and armored infantry companies. I did the first inspection myself in each of the three combat commands, requiring the pertinent combat command and battalion commander to accompany me and even assist —so they might see what was required of the tested company and be prepared to conduct subsequent, almost identical inspections themselves. In combination we tested every combat company in the division twice each year, with marked signs of improvement in company performance.

I used only two young assistants, my aide and one other. The company (with an artillery forward observer) that was selected at random for test had a day's warning to report to me (when I was the inspector) at a designated crossroad in a training area at maximum possible strength (all passes, dental appointments, and the like being canceled) and in full battle gear. We began the "tactical" inspection by putting each platoon through a different series of about four simple exercises, each of 30- or 45-minutes duration, with the company commander watching. Sample mission: "Your platoon has been moving all day against a slowly retreating, hard-fighting enemy tank and infantry force. Your company commander had just told you by radio that some enemy forces are between your platoon and the rest of your outfit. Only a half hour of daylight remains. Your mission: put your platoon into this patch of woods for the night, with the function only of *surviving* the night. I'll be back to look at your dispositions 20 minutes from now."

After all such little platoon exercises (some of them very much out of the ordinary, to test the platoon leader's ingenuity), the company commander was told to put his company in tactical bivouac, posting the proper security, for supper and a night's rest. Of course, my two assistants and I attacked the company with machine guns shooting blanks as soon as it got bedded down, and then got everybody up for a series of night marches (which we ambushed and otherwise harassed) and night combat exercises until the sun came up. And then the company was given an attack mission involving lots of maneuver and tactical know-how to take three successive objectives. By 11 A.M. , when I called everyone in to listen to an on-the-spot critique, the company had been working very hard, physically and mentally, for about 24 hours without sleep and with no more than one hurried meal of C-rations.

At the critique, attended by the entire company, of course, but also by the appropriate brigade commander and battalion commander, both of whom had been with me the whole 24 hours, I discussed mistakes and inadequate performance in some detail, rendered compliments as appropriate, and then rated the company as Ready for Combat or Unready for Combat—just that simple.

Never did I get an argument or hear an objection when, as I often did, I rated the company tactically not combat-worthy. How could one argue? The company had just demonstrated, for all to see, whether or not it could cut the mustard.

It was a pretty exhausting procedure for everybody, including me— 24 hours on the go, hard. But the combat tactical inspection, done semiannually, did much to bring Hell on Wheels (the division nickname) into condition as a first-class combat-ready division. We had deficiencies, of course, but we eventually came to the point at which I knew the division could fight, and so did everyone else.

One day I decided that I would like to fly. Qualification as a pilot was a formal matter requiring proper authorization, so I did no more than learn the ropes in a two-seater light military reconnaissance aircraft known as the Cessna L-19. The division aviation officer arranged for this, providing me as an instructor one Capt. Jim Hamlet, one of the most personally capable and likable individuals it has been my pleasure to know. He retired, very much later, as a major general.

So we wouldn't bother anybody we did much of our flight instruc tion at a little grass field out in the country near the town of Finthen, not far from the Rhine River. It was great fun and I became, if I say so myself, very proficient. But though I made countless landings and take-offs and did the aerobatics I never made a solo landing—a very proper restriction. But I had the bug.

Bad Kreuznach was a wonderful spot for my family. Mary and I studied German pretty religiously under a civilian instructor, one Herr Stra-donsky—sounds Polish or Russian, but he wasn't. He had lunch with us twice weekly, followed by an additional hour of instruction. I per-sisted in this for one year, Mary for two. I became reasonably capable in Jaeger Deutsch (hunter German) and in casual conversation with the servants, shopkeepers, and local acquaintances, but she became pro-ficient even in fairly abstract social conversation—a much severer test. On one occasion, however, she did rush out of the house in a big hurry, throwing out over her shoulder to Liesel, the maid, "Be sure to eat the dog!"

We made a number of friends among the Germans, many of whom were very agreeable, cultivated people. The typical German salesclerk speaks clear, grammatical German and writes in a firm, beautiful hand that few of our business executives could match. So did our maid.

Impressive also were German schoolchildren, always scrubbed clean and always, girls and boys, in simple attractive uniform. It was quite common to see columns of such children being led around the town streets by teachers. The very apparent state of order and discipline seemed to guarantee solid, productive education. And indeed, I'd guess that's what the children got. I venture the thought that our badly ailing American school system cannot be retrieved without the institution of something approximating the German variety of discipline.

Mary and many other officers' wives did charitable work among the German townspeople who, though they had partially recovered from the frightful desolation wrought by World War II, still needed help as respects medicine and refugee and crippled-child care. Mary organized an American woman's club in Bad K for the purpose.

One good German friend was the owner of a leather goods business: he had a tannery and made the finished product—suitcases, handbags, and the like, all of fine quality. We remember him for three things: (1) The RAF had bombed and destroyed his primary plant in Germany; (2) the Luftwaffe had bombed and destroyed his branch plant in London; and (3) as an elderly reserve officer in the German Army, he was in the last stages of the war given command of a hastily trained lot of young boys, armed with rifles, and told to march them westward from Bad K to delay, in his designated sector, the advance of the American armored divisions. In pursuit of this mission, he told me, he first put his charges into formation and inspected them very carefully; he then marched them westward through town and thence onto the bridge crossing the Nahe River just out of town, where the water was deep. He halted the boys on the bridge, gave them "right face," and then, on command, had them throw their rifles and ammunition into the river. He then marched them smartly back into town and sent them home.

There was no golf course near us, but there were excellent tennis courts that we used almost daily during the very long summer evenings, after work was done. It was delightful, and equally delightful were the weekend family picnics with our still small boys (usually with Liesel along) in the lovely wooded hills within a few miles of our house. Every German wood, whether it be a national or state forest, or one belonging to (and inevitably named after) a small town, is faithfully tended by a Forstmeister, who, with or without assistants, cleans out undesirable underbrush and dead timber and otherwise keeps the wood neat and tidy. And the woods—and indeed the cultivated plains—of Germany are full of game, all because of systematic wildlife supervision and care.

Hunting in Germany is extremely good—pheasant, partridge, duck, deer (including a very large red deer of nearly the size of our elk), and boar. I did all except the boar. We at Bad K had a particularly good deal whereby a small Navy launch belonging to the tiny U.S. Rhine River Patrol at Wiesbaden came downstream each Sunday, during the very long shooting season, to Bingen, just 17 miles from Bad K. About five of us piled in the boat to hunt through the brush and small trees overhanging the water along the river shore and near little islands. This system isn't legal in the United States, but was then in Germany. We had superb mallard jump shooting.

On one occasion, however, when we spied an enormous flock of mallards on a gravel bar, we approached it, all hunkered down in the slowly moving boat, until we ran aground only 20 yards away—unusually close to the quarry. Our man in the front whispered, "Okay! When I count three, everybody stand up and have at it!" We arose at the count of three: the ducks just stared at us. Our gallant leader whispered again: "Okay! I'll shoot over their heads. Then get 'em!" He shot; the startled (and highly offended) ducks jumped a couple of feet vertically into the air, and back down onto the gravel bar. We bade them goodbye—we had encountered a flock of city-park ducks on migration north.

Things were so pleasant in Bad K that holiday was hardly necessary, but occasionally we took leave for a week or so to go on auto trips over the lovely southern German countryside or down to Garmisch, a beautiful and then still quaint resort town snuggled in an Alpine valley, or to the Kleinerwalsertal (meaning the Valley of the Little Wals River) a smaller, remote equivalent of Garmisch, or to Austria, from Salzberg to Vienna. My wife and I have seen most of the lovely mountains of America, too, but the Alps are in a class by themselves, partly because of the width and length of the snow- and glacier-clad mass of peaks—hundreds of them—and partly because the mountain chain, unlike most of ours, springs not from a mile-high plain but from farmland only a few hundred feet above sea-level.

And once, leaving our boys with Liesel and the cook, we motored down to Naples to pick up my 80-year-old mother, arrived for a month's stay. The trip and the ensuing visit were most enjoyable for all of us. But the highlight of her visit for my oldest boy, then 8, came at her departure. He sat on the lap of the German engineer of a small, luxurious private train, inherited by our senior command in Germany from Hermann Goering, by then deceased, and lent to me to take my mother to her ship up at Bremerhaven. Bill, the boy, ran the train up and back for a total of 18 hours, sitting on the lap of the engineer. He wouldn't leave that lap—we had to send meals up to him.

A cruel (I thought) interlude for me was six-weeks' duty as the next-to-senior member of a nine-officer court-martial trying a bunch of quartermaster reserve officers for wholesale theft in conjunction with a crooked German wholesale coal merchant who had enormous contracts with American forces all over our sector of Germany. There were some eight charges and about 150 specifications backing up the charges; all the supporting exhibits had to be laboriously introduced, one by one, into the evidence, admissibility being argued in each case by a defense counsel. He, also a reservist and a stuffy one, was obviously overcome with his own importance. The law officer, also an unusually pompous character and another reserve legal-eagle, would countenance no short-cuts in this interminable process.

The reader may judge unseemly my heavy criticism of the legal specialists. First, let me say that I have no prejudice against reserve officers—a great many of the company-grade officers of the 2AD were such, and fine people. Reserve *law* officers, however, are accustomed to the complicated and obfuscating procedures of civil law and will really mess up a court-martial. Indeed, our modern procedures of civil criminal law have, as of this writing (1995), given to the U.S. public the highest rate, in all categories of crime, among all the world's developed countries.

There followed in our court-martial all the oral testimony, all the lofty objections by counsel, and all the pontifical rulings by the law officer. The exhibits, mostly falsified invoices and ledgers, amounted to a pile of paper about two feet thick, and with weeks of testimony and argument thrown in, the whole issue became much too complicated for comprehension and memory. Accordingly, I requested that all the stuff be given me to study in my room, and after many nights of such study I arrived precisely at the manner and size of the fraud in a way no other court member could manage.

When the sessions, lasting nearly six *weeks,* were finished, I was able to lay out before the deliberating court the nature and magnitude of the crime. But when voting began, I was dumbfounded to hear a "not guilty" vote on many of the specifications and charges. I called a halt, and though I didn't know exactly what my prerogatives were I refused to continue in what was about to be an outrageous miscarriage of justice. The court's president agreed, so we threw out all the previous vote and began again. With the benefit of the exhibits I reviewed the evidence to support the countless specifications. So we ultimately arrived at reasonably correct decisions on almost all of the counts of malfeasance, and ordered good solid multiyear sentences in the pen for all the defendants. I wished we could have done the same for the law officer and the defense counsel.

Our verdicts and sentences apparently infuriated the law officer who, I found some months later, preferred charges against me for illegal influence on members of the court. I was visited and "investigated" as a matter of form by a captain from the Judge Advocate General's Department in Washington. He recommended that the charges be dismissed, as they were.

One more aspect of the coal fraud. The court members worked ten-hour days six days weekly, but on each cold and frequently wet Sunday we went duck shooting on the Weser River, not far from Bremerhaven, in small decrepit rowboats fitted with outboard engines. All were rented from local riverside farmers. We found that the outgoing tide was downright scary—something like 12 knots; and when it was out, some of the multiple river courses went almost dry. We killed lots of ducks, drank a little whiskey, and had a great time (mostly because we weren't in a courtroom), but occasionally spent an extra (and extra cold) six hours or so in the reeds on the wrong side of one of the river channels.

In the late fall of 1953, shortly before I left the division, we participated in a large field maneuver, allied with some and against other American divisions and Air Force Wings in Germany. It was valuable training, but at the same time depressing because of what we did to the land. The crops were all in, but tanks do dreadful things to soft farm soil and also to small macadam country roads.

But the division did well. I'm proud to say. For a reason I've forgotten, my division commander, Chubby Doan, for one 24-hour period was diverted to other duty, resulting in my being in command of the division for that day of intense maneuver activity. I greatly enjoyed the brief experience.

After a year and a half in the 2AD I was ordered to Seventh Army Headquarters, then near Stuttgart, as the Deputy Chief of Staff for Operations. Mary and I hated to leave the division and the little town of Bad Kreuznach. My new boss and the Army Commander was Lt. Gen. Anthony McAuliffe, who as the assistant division commander of the 101 Airborne Division at Bastogne during the Battle of the Bulge of World War II scribbled "NUTS!" on a written demand for surrender by the commander of the besieging German forces. This earned McAuliffe much not-very-meaningful fame, but in truth he was a most capable commander, in combat and peacetime, and a very likable one.

Stuttgart is an attractive and very substantial city in the bottom of a river valley with pretty steep sides. We were assigned a large, lovely house and garden on the west side, overlooking the valley and the city. A gardener and two house servants awaited us, and we brought Liesel along for good measure. A tree which on our arrival was absolutely laden down with the most delicious cherries decorated our new front yard—I, in full uniform, occupied its branches for perhaps 20 minutes each time I came home from work.

Unlike Bad K, Stuttgart had been very heavily punished by American and British bombers, and by artillery fire, during the war. Most of the debris had been removed (in the course of eight years) from downtown and was stacked in a huge pile on our ridge a couple of miles to the south. This was known both by Germans and Americans, aptly enough, as "Hitler's Denkmal." *Denkmal* means "monument."

Stuttgart is part of southern Germany, and all southern Germany is beautiful. The beauty of rural Germany is due largely to the luxuriant growth of woods and crops and the great proliferation of flowering fruit trees, but also to the clustering of farmhouses in villages—close-knit, quaint, attractive villages, as distinguished from the scattering of individual houses, barns, and silos (and often rusting machinery) on the farmland of America. German farmhouses, mostly cream stucco with orange-red roofs, are themselves attractive parts of the landscape.

Seventh Army headquarters were near a pleasant town, a suburb of

Stuttgart, called Vaihingen. Vaihingen is distinguished by being the sauerkraut capital of the world—an honor if there ever was one—and demonstrates its right to the title by producing an infinite quantity of enormous cabbages.

My primary job, in part self-imposed, as Deputy Chief of Staff (Operations) was to preside over the rewriting of the operational plans for the defense of the southern half of Germany against possible Warsaw Pact attack. The Seventh Army general staff did the writing; I was required to lay out the tasks for the several staff sections, provide the coordination, and review the product for further coordination with the French (who, despite having withdrawn from NATO, had a force of several ready divisions in Germany, not far west of us) and submission to the Army Commander. On his approval it was to go on up the chain of command.

The defense of our sector promised to be a daunting task, given the superiority of the enemy forces, the possibilities of surprise, and the recent withdrawal of France from NATO. Mind you, the French corps under General Juin, its divisions, and its supporting air squadrons, were altogether enthusiastic and cooperative in the drafting of the new plan, and given the order by President de Gaulle they would have been entirely cooperative with us in case of Soviet–Warsaw Pact attack. But there was a doubt remaining: Would de Gaulle, unpredictable and habitually suspicious of his allies, withhold his participation in another war if the circumstances didn't suit him? We thought he might, and so did our masters in NATO and Washington.

As I pondered our necessarily complicated plan, during its months of preparation, I devised a scheme of attack that the USSR and its allies might execute with enormous effect. There was nothing complicated about it: the enemy need only take maximum advantage of surprise. Surprise is often the single greatest ingredient of victory on the battlefield, as witness the smashing success of the opening German attack in 1940 on the combined armies of Britain, France, and the Low Countries—almost a year after war had been declared. Witness also the initial success of the later German attack on the Russians.

To attain that sort of surprise in 1954 (and indeed, until 1989) the enemy needed only to launch his initial attack not with his entire panoply of force but simply with selected elements: to wit, short-range nonatomic missile units and fighter squadrons, all with the mission of:

1. Taking out of action the NATO fighter squadrons within 200 miles of the frontier. This could have been done in the same way that the Israeli Air Force destroyed the large Egyptian Air Force in a single morning of June 1967: that is, by destroying the aircraft on the ground, by cratering the runways with "concrete dibber" bombs, and by blowing up the hangars. The location of every airfield in Western Europe was at the time known to the Soviet Air Force to the nearest meter.

2. Neutralizing the command structure of the allied forces defending the frontier in Germany. The location of every air force, air division, and air wing headquarters; of every field army, army corps, and combat division headquarters; of every logistic headquarters; and of every ammunition and other supply installations of the Allied Forces in Europe—*all* of these were known precisely to the Soviet Air Force. The effect of destroying these installations by surprise attack could be described by a single word: paralyzing.

Such an attack would have surprised the great bulk of the Warsaw Pact forces as much as it would ours. Soviet and other Warsaw Pact air wings and ground divisions would have had to gather their wits and leap to arms just as ours would—but with what a difference! Their forward airfields, their major headquarters, and major supply dumps would have still been intact and functioning. Ours would have been flat, and largely without communications.

Although the situation scared my pants off—and I was the senior planner for Seventh Army—the official position of the Intelligence community in Washington was that we'd have several days of warning, that estimate based on the estimated time necessary to alert and prepare the bulk of the enemy forces for a general ground, air, and submarine attack. We would have detected all that activity and have had time to prepare for it. But if I were the Russians I wouldn't have planned to do it that way.

Given the current situation in the Soviet Union and the ex–Warsaw Pact countries, this matter of warning is, of course, no longer of importance. But it was until 1989.

Life in Stuttgart was pleasant, in part because we belonged to the German American Club, in part because of the beauty of the countryside—and its interest. The shooting, particularly pheasant and partridge, was superb. One German friend with a large and productive *revier* or preserve allowed me simply to call his gamekeeper to arrange a hunt. A special feature of his preserve was a lovely meandering stream bordered by trees—walking up on mallards there was simple delight. In many ways I think it's too bad that we in America don't adopt some of the procedures and traditions associated with hunting in Germany. Seasons are long—the duck season, for example, runs from August through mid-February.

The terrain of Germany is divided into thousands of hunting *reviers,* the hunting privilege on each revier (comprising one or perhaps several farms) being sold, as I remember, once every three years to an individual. Who owns the land itself is immaterial: a farmer may not shoot game on his own land unless he purchases the hunting privileges on it. This is accepted because the very considerable money the state gains from selling the hunting privilege is deducted from the farmer's annual real estate tax. The revier's temporary owner (the hunter) literally crops his revier of game, in many cases retrieving part or all of the cost of the revier by selling the game to meat markets—all quite legal—and, if he wishes, by charging guest hunters (who expect this) a fee for each piece of game they take.

And believe it or not, a farmer may not let his dog or cat run loose on his own farm; if he does, the revier owner is privileged to shoot it. On the other hand, should a roving herd of wild boar (which can move across several large farms in a single night) root up a farmer's beet field the revier owner is required to compensate the farmer for the damage.

Hunting in Germany is much influenced by tradition, and some procedures are formally observed. The visiting sportsman should be aware of this. The German hunter wears something close to a uniform: rough green knickers and stockings and a green shooting coat and hat, the latter usually with a duck or pheasant feather in its band. If you kill a deer, your companion will carefully select and cut off a pretty sprig of evergreen from a nearby tree; this he dips lightly in the deer's blood and then places in the fold of his hunting hat. He then approaches you, clicks his heels, says, "Weidmann's Heil!" ("Hunter's salute"), bows deeply, and presents you the sprig, cradled in his hat. You take the sprig, bow, say "Weidmann's Dank!" ("Hunter's thanks!"), and stick it in the band of your hat.

A similar routine is followed when the first drake mallard is shot on a duck hunt. A special little dark-green feather taken from under the bird's wing is presented, with all due ceremony, to the successful shooter. And the same ceremony is followed for the first cock pheasant.

It is not unusual to take Hungarian partridge (slightly larger than our quail), pheasant, *kniche* (bunny rabbit), European hare, and even duck and geese on the same day. Periodically, the hunt stops for everybody to have a pretty large silver jigger of schnapps and to view the game taken, which the gamekeeper lays out in long rows of two—two pheasant, two hare, and so on. The hunters, as they sip the liquor, walk up and down the rows, commenting favorably on the beauty of the birds and congratulating one another on his skill—if and when displayed. Never does a hunter walk across the line or lines of game, that being a discourtesy.

It would be hard for me to convince American hunters that these formalities add to the pleasure and sociability of hunting and, in a way, do honor to the game one has taken. But it is somehow more attractive, at least to me, than simply throwing the carcasses into the back of a pickup.

I would add here a word of advice: if you want a good European hunting dog, buy a Drathaar, meaning "Wirehair." They are uniformly ugly but amazingly good on all varieties of game, including hare, and can switch from one variety to another without losing stride. The Germans raise lots of Weimeraner, too, but mostly to sell to Americans.

One feature of life overseas in a major military headquarters is the recurrent appearance of U.S. congressmen on what some irreverent taxpayers call boondoggles. We had them in Stuttgart. On one occasion a congressmen actually requested, on arrival, that he be shut away in a comfortable apartment, under the supervision of a sergeant he knew, for a three-day drunk. We accommodated him. Occasionally, too, we took a group, including wives, on one of the luxurious German private trains for a tour of our sector of Germany. I remember one visitor sipping booze without interruption, save for eating and sleeping, for an entire weekend.

Two trips with General McAuliffe are worth mention.

One took us to a command conference with the French (subject: the new defense plan we'd just completed) at their headquarters in Baden-Baden in the Black Forest. Baden-Baden is unquestionably one of the most beautiful towns on the surface of the earth. Our conference was held in an enormous manor house surrounded by broad grounds largely covered by rhododendron in bloom: huge bushes, huge, fragrant blossoms. Breathtaking.

On one of my evening strolls through this magnificence I encountered a really charming girl, just off the boat from America and the wife of one of our young officers. She had a question: Why were cuckoo clocks constantly sounding off the hour in this part of Germany? I had to tell her that she was not hearing clocks, but live cuckoo birds. It took some time to convince her I wasn't kidding.

On an another occasion I accompanied General McAuliffe to Paris and a CPX (Command Post Exercise) in which only military headquarters participate, the troops remaining in their barracks. The British call these TEWTS (Tactical Exercises Without Troops).

This CPX was special because British Field-Marshal Lord Bernard Montgomery, then holding the post of Commander of NATO Ground Forces, conducted it. All attendees anticipated something different, and got it—in the shape of a one-man show, starring Monty. Most CPXs have various presenters and other active participants, but not this one.

Monty operated on the floor of an oblong indoor stadium holding perhaps 300 persons, not far from Napoleon's Tomb. Most of the floor was covered by an elaborate contour map of the line of contact between Warsaw Pact and NATO forces in Western Europe, all major military units being carefully represented. Ample space was available around the map for Monty to walk about—which he did, without pause in walking or talking, for all three days of the exercise.

A number of very high ranking generals, Army and Air Force, and Navy admirals, of all the NATO nations were present. Monty addressed them rather like he would schoolchildren. He first forbade them—no exceptions permitted—from talking, coughing, or sneezing. A severe cold, or presumably even a potentially fatal onslaught of bronchial pneumonia, was no excuse. Monty had hung on his Sam Browne belt two enforcing devices—one what we'd call a company officer's whistle, the other a dinner bell. When any attendee dared cough or sneeze Monty instantly stopped talking, stopped walking, rang the bell or tooted the whistle, and then pointed at the culprit, fixing him with an accusing stare and sometimes chiding him on his behavior.

Very senior British officers are marked by their strong personality and aplomb. None of those officers present, however, survived those three days with much of either left intact. Monty embarrassed them down to the soles of their boots.

About five months before our three-year tour in Germany was due to end I got orders for immediate return—to the Pentagon. We managed to postpone our departure for two weeks, but then had to go. The cause of our leaving was "Gentleman" Jim Gavin, a lieutenant general and one of the ablest—and certainly one of the bravest—officers in the Army. He had graduated from West Point in 1928, and during the war rose to the rank of major general and to the command of the famous 82nd Airborne Division, which he led with great gallantry in much severe fighting. He had selected me, I judge because of my demonstrated emphasis on mobility in the tactics of ground warfare, to become the first director of Army Aviation. I didn't relish returning to the Pentagon, but if I had to, going to Aviation seemed the best.

Believe me, it was hard to leave my job, Germany, and the delightful life we led there. Especially hard it was to leave Liesel and the other servants, our German and American friends in Stuttgart, the shooting, the travel, and the beautiful countryside. General McAuliffe had been a splendid boss, who didn't object to my long workday lunch hour during which I played two sets of tennis or, in winter, squash. He was also kind enough, and errant enough, to put on my efficiency report that I was the best brigadier general in the Army. That was not correct, but was nice to read and did me no harm.

We were given a special train again to take us to Bremerhaven, and in the military part of the dock area were put up for the night in a suite of one living room and six bedrooms, each with two beds—part of an old but refurbished German military wartime hospital building. We had dinner at the mess, and something they ate poisoned both little boys. We were up with them repeatedly all night, but seemed never to manage to reach them in time to keep them from destroying, utterly and I suspect forever, one set of twin bed linen after the other. As I remember, they accounted for a total of five pair.

Our return across the North Atlantic aboard the beautiful new SS *United States,* being in midwinter, was rough as a cob but nevertheless delightful—except sometimes. And in the drive from New York down to Washington we were struck by the rise in the cost of hamburgers in the three years we'd been abroad—as I remember the price had risen to something like 40 cents a burger.

ARMY AVIATION

15 On arrival in Washington in early February of 1955 we bought a house—our third one in Falls Church, Virginia—and resumed our close relationship with Maj. Gen. and Mrs. Guy V. Henry, retired, Mary's parents living in Kenwood, a part of the Bethesda suburb of Washington, and with my mother, living in the District. And I reported for duty to Lt. Gen. Jim Gavin in his office in the Pentagon. He was cordial and brief: my new appointment was due to my lifelong demonstrated interest in battlefield mobility. Aviation in the Army had a bright future, but needed direction: I was to carry on as its first director—that being, it should be said, no more than a staff title. I told him I wanted to fly, mentioning that I had already a pretty good, if irregular, start. Jim Gavin said I should do so.

I would note here that James Gavin had contributed and continued to contribute very greatly to the battle performance and general effectiveness of the Army, not only by his exceptional combat leadership—amply demonstrated in World War II—but by his imagination and insight into the changing complexities of battle tactics and technique, with particular reference to mobility. The Army is and will continue to be much in his debt.

I arranged immediately for a flight physical examination. The Army doctor found out I couldn't see worth a whoop without benefit of glasses, gave me what he called the biggest waiver anybody had ever given to any prospective military pilot, and I became what I suspect was the first flight student with station in the Pentagon.

I take a perverse pride in reporting that I did all my flight training (except for night flying, of course) during Pentagon duty hours, not after work or on holidays or weekends. For all my instruction, ground and air, I had to motor about 45 minutes down to Fort Belvoir's Davidson Army Airfield. My initial aircraft was once more the Army's little L-19, on which I had had many hours of bootleg instruction while in Germany; as might be expected, I soloed very quickly. My instructor in this ship was Capt. Jim Leffler, a fine aviator in all respects though he snored terribly—as I found out on a hunting trip. After initial solo I had lots of additional instruction in acrobatics, emergency landings on roads and rough fields, and emergency procedures. I also spent many pleasant mornings and afternoons flying alone over the Virginia and Maryland countrysides, dropping in on the little civilian fields to swap lies with the private pilots lounging around the hangars and flight offices.

To get my wings as a single-engine pilot I had to do a solo cross-country: mine was from northern Virginia to Fort Rucker, the newly established Army Aviation School in southern Alabama. At Rucker I was checked out on another Army airplane, the Cessna L-26, sometimes known as the Blind Bat because the big radial engine completely concealed, from the pilot, the follow-me jeep, the taxiway, and everything else below cloud level when the ship was maneuvering on the ground. I was also given an intensive week of night flying (mostly night landings and takeoffs), road landings on not-too-straight country roads running through woods, emergency landings, acrobatics—and a ground course on aviation weather. I was then presented my wings by my West Point classmate, Brig. Gen. Carl Hutton, Commandant of the Army Aviation School.

Gad, it was fun—light aircraft operations being so much less formal, less requiring of preflight preparation, safety precautions, and routine than high-performance stuff. On my way home to Washington, happy as a clam at high tide, I ran into a heavy weather front I knew was beyond my ability to fly through, and asked the tower operator at Donelson Air Force Base, North Carolina—an installation occupied by a heavy bomber wing—for permission to land my little craft and spend the night. He cleared me to land on runway 28 or some such, into a very strong headwind. I put my wheels down just short of the bottom of the huge figure "28" painted on the end of the runway, and braked to a halt at the top end of the same figure. The tower operator, obviously amused at this little gnat of an airplane, told me the nearest turnoff onto a taxiway was 8,000 feet (a mile and a half) dead ahead. Just to show off I took off and flew down at about a 10-foot altitude, landed again, and made the turn off quite handily—but this time was politely but unmistakably bawled out by the tower for improper procedure.

When I moved on to twin-engine and instrument instruction my instructor was Capt. Bill Rutherford, another magnificent pilot. One time, as part of my instruction in emergency procedures, he killed power on one of the two engines (by pulling its mixture control lever all the way back) shortly after I lifted the ship off a little deserted (but paved) field out in the Maryland woods. I knew I should cut the ignition on the dead engine and feather its prop, but what I *did* do at about 100 feet off the ground was turn off the ignition on the other, working, engine. This stunt instantly brings about a deathly silence in the cockpit—nothing going on—and is not a habit-forming experience. The veteran Rutherford grabbed the wheel, announced that he had "got it!" and turned hard to land on the median (which had a big ditch down the middle) of the very busy Baltimore-Washington Parkway. But he also switched back on the ignition I'd cut off: the engine caught, fortunately, and then the second one was brought back to power and we sailed away—with one highly mortified flight student aboard.

Later still, when I undertook helicopter flying, my again very skillful teacher was a civilian employee of the Army and a member of the flight safety contingent in my office—Mr. Paul Greenway. An airplane, I had learned, is stable: it wants to stay upright and fly properly, but a helicopter's fervent and unequivocal desire is to go bottom up and crash. For my first six hours of instruction the proposition looked hopeless, but then it occurred to me that a helicopter is much like a fractious horse—it does silly things, like shying at blowing newspapers. After this became obvious, things came under control (I knew all about horses) and helo flying became almost an obsession. Its charm lies in its close association with the ground—the pilot finds multiple opportunities to land—to have a nap, say, or to visit with the locals, or just to scratch his bottom and have a sandwich.

I was blessed to have in my office, the Army Aviation Directorate of G-3, an excellent staff (Dutch Williams, Glenn Goodhand, Carl Rowan, Ford Alcorn, Trigger Trigg—also known as "Bugs Bunny" because of his big toothy grin—Jim Wells, Paul Greenway), all seasoned pilots, smart, good-humored, tolerant of a beginner as a boss, and full of beans—true believers in Army Aviation. All of us were aware that the U.S. Air Force had in effect "flown away" from the Army, having become strongly preoccupied with the new super firepower afforded by atomic fission and with the new means of propulsion—the jet engine—and with what these things made possible: very high altitude, supersonic speed, and (for bombers) intercontinental range with devastatingly effective bomb loads. The Air Force, convinced that it had all the tools necessary to win the next war, had lost interest in the slow, low regime of flight—flight close to the treetops.

In result something gradually dawned upon certain perceptive officers of the Army: maybe all future combat would *not* necessarily be atomic or at transoceanic ranges—that, indeed, many things useful in combat could be done in the air at low altitude. And the Army, after a great deal of persuasion from within, made up its mind that it was the service to fill the gap.

Extended operations in the field of aviation require lots of support: budgeting; research, development, and test of aircraft and supporting equipment; aircraft procurement and maintenance; pilot and mechanic training; safety training; airfield development—and countless other things. In early 1955 the Air Force, already set up and operating in the aviation business, of course, was doing many of these jobs for Army Aviation, and doing them generously and effectively but, it should be said, not without some suspicion as to what we were up to. By mid-1955 the Army—mostly the Transportation Corps—had started taking over all these functions, and within perhaps a year and a half we had 'em all as they pertained to Army Aviation.

Gary Air Force Base at San Marcos, Texas, for example, where the Air Force had trained, along with their own, all Army rotary wing pilots, was turned over to us: for some months we continued training helo pilots for both services, but then closed Gary in favor of doing the job at Fort Walters, Texas.

In 1955–57, Army Aviation was still constrained by agreement with the Air Force and the dictates of the Department of Defense to the procurement of fixed wing (not rotary wing) aircraft with an empty weight of no more than 5,000 pounds. That's a pretty small craft. We argued that our procurement should be determined by our approved mission, not by an arbitrary weight figure. We eventually won, but it was a long, hard argument. Before I left the job, we had under procurement the twin-turboprop Grumman Mohawk (something like 12,000 pounds empty weight) surveillance aircraft and the Canadian de Havilland twin-engine light cargo aircraft (the Caribou, with an empty weight about 17,000 pounds)—a big step forward. Both aircraft eventually saw extensive (and very valuable) service in Vietnam.

I can't judge just how important any of my functions were, but the one I conceived to be most vital was the selling of the whole Army—all of it—on the value of organic aircraft to the function of every one of its combat branches and many of its service branches. It wasn't a matter of revolutionizing combat and combat-support procedures, but simply that of making both of them easier to do and therefore, in many instances, far more effective.

In the course of this endeavor I gave birth to an idea, and in pursuit thereof wrote the Army's Command and General Staff College, at Fort Leavenworth, Kansas, for copies of the combat problems it was currently presenting to its students for analysis, discussion, and solution. Each of these problems I was able to present in much abbreviated form to Pentagon audiences—large or small, anyone who would listen—in two ways: one in the way the C&GSC presented it to its students, and the other changed only by the addition of no more than a very few aircraft of two or three standard types to one of the two contending forces—but not the other.

The effect these few aircraft would have, almost inevitably, on the outcome of each battle was simply amazing. The commander of one side would have far better information of the enemy than the other would; one commander could move parts of his force quickly—with surprise—across a lake, swamp, river, or cliff, and the other couldn't; one could put artillery fire down much more accurately than the other; one could achieve surprise in the direction, timing, and location of his attack and the other couldn't; one could move vitally needed supplies much better than the other; one could evacuate casualties much more readily; one could pursue a retreating enemy better, and sometimes even ambush his retiring forces.

Etcetera. It was easy to demonstrate that a few light aircraft immediately available to the ground commander of one side would very often have *decisive* effect on operations.

To whom did I preach that sermon? Well, to my fellow inmates of the Pentagon—in fact, essentially to any Army staff section that left its door unlocked, and some that didn't. But also to the Chief of Staff, Gen. Maxwell Taylor, and the chiefs of the various Army General Staff sections, all lieutenant generals. And to the Army's Chief of Research and Development, for he could and did do a great deal to help us. And even to the secretary of the Army and the secretary of defense, "Engine Charley" Wilson, when I had to ask approval for the purchase of aircraft that exceeded the 5,000-pound gross-weight limit. And most important, I gave my spiel to the tactical departments of all of the Army's prestigious combat branch schools, infantry, armor, and artillery; to the Command and General Staff College at Leavenworth, and to the Army War College at Carlisle Barracks, Pennsylvania.

It should be noted parenthetically that this was a time—1955–57—in which this country was the only one that had in its ground forces the beginnings of tactical aviation, or was even thinking about getting it. Now, as I write this, all military powers of any consequence do. This matter—the implications of the *worldwide* spread in the development and acquisition of Ground Forces organic aviation—will be undertaken in a later chapter.

I traveled a lot during this three-year tour as director, partly to find out what was going on in the civilian and military fields of light aviation (and there was a lot), partly to spread the word among Army headquarters, at home and abroad, of the manifold command, combat, and combat-support capabilities of such aviation. The domestic part of this travel was a delight because I could fly myself, though with a copilot aboard. And visiting abroad has always been pleasant and interesting to me.

The Army was and always will be intensely interested in the science of vertical takeoff and landing (VTOL) and in flight at very low altitudes (in the "nap of the earth," so to speak), and in operations at night and in inclement weather. In my travels I was astounded to see how many ways had been developed to lift an aircraft and its cargo vertically off the ground—many of the aviation manufacturing companies I visited had an experimental candidate aircraft to show me. In one case a man's body constituted the aircraft's fuselage: with small rockets attached to his back, he could take off in a great cloud of dust and flame, fly 100 yards or so, and land on his feet. There were other pretty wild and very innovative approaches to the problem, but most, in the nature of things, were destined for eventual oblivion.

Even so, all of them were worth doing experimentally, constituting some addition to our knowledge of flight. Although no other VTOL could match the helicopter in agility and overall flight efficiency, it was interesting—indeed fascinating—to see what had been done experimentally, almost always at great expense. I was impressed especially by Bell Helicopter Company's stable and readily maneuverable tilt-rotor, the XV-3—an experimental aircraft, funded by the Army, which had flown regularly and dependably since 1953. At this writing the tilt-rotor seems destined for eventual success both in military and commercial fields.

Instructive, too, were my visits to aircraft manufacturing companies abroad—Boelkow in Germany, Aerospatiale in France, and Agusta in Italy; Hawker Aviation, Westland (which made helicopters on the Sikorsky design) and Rolls Royce (which makes aviation engines) in England; Scottish Aviation in Scotland; and de Havilland Aircraft and Pratt & Whitney Engines in Canada.

Of all short takeoff and landing (STOL) manufacturers, de Havilland of Toronto in my time was at the top of the ladder, and may still be. In Scotland, Scottish Aviation allowed me to fly their excellent STOL experimental light transport (designed mostly for use in back-country

Malaysia and other parts of Southeast Asia) for 30 minutes or so, and on landing I congratulated the company's officers on the product. But I added that I thought the de Havilland models seemed a tad more capable, upon which my hosts just folded up their papers and, in all good humor, bade me goodbye. The inference was that no one could compete successfully with de Havilland in short field operations.

I made special effort to see the president of every U.S. company I visited because one of my self-appointed functions was to make certain that Army Aviation became known as a new and not insignificant addition to the market for aviation products. My endeavor in this regard was aided by my promotion to major general—that rank, throughout the industry, being one of the criteria for getting in to see the boss.

My new rank did me no good in one respect when I visited Hughes Aviation Company in Los Angeles—a part of Howard Hughes's industrial empire. I expressed to the company's president an interest in seeing the *Spruce Goose*—an irreverent nickname for Howard Hughes's gigantic plywood amphibian experimental airplane which he, as the pilot in a taxi trial on a protected bay near Los Angeles, had actually lifted a few feet into the air for a mile or so. That was the ship's first and last flight; in the years following the eccentric Mr. Hughes had kept the ship locked up tight in an immense hangar. My host replied to my request to see the ship as follows: "My dear sir, if you were the President of the United States we *might* be able to get you into that hangar. But as things are . . . "

For all his billions, in his declining years Hughes became a bit eccentric—among other things, neglecting to shave his beard or cut (or comb) his hair. How he managed his enormous business empire is hard to fathom. At a big civil aviation clambake in Las Vegas, after I'd retired, I asked the president of Hughes Tool Company (Helicopter Division) where he was staying during the convention. "Out at the ranch," he said, meaning Hughes's luxurious ranch house outside of town. But he said that not only did he see neither hide nor hair of Howard (though he was there), in the last few years he'd spent many hundred millions of Hughes's money on the basis of only four or five phone calls, each initiated by Hughes at two or three in the morning. Never had Hughes answered my friend's letters, reports, or queries.

I also took some hunting and fishing trips as the guest of some aviation and engine company officers doing business with the Army. I found this very pleasant, I must confess, and useful in my becoming better acquainted with people in the industry. But this sort of thing, once very common, has long since been declared illegal—properly so. I can and do, however, state without reservation that these trips never on any occasion influenced my judgment in any of the multiple contacts I had with civilian corporations. But yes, they should remain illegal.

There's something fascinating about flying an airplane—interesting things, unusual and pleasant things, happen to you. I made two flights (with many stops) as pilot from one of our oceans to the other—a perfectly beautiful thing to do when you have the tremendous visibility afforded by the cockpit windshield—especially at night, when every hamlet, town, and city decorates itself with thousands of multicolored lights.

Our flights were frequently enlivened by my friend Bill Rutherford's conviction that successful flight through thunderstorms was simply a matter of experience. On our cross-continent flights, therefore, we deliberately sought out thunderstorms, especially at night, and flew through the dead center of them. It was exciting, often blinding, and always very rough, but not nearly so scary in the cockpit as it would be in the back of the airplane. I'm not sure that looking for thunderstorms is still the accepted wisdom, but I was thankful for the experience.

On the other hand, Bill and I once were about to take off in a pretty heavy snowstorm from the Bell Aircraft home plant in Buffalo, New York. Larry Bell, founder and owner and one of the most prominent pioneers in the American aviation industry, came out on the hardstand to see us off. Looking at the weather, and having heard the aviation weather forecast, he rather earnestly urged us not to go. "No sweat," we said, climbed in, and took off. A bit later we were circling not far above the rooftops of Wilkes-Barre, Pennsylvania, which fortunately sits in a valley. I flew the ship and dodged the lowest clouds while Bill called Flight Service for an IFR clearance. During all this I was aware of Larry Bell's parting words: "You can beat the weather ninety-nine times out of a hundred. But it has only got to beat you once."

I also enjoyed flying, with a company pilot aboard, several special experimental aircraft—one attractive one being a sporty little Goodyear Tire Company amphibian, which the pilot could land on smooth water by setting power and trim for an approach and then just sitting there until the little ship was afloat on the river. (It was a *little* smoother if one used just one finger to pull the stick back when five feet above the water.) Goodyear Tire, as a matter of interest, built several thousand Navy Corsair fighters during World War II.

I also enjoyed flying an AeroCommander L-26 down into Baja, California, landing on a stretch of beach sand (marked by an Army helicopter crew) where Donald Douglas, president of Douglas Aircraft; his son Douglas Jr.; Dr. Paul Dudley White, the famous Boston heart specialist; and the president of the company that manufactured the Electro-Cardiograph machine were in combination, under the auspices of the *National Geographic* magazine, trying to record the heartbeat of the gray whale. Medical science, you see, already had on record the heartbeats of mammals all the way from the mouse to the bull elephant, but the heartbeat of the whale, the largest of all mammals, was necessary to complete the spectrum.

Hundreds of grey whales come down from Alaskan waters each winter to breed and (a year or so later) to calve in a couple of big, shallow lagoons ("Black Warrior" and "Scammon's" by name) about halfway down the Pacific coast of the long Baja peninsula. Each year the lagoons are alive with the huge mammals, and in the shallow water their backs are exposed to the air for much of the time. The heartbeat was to be taken by shooting into the exposed back of a basking whale, by means of a pair of very low velocity rifles mounted in the door of a light Bell two-passenger helicopter, a couple of arrows—light aluminum arrows trailing wires to an Electro-Cardiograph machine mounted in a small unmanned glass-bottomed boat. Immediately upon shooting the arrows the boat was jettisoned—at very low altitude—from the bottom of the hovering chopper. A radio transmitter also in the boat was to relay the whale's pulse to a recorder on the shore under the personal on-the-site management of the president of the company making the EKG machine.

All simple and very scientific, but one of the assumptions was that a great big ol' papa or mama whale wouldn't mind the insertion of a couple of .45-caliber arrows a couple of inches into its hide. In the actual event it minded, on each occasion, very much indeed, and would take off over the surface of the lagoon like a runaway train—its bow wave often threatening to overturn the dingy I was in. The little glass boat in tow by the whale aquaplaned over the water in a series of long violent leaps until the electric wires, which were quite heavy, broke, at which time Donald Douglas Jr., who was the gunner in the chopper, his father, and the *National Geographic* staff would revert back to the tactical planning stage.

I was on site (at night in the Douglas yacht, anchored in one of the deep tidal channels of the lagoon) for only two days, leaving before the problem was solved. I later received a movie of the expedition in which victory—a successful record of the heartbeat—was claimed, but I don't know exactly how it was done. I imagine that the record consisted of only three or four beats taken before the racing whale once more detached itself from the little glass boat. As I remember, the film said that the whale had a pulse of something like eight a minute, against the elephant's thirteen.

America in the 1950s had an annual National Air Show, each year at a different city. Air Force and Navy stunt teams and displays were main attractions, small low-and-slow flying Army aircraft having nothing competitive to offer in the way of thrills. But the Army did do a helicopter square dance, and it was a crowd charmer.

Each little helo had a large smiling male or female face, in cartoon, painted on the bubble, a red hat on top of the bubble and a huge ear on each side. And each craft wore a bright calico skirt or black pants. To a caller's voice and music over the loudspeaker system the little ships bowed to one another, circled right and circled left; then opposite helo pairs would approach, bow, and retreat; then take hands, do the do-see-do, and otherwise simulate the regular square dance. It was an enchanting little performance, though a bit noisy; it also nearly tore off the skirts of ladies close by in the audience.

During my tour as Chief, the Combat Developments Department of the Army Aviation School was doing all sorts of useful things in respect to the development of helicopter flight procedures close to the ground, often between the trees, and at night and in marginal weather; there were no established blind-flying techniques for helicopters at that time. We sent school flight instructors to learn special helicopter mountain-flying techniques from the Okanagan Helicopter Corporation in British Columbia, since there were no mountains in Alabama.

And our people also strapped onto helicopters every variety of light weapon they thought might not blow the ship out of the air: all sorts of machine guns, including .50-caliber (which on our cobbled-up mount nearly shook the helo to pieces), 75mm rocket launchers, and 40mm grenade throwers. We even pushed fused 81mm mortar bombs out of the side of our Hueys with our feet, being careful not to go out with them. This was all a bit illegal, but we were demonstrating for the first time that a helicopter could be made (ultimately, with the application of money, engineering, and weapon expertise) into a formidable fighting machine.

An "unrated" colonel (meaning that he was not flight qualified) by the name of Jay Vanderpool at the Aviation School was one of the prime instigators of this sort of experimentation. He did us lots of good.

During my years in Washington we devoted much time to the Model H-40 experimental helicopter being developed by Bell Helicopter Company, Fort Worth, on our behalf but under the cognizance of the Air Force. The H-40 (ultimately to become the UH-1, or "Huey") was, most important, designed at what we believed to be the right size to carry an infantry rifle squad, and in the right shape—shape being important, for we sought a low profile so that, among other things, we could transport it in a C-130 and hide it under a tree. The cargo weight goal—the infantry squad—was never fully realized even after enlargements and greater engine power in later model numbers. That's the way aircraft design and construction goes—or at least went in those days—as any aeronautical engineer will tell you. A new ship rarely met expectations in every respect.

Before the first H-40 experimental model was delivered, the Air Force recommended that the whole project be scrubbed because of prospective manufacturing problems with the blade. This was devastating news—the future of Army Aviation hung in large part on our getting a ship of this size and capability into our inventory. After much debate and effort at persuasion, on our part, the Air Force relented: the difficulty was overcome and the helo reached production. In its several models the Huey became the aviation mainstay of the Army, which over many years bought about 12,000 copies. Counting purchases by other U.S. services, American civilian sources, foreign coproduction, and licensed production, more than 16,000 copies—an astonishing number—were made. Of all the world's aircraft, it became one of the most prominent—thus justifying the decision by our little office in the Pentagon to persevere in its development.

What's more, the Huey dynamics—engine, transmission, and blades—formed the basis for the production of an additional 2,000-plus Cobra helicopter gunships. I remember the Cobra on display, on the ground and in the air, at the Paris Air Show shortly after it was introduced. Soviet official photographers could not keep away from it—they practically photographed the top layer of paint off.

Although the ship has to be considered a very great success, the Huey had its faults, as all aircraft do. One fault was serious: blade slap, the loud, distinctive, rapid "plop-plop-plop-plop" that telegraphs the ship's approach to any destination three or four miles before it gets there. In Vietnam this alerted the enemy, very undesirably.

The phenomenon arises in the speed of the forward-moving blade: at cruise speed that blade cuts the air at very near the speed of sound—the speed of the ship plus the rotational speed of the advancing blade tip. That makes the loud "plop." As the ship passes overhead, that "plop" in the ear of the ground observer instantly disappears, but the damage (in alerting an enemy) has been done.

All this is because the Huey grew from a lighter H-40 and the rotor diameter was increased to provide greater lift. The increased rotor diameter resulted in higher tip speeds, which increased the severity of the "plop."

I did a great deal of speechmaking, in Washington and elsewhere, before all sorts of societies and other organizations and before the press. Although it increased my workload I never refused an invitation because of the widespread interest in Army Aviation—a new bird on the roost. It also made me formulate specifically, for civilian consumption, the theory and battle doctrine of this new endeavor. My appearances on the platform were so frequent, however, that I often resorted to a special device: I'd start my talk with a very few introductory paragraphs and then throw the subject open for questions by the audience. It worked like a charm—there were lots of questions and no complaints.

There were a large number of outstanding individual Army aviators, but the activity was so new that there were few of any rank. I felt quite strongly, therefore, that our interests should be represented better in the higher echelons of command. After getting approval of the proposition, I wrote or otherwise got in touch with a number of fine colonels of my acquaintance—all of them line officers and outstanding prospects for high command—and asked if they were interested in taking flight training. They *all* were—at least all that qualified physically—and each one so qualified made the grade in flight school and did us much good. One of them, "Bugs" (for Bogardus) Cairns, had served with me in the 1st Armored Division in World War II, as previously noted. He soon became a major general and Commandant of the Army Aviation School, and was killed in that job when the helo he was flying went down in the Alabama woods.

What else happened? Well, on one occasion, Col. Glenn Goodhand came into my office to ask if I would approve of the creation of an Army Aviation Association of America (AAAA). After maybe a half-minute's consideration I said sure, sounded like a great idea. Within a few years the "Quad A" had become an enormous, very active, and influential organization, whose annual convention now fills thousands of hotel rooms and whose industry exhibits, put on by scores of nationally known aviation, electronic, and weapons manufacturers, fills acres of indoor floor space. Little did I know! After my retirement, I became one of its succession of presidents.

While still in Washington I became a "Man of the Month" of the National Aviation Club and a permanent dues-free member—an honor that vastly inflated my prominence as an aviator. And I otherwise met, got to know, and received strong encouragement in what we were doing from such aviation greats as Eddie Rickenbacker, Igor Sikorski (virtually the inventor of the helicopter), Gen. Jimmy Doolittle, and Adm. Arleigh ("39-knot") Burke, Chief of Naval Operations.

All good things come to an end—though I never thought I'd say that about a tour in the Pentagon. A prime good thing about this tour was that I didn't spend too much time in that renowned building—being out of town much of the time—and another was the interest generated by the act of encouraging and guiding the development of a brand-new and highly influential addition to the tactics and techniques of warfare. It had been a great privilege and a source of abiding interest. But whatever my regret at leaving the job as the first Director of Army Aviation was mitigated by the announcement of my new one: the command of the 82nd Airborne Division, one of the great combat divisions of the world.

THE 82ND AIRBORNE

16 My first 11 years in the military were in the old Horse
Cavalry. Although the Army's Airborne Forces undeni-
ably originated in the Infantry, and though their outstanding World War II leaders were mostly ex-Infantry-
men, they nevertheless seem to me to have inherited the tradition and
esprit of the Cavalry. I think this is because military esprit is in part derived from mobility: forces inherently able to move faster have options
and capabilities slower forces don't have and therefore feel better about
themselves.

Airborne esprit is further enhanced by the soldier's knowledge that
he repeatedly does something that many men cannot force themselves
to do: jump out of airplanes. That act (at least in peacetime) is an eminently survivable one—only two were killed by airplane jumps in my
two years with the 82nd Airborne Division—but when one is standing
in the airplane's open door, about to jump out of it, that survivability is
not totally apparent. And when an airborne company turns out for drill
each morning it is likely that a couple of troopers will be sporting plaster casts.

Basic airborne training also makes good soldiers partly because it is
vigorous and strength-building, partly because it builds teamwork, and
partly because of its straightforward discipline. When an airborne
trainee goofs off even slightly, the NCO instructor doesn't write him up
or report him to anyone: he just points to the ground. The trainee, usu-

ally with parachute harness on his back, drops instantly to his hands and does ten loudly counted push-ups, plus *"one for Airborne, Sir!"*

This is outstandingly effective discipline: requiring no reporting to the first sergeant, nothing on the record, no hard feelings—all over and done in 20 seconds. What's more, it builds in each airborne trainee arm, shoulder, and belly muscles useful in his business as a fighting man. The Airborne soldier in 1957 took special pains to keep his uniform starched and immaculate and his uniquely patterned boots at a high shine; so, many years ago, did the old horse soldier. And the men of the 82nd accompanied their salute of an officer with a lofty bellow: *"All the way, Sir!"* practically forcing their salute's return.

In my time with the 82nd it and certain other divisions were organized "pentagonally"—no regiments, no battalions, just five "battle groups" of five large (over 200 men) infantry companies each, a division artillery of five batteries of six guns each, and a reconnaissance battalion incorporating an aviation company—mostly light helicopters. There were two brigade headquarters, under which combinations of battle groups and artillery batteries could be grouped on an ad hoc basis. All this was an experimental organization with some obvious weaknesses, but we didn't lose any sleep over it because we knew we could make it work in combat if we had to.

Fort Bragg is a very attractive post in an attractive part of North Carolina, with good weather and a good sandy soil that doesn't get muddy from a rain. That's important to a soldier. And perhaps most important, Bragg's training area is superb—large, varied, and covered mostly with long-leaf Southern pine and Loblolly pine. We had lots of quail, and our deer population was estimated at about 3,000. (We had too many does, however, many of which were fallow. I thought the North Carolina wildlife people were shortsighted in refusing our requests to shoot them. Our deer were individually too small—not enough feed for the large population.)

We also had North Carolina ticks and North Carolina gnats ("no-see-ums") with long razor-sharp fangs full of poison. But no place is perfect.

In the old days a senior military commander had his horse delivered to the front door of his quarters every workday morning, said horse providing him the mobility to allow him to have a good look at his troops in training. Instead of a horse I used a light helicopter, again delivered to my front door by a pilot who then departed in a jeep.

With exceedingly rare exception, I took off every morning, usually with a passenger (the division Chief of Staff, or a staff officer, or one of the two assistant division commanders, or perhaps a visiting officer from higher headquarters), for the training area, where I dropped in on several companies or batteries in training each day. Needless to say, I had specified that officers and NCOs of line units be schooled on how to guide a helo, by hand signals, on a safe descending path.

And on the ground I had a damned good look on how training was being done, asking multiple questions, particularly of the NCOs, and minutely checking the siting and fields-of-fire of weapons. Our Army strives hard, as it should, to bolster NCO morale, but in many respects it is not sufficiently demanding of NCO performance.

No doubt there were jokes among members of the division about this habit of the division commander—descending on them out of the sky. In defense of that routine I can only say that no other CG ever had a broader or more frequent look at training activity. I recommend the practice.

But I tarnished my record badly on one occasion when, with the division Chief of Staff, Col. Bob Linvill, aboard, I descended in my chopper to have a look at an infantry company in training alongside a narrow dirt road—across which stretched a very heavy gauge uninsulated red copper telephone wire, invisible to both Linvill and me—partly, no doubt, because it was exactly the color of the road. Well, my rapidly spinning main rotor blade jerked a substantial length of that wire plus a heavy glass insulator off the telephone pole and wrapped the whole bloody mess in a tight bundle around the main rotor shaft. The insulator, en route, went through the bubble of the helo with a loud crash, showering Linvill and me liberally with pieces of Plexiglas.

This was a reportable accident, and aircraft accidents are not popular with the very high echelons of the Army brass. Moreover, my immediate boss and good friend, Lt. Gen. Bob Sink, CG of the XVIII Airborne Corps, indulged his sense of humor by ordering the creation of a nice new portable board listing Corps aircraft accidents so that my name could appear at the very top of the list and stay there for the maximum number of months. This board was a regular exhibit at the Corps Commanders' Conference, held monthly.

I did not enjoy the publicity, but I did require that gallon cans, with the bottoms taken out and the outsides painted bright red, be hung on all wires crossing roads on the Fort Bragg reservation. Naturally they became known as "Ham Cans." So far as I know, this was the first instance (helicopters in those days still being rare animals) of marking overhead wires or cables so aircraft wouldn't fly into them.

Col. Jack Marinelli, a longtime and highly skilled pilot, made me feel better with his wire from Washington: "ONLY PILOTS HAVE AIRCRAFT ACCIDENTS." I was sorry it happened, but I said to hell with it.

I shall take a page or two to describe certain practices I instituted with what I believe to have been of much benefit to our battle readiness.

Every combat unit in the Army suffers from understrength—not enough soldiers available each day for really adequate tactical training. I went some distance in solving this by pairing line companies, one with another. While, for example, Company A trained on Monday and Tuesday, Company B took all the special duty, KP, fatigue details, and dental appointments, for both companies; on Wednesday, Thursday, and Friday of that week, the roles would reverse. This sort of pairing was put in effect throughout the division. Half the division (comprising what I dubbed the X units) would leave their barracks for the training area by 0800 Monday morning, spending all that day, most of that night, and the next morning at training, returning to barracks after noon. The other half (the Y units) would leave barracks by 0800 Wednesday and return no earlier than Friday afternoon, giving them two and a half days and two usually active nights in the field. Next week the X units would trade training days (and nights) with the Y.

This system appreciably increased the size of platoons and companies at training. With a bigger proportion of their units present, officers and NCOs could train their commands *much* more effectively. Moreover, the scheme greatly increased our time spent in night training, an acknowledged advantage, and it increased training variety and interest, perhaps the biggest benefit of all. And the total number of man-hours at training increased, not decreased.

If there was another side to the coin it was this: I often had to explain to visiting senior officers why they could always see line companies playing baseball and soccer on workday mornings, and I had to listen occasionally to officers' wives explaining their husbands' absence at a dinner party by saying, "Oh, he's out in the woods, *X*'ing and *Y*'ing."

I thought the division did well in corps and field army maneuvers, but I will say very immodestly that our best and therefore most instructive maneuver was one held altogether within the division. I divided it into two equal, opposing halves, with one assistant division commander, Brig. Gen. Clifton von Kann, in command of one half, and Brig. Gen. Chester de Gavre in command of the other. Both were absolutely outstanding individuals—and it occurs to me, as I write this, the maneuver pitted a German (by descent) against a Frenchman. They both performed, as expected, extremely well.

The maneuver was different from any other of my experience in that umpiring (I being the head umpire) was unobtrusive—each side being allowed almost total freedom of action. When opposing units got a bit tangled with one another, we simply declared a two-hour truce to correct the situation. We also made casualties stick, avoiding the usual process of resurrecting the dead—in other words, a successful action gave the successful side a lasting benefit on which it could build. The maneuver lasted only about two and a half days, in which time no one got more than a few hours sleep.

I also instituted the system I used in Germany, that of requiring that each platoon leader, officer, or NCO be given command of his platoon for one unsupervised training period of at least 24 hours, out in the field, each month—unvisited by any senior officer, even his company commander. Of course I might unknowingly descend on the platoon by helicopter, but that rarely occurred and wouldn't make any difference anyway.

In a remote corner of the big Fort Bragg reservation I laid out a combat firing drill for a parachute infantry company reinforced with a recoil-less rifle section and supported by a battery of artillery—the latter as a matter of economy firing only one gun of its six to represent a three-round battery concentration.

This drill—and it was strictly a drill—was a honey, if I say so myself: a set piece involving a succession of platoon and company objectives carefully laid out by me (but carefully critiqued by my staff) to illustrate, as perfectly as our combined intellects could make it, infantry company assault tactics. The company commander, provided in the assembly area with a mounted 10-by-10-foot painted sketch map plainly showing contours, routes of approach, platoon and company objectives (of which there were several successive ones), and artillery concentrations, carefully explained to all his men the logic of the tactical plan and how all elements would coordinate their efforts with those of the others. He then began the approach march and the execution of the exercise, which took two or three hours. Not all that detailed explanation would be possible in combat, of course, but the purpose here was instruction—to demonstrate in the plainest way the interplay of all the forces involved in the execution of a company attack on a succession of enemy positions, and to give men some experience in the sounds of battle.

The drill was "set" for another reason: we could push up hard against the safety rules binding on all live-fire exercises, since the dangers of misunderstanding and mistake could be largely eliminated. Designated Safety Officers, who were warned to be inconspicuous, could if necessary stop the exercise instantly by firing a red rocket into the air. It was never necessary, and never did we hurt a soul despite the liberal use of live ammunition, sometimes in pretty close quarters, and much troop maneuver.

And finally, weapons competition. Our energetic young troopers in my view did well enough in the prescribed marksmanship courses but were not at all impressive in the more practical art of field firing. I therefore set up semiannual field-firing competitions in *all* division weapons—rifle, .30- and .50-caliber machine guns, recoil-less rifles, antitank weapons, and artillery pieces. I'll not take the time and space to describe all these competitions, making do with the statements that they were as realistic as we could make them and that no allowance whatever was made for the nonfunctioning gun, which simply made no contribution to the company score. Moreover, all riflemen and gun crews had to use their regularly *assigned* weapons, not borrowed ones, and all firing was against time (thus requiring very prompt adjustment of fire) and at tactically displayed field targets.

At the firing site, a careful tally of target hits was kept and displayed on a prominent scoreboard, and a running record of every company's performance to date, in order of merit, was published every week in the division newspaper. Every trooper knew that the competition was fair and a reasonable close approximation of the sort of shooting he and his fellows must, for success, do well in combat. He could also see—and know that every other trooper in the division could also see—if his company could or could not hold up its end in the destruction of an enemy, that being what combat units are for.

And it became very apparent that good young paratroopers and their noncoms didn't like to see their outfit unfavorably compared, in this respect, to others like it. As a result, our capabilities in field firing took an enormous jump each six months—that being the cycle for the competition. In a word, we really learned to shoot.

One February, I guess as a sort of show of force in Central America, the division was required to put a battle group (about 1,400 officers and men) into airplanes and, for the enlightenment of a large Panamanian civilian and military audience assembled in a training area about 50 miles north of the canal, jump it into Panama. It was suggested by the Pentagon, which laid this show on, that I go with the battle group and jump first, so I did. We bundled into a flock of C-130 Air Force four-engine transports at Pope Air Force Base, right alongside Fort Bragg, and on a very cold night took off for the deep south at about 11 P.M. Only trouble (for me at least) was that in the cargo compartment of my ship the heaters weren't working, and all of us aboard agreed that eight hours of that in cotton fatigue clothing at 20,000 feet on a bitterly cold winter night wasn't the best way to spend your time.

But finally the sun came up and all the aircraft dropped down to jump altitude (1,200 feet—where it was much warmer) and we headed in over the Pacific toward the DZ, or drop zone. When parachute forces jump onto an objective, some designated troopers must carry extra canvass-wrapped loads—field radios for example, or extra ammunition—each weighing maybe 20 or 30 pounds. The trooper jumps out of the plane carrying the load—but so he doesn't have to bear on his feet and legs the landing shock of the bundle's weight added to his own weight, he can by pulling a simple release, as he approaches the ground, allow the bundle to drop away from him to the end of maybe a 40-foot rope. It is still attached to him so he can find it after landing, even if it's dark.

Well, a sergeant in a plane behind mine was standing in his aircraft's door, still well offshore, as I was in mine; but he had an extra bundle attached which he inadvertently let fall out the door and into the airplane's slipstream. The bundle jerked him out as though he were a loaf of bread. His parachute opened okay but it and his body, weighted down with gear, were never found, though a search was made of several square miles of seawater.

A loudspeaker announced to the several thousand people witnessing this "show" jump that the division commander would be first out the door. Through an error somebody in another plane (not mine) kicked out, too early, a door bundle—this time with a parachute attached which did not open. The bundle fell like a rock and hit the earth with a dreadful thump—the audience, of course, assumed that it was me. I'm glad my wife was not there. Actually I jumped a few seconds later and landed happily along with everyone else. I was picked up in a jeep and brought over to the stands where all the big brass and the press were and where I became a curiosity because my uniform, in that blazing tropical heat, was still cold to the touch.

Despite the glitches the rest of the show went without incident and I guess the Panamanians were impressed by the hundreds of parachuting soldiers. I was also impressed: it was a good show, if a bit artificial for the benefit of the spectators.

My twin Beech airplane was waiting for me, and after I shook hands with all the dignitaries I enjoyed flying it back, over all that water, to Fort Bragg. We had to refuel in Kingston, Jamaica, where all the locals we dealt with at the airport spoke excellent English in a broad British accent.

One day I conceived the idea of writing the parents of every young soldier in the division to tell them how proud they should be that their son had qualified for airborne duty and also suggesting that it would be very good for him if he went to chapel, at Fort Bragg, on Sunday mornings—which Mary and I did, rotating among the five or six chapels in the division area. I was embarrassed to get a whole mountain of replies from the parents, many of them thanking me for having made friends with their child (which I had not done—there being nearly 15,000 men in the division) and suggesting that he be advised to write more often. And I regret to say that Mary and I couldn't see any very perceptible increase in chapel attendance.

One of our chaplains had a better idea—early on each Sunday morning he invaded one of the company barracks, routing the men out of bed and sternly encouraging them to come to his service. It worked—but on one occasion Mary and I went to hear him preach. For his sermon he abandoned the pulpit altogether, walking up and down the transept of the chapel shouting at the young troopers about "love"—which I must say kept everybody's interest. But then he launched into a story about the wife of a faithless husband who stuck a butcherknife into the belly of said husband—and then he asked, at the top of his voice, "You call that *love?*" All the young lads shook their heads—no, they decided, that wasn't love.

I decided then and there that I was out of my field and turned the problem of church attendance back to the division senior chaplain, who incidentally could do twenty-one one-arm push-ups.

One day we got orders to send our 504th Airborne Battle Group, intact, to Germany, for permanent station—in return for which we'd get an equivalent number of airborne officers, NCOs, and specialists, and about 1,000 recruits freshly qualified as parachutists. I selected an outstanding colonel, Don Clayton, to command the new outfit, and sent him, his officers and NCOs, and new troopers into the woods for six weeks—with the requirement that the unit at the end of that time return to barracks ready to go, if necessary, into active combat.

Food, ammunition, and mail were sent to this outfit, but visitors (with the exception of a doctor once daily, a daily mail truck, a twice-weekly Post Exchange truck, a chaplain on Sundays, and me) were forbidden. I greatly enjoyed visiting because of the extraordinary interest shown by the new young soldiers—each one took notes during instruction, and all knocked themselves out on all the physical things—including parachuting.

At the end of the period all the young recruits were still short on experience and would in combat have made mistakes. But believe me, by enthusiasm and energy alone they would have given any enemy a run for his money. It was heartening to see how quickly and well this battle group developed into an effective military combat unit, and further reinforced my conviction that the new recruit (especially if he has had airborne training) is usually very highly motivated. But he loses that motivation very quickly if he is put in an understrength (and therefore *inevitably* undertrained) unit, or into a poorly led unit.

To sum up this training experiment—and that's what it was—its success lay in the quality and hard work of the commander, officers, and NCOs, certainly, but also in a system that kept the whole outfit in the woods, undistracted, for 42 uninterrupted days. The secret of an *army's* success lies in the application of the same principle, realistically modified to fit each situation.

We learned one day that Lt. Gen. Jim Gavin was retiring from the Army and desired that the traditional retirement review in his honor be conducted by his wartime command—the 82nd Airborne. This was altogether fitting—we were glad for the opportunity. Some distinguished visitors came too, notably retired Generals John Hodge and Matthew Ridgeway, the ex–Chief of Staff and, more important, the man who turned military disaster in Korea, bequeathed to him by General MacArthur, into something close to victory.

I was again impressed at how very inadequate and inappropriate was the new infantry drill, in which units (including the Corps of Cadets at West Point, which used to look so splendid on parade, and now looks terrible) march by in order of masses—men clomping by in great blocks within which individuals are lost in the crowd—nothing but blobs in a sea of blobs. This violates a basic principle: the officer taking the review can't see most of the people he's reviewing. You could put a chimpanzee at the far end of one of the ranks and an observer would never know it.

Moreover, a unit the size of a division takes forever to go by in review.

I lessened that fault by half by inventing a system of two companies coming by abreast. This took some double-timing, which paratroopers are used to. In any event, the division looked as good as it could in double column of masses and Jimmy Gavin seemed pleased.

In the Army, one keeps a command for a maximum of two years—a good rule, but one that lost me my job with the 82nd in favor of that of Chief of the Army's Korea Military Advisory Group (KMAG). With our two boys, in a car without air-conditioning, we drove, sweltering, cross-country via the northwestern states to San Francisco for transport by civil aircraft to Korea, via Honolulu and Tokyo. On our auto trip we had to make a 50-mile detour so the boys could say they'd been in Utah. They'd already made most of the other states.

KOREA

17 Our little family of four was met on the tarmac of the airport in Seoul by the U.S. ambassador and his wife, by CINCUNC (Commander-in-Chief, United Nations Command, a four-star U.S. Army general), and by the Chief of Staff of the Korean Army, "Tiger" Song (his proper name was Song Yo Chan—in Korea the family name comes first) and Madame Song, who went by the name of Sally. Also present was the Korean minister of defense and a number of other dignitaries—and most obvious of all the razor-sharp Korean Army Honor Guard and the Korean Army Band.

Because this sounds like a heavy reception committee for a mere-smear American major general I must explain that the Chief of the Korea Military Advisory Group (KMAG) in the 1950s had very great influence on the amount and distribution of U.S. military aid annually allotted to Korea—in my time figured at several hundred million dollars—and also on the organization, equipping, and training of the very large (about 550,000 officers and men) Korean Army, vital to the maintenance of peace in the Far East.

In our time in Korea, which started only six years after the 1953 armistice ending the Korean War, much of the war's damage was still apparent and the vast majority of the people were dirt poor, the national per-capita income being in the neighborhood of a couple of hundred bucks.

Even in Seoul, the capital city already with about 5 million inhabitants, the vast majority of houses in town had no running water—everywhere women could be seen carrying water (invariably in square five-gallon cans, usually suspended from both ends of a six-foot pole) from hydrants at streetcorners to their homes. And even on bitterly cold winter nights, thousands of the tiny stores lining the city streets were without glass, open to the weather—their proprietors bundled up and huddled over little coal stoves.

The homes in the cities were almost all of adobe, cement block, or field stone; those in the country (also without water or plumbing) were sometimes of stone but mostly of adobe, and nearly all had thick rice-straw roofs, which were good insulation but which, under the heavy winter snow, sometimes collapsed and smothered the family within. Straw roofs had a useful life of only two years.

Most country dwellings were heated by the *ondol*—a tiny outside stove burning molded coal briquettes. The stove's chimney (sometimes via two or three channels) ran horizontally under the clay floor, heating it, and thence up the opposite outside wall. The briquette smoke was lethal, and when a chimney leak occurred under the floor at night the smoke could sicken or kill the inhabitants.

Until about 1965 the Korean countryside smelled, dreadfully, from the extensive use of nightsoil as fertilizer. When Bob Hope got off the plane on his first visit he asked what the terrible odor was. He was told the source of it—and he said, "Yes, I understand, but what do they *do* to it?"

One can't speak of life in Korea without mentioning kimche, a food included in every Korean meal—three times daily. Every farmhouse and most town houses boasting a yard of any kind has a large—about 20 gallons—kimche jar buried nearby. Kimche consists of a mixture of chopped-up salad vegetables: Korean varieties of radishes, cabbages, turnips, beets, and certain other things unfamiliar to Americans—plus a generous quantity of hot red peppers—which combination, in the buried jar, over a period of a few weeks ferments into something not too dissimilar to what American farmers call silage—with a small alcohol content. The alcohol keeps the kimche free of bacteria.

In our time in Korea, and perhaps still, the Korean—whether a soldier, laborer, Navy admiral, or rich manufacturer—ate kimche with every meal, and in result carried a strong and (to non-Koreans) very unattractive odor on his breath. But kimche has contributed very significantly to Korean health—it is the local substitute for American canned food, providing vegetable nutrients to the population over I don't know how many hundred years. Koreans have, I would guess, the world's best teeth—white and straight—that being, I'm sure, one of the benefits rendered by kimche. But Americans—this one in particular—can't stand its taste and used to deeply regret its odor on someone else's breath.

South Korea is very mountainous. Civil travel between the cities, even at the end (1965) of my second tour there, was by train, aircraft or, for those very few who wished to endure it, by jeep over unmaintained dirt roads likely to break the jeep's axle or, after a heavy rainstorm, likely to drown the jeep's passengers, for many of the waterways were not crossed by bridges. Nowadays, of course, the cities of South Korea are connected by eight-lane, concrete, high-speed highways.

The study of English is mandatory throughout the Korean public school system. Why? Because the world's knowledge is recorded in English-language books, and not, I assure you, in Hangul—Hangul being the Korean written alphabet, a modern phonetic substitute for the Chinese character. Korean schoolchildren are uniformed, disciplined, and smart. To go from grammar school to middle school, and from middle school to high school, and from high school to a university requires that the child pass a rigorous written examination. If a child fails at any level he is put into a vocational school—no ifs or buts. During the time these examinations are being administered the anxiety among the Korean adult population—the parents—is palpable.

At the time, Korea was notorious for petty thieves, who preyed mostly on "rich" Americans and on military supply depots, big and little. They were a terrible nuisance but a diminishing one as we learned to cope with them and as the country gradually became more prosperous.

In my job as Chief KMAG, my colleagues and I devised ways of reducing our losses. I once assembled all the tire manufacturers in Korea to tell them that they were cutting their own throats by making tires for sale to civilians with the distinctive military tread. I persuaded them to change the tread—which, of course, over a period of time allowed our military police and the Korean civil and military police to identify, on Korean civilian vehicles, tires stolen from U.S. or Korean military units. As another example I—we—also brought over American boot manufacturers to show Korean shoe-makers how to make military boots, which they did, thereby reducing by just that much the cost of American military aid while it boosted the Korean economy.

But my main job was the continued improvement of the very large Korean Army, and in the company of more than 1,000 good U.S. Army officers and NCOs of KMAG (supported by 100 Department of the Army civilian technicians, such as electricians and plumbers) we did that, largely by taking the nonsense out of some of the training methods then in effect.

These were mostly Korean-invented practices, pseudo-military sound and fury designed to impress the American visitor or inspector. We simply showed up the perpetrators of this sort of nonsense—being careful however not to humiliate anybody, for the loss of face in the Orient can lead to violence and catastrophe. By and large, however, we came to like and very often admire the Korean military man—in most cases he was intelligent, energetic, tough, full of good humor, and a pleasure to work with. If you told him correctly how to do something, he would do it right forever; if you told him wrong, he'd do it wrong—forever.

I instituted the first annual physical examination in the Korean Army officer corps—as a starter, for general officers only. Among them the doctors found numerous cases of tuberculosis. And a substantial majority of all Koreans were infested with worms, due to pollution of village water wells. Worms or no worms, however, it didn't seem to sap their energy: I've seen a battalion of Korean soldiers, with packs on their backs and rifles in their arms, practically run up a steep mountainside.

But I nevertheless had my staff engineer conduct a sampling of village water wells; after a few weeks he reported that of 984 wells inspected, 984 were polluted. Korean well-diggers in those days were sublimely indifferent to the proximity of outhouses—there being no toilets in the rural areas. It was safe to assume that every village (some of them several hundred years old) had polluted the whole area surrounding it.

As is true in many other countries, long centuries of human habitation had denuded the Korean countryside of trees. The Korean government had, by 1959, already instituted a reforestation program. On Arbor Day a very large proportion of the population, including all the schoolchildren, turned out to plant seedlings furnished by the government—another example of the Korean national trait of cooperative effort. Coincident with this was police enforcement of the law prohibiting the use of even small tree branches—if they were cut from living trees—for firewood, wherefore numerous poor rural families suffered both from cold and for lack of fuel for cooking. I remember still, with sadness, reading in the Korean English-language press of a man who killed his wife, children, and then himself because he had been punished for the use of a few bits of wood, cut from trees, for cooking purposes.

As I write this, all the above has changed greatly for the better—partly because of general prosperity, partly because of highly motivated, intelligent programs directed by the national government. When I visited Korea in 1981, as a guest of the government, the rice-straw roof had all but vanished from the countryside in favor of tile, walls were mostly concrete block instead of mud, and almost all farmhouses had at least a water tap in the kitchen or nearby—the water coming from deep, government-dug, presumably sanitary wells. And the mountains were covered with thriving forests.

I continued flying in Korea, using fixed wing twin-engine aircraft for the longer trips south to Taejon, Taegu, Kwangju, Pusan and Cheju-do, and the UH-1 Huey helicopter for my almost daily visits along the northern front. From the air the land was simply beautiful, summer, winter (with its heavy snows), spring, and fall. And from the air you couldn't smell the fertilizer.

That front, just mentioned, consists—still—of a three-mile-wide "demilitarized zone," or DMZ, established at the end of the Korean War. Nothing is in that zone legally: it is uninhabited and unused, the old villages rotting away, the roads and railroad tracks unused, the old farms overgrown with brush and trees. Occasionally the North Korean side will, illegally, put a patrol in the zone, and in the four decades since the war's end the North Koreans have made some fairly sizable raids across the zone and into South Korea—one, apparently, with the mission of killing or kidnapping the South Korean president. This raiding party was, incidentally, intercepted and almost completely destroyed by ROK (Republic of Korea) infantry.

The DMZ has always been the world's tightest border—far more so than Europe's Iron Curtain ever was. No one crosses it legally, though some spies do illegally. There is no mail, telegraph, or telephone connection between North and South Korea, even via a third country. My wife and I came to know several families in which brothers and sisters, parents and offspring, and sometimes even husbands and wives had neither seen nor heard anything from or of their relatives since 1950—this in an area where people on one side of the line are indistinguishable in language and appearance from those on the other.

Korea used to be known as the "Hermit Kingdom" because of its isolation, and our first (and very tenuous) connection with it started with an American naval vessel's visit in 1881. Our connection strengthened somewhat later, however, because of the Russo-Japanese War in 1905, in which a Russian fleet, after an extremely long and difficult trip from European ports, was decisively defeated by the Japanese in the western Pacific. Through the initiative of our president Theodore Roosevelt this war was terminated, believe it or not, by the Treaty of Portsmouth, New Hampshire, where the negotiators met, with Roosevelt in attendance. That treaty gave Japan political hegemony over Korea—replacing that of the Russians. Americans, including this one, tend to admire Teddy Roosevelt, but one cannot say that he did well in Portsmouth.

Japan occupied and severely exploited Korea from 1905 until Japan's surrender to us in 1945. The Japanese administration was a repressive and sometimes brutal one, denying Koreans personal freedom and the opportunity for modernization and development. This became evident in the years immediately following 1945: both Korean industry and the Korean military suffered, for some years, for lack of middle and top-level management. The Japanese had not allowed it to form.

But to go back a bit: at war's end a very large number of Japanese troops were still in China, Manchuria, and Korea. Until Hitler's fall, the Soviets had paid little attention to the Japanese occupying Manchuria, on their eastern border, but toward the end, Soviet forces, reinforced by some of those who had been fighting in Europe, inflicted defeat on the Japanese in that area. Indeed, the Soviet account of the war that I consulted gave me the strong impression that the Soviet Union, with no more than inconsequential help on the part of the United States, was responsible for the defeat of the Japanese empire in World War II. That's not quite the way most Americans remember it.

Even so, there had to be some agreement between the United States and the USSR about who would do what with the hundreds of thousands of Japanese soldiers and airmen on the Asian mainland north of China, so a meeting was called—our side being headed by none other than Gen. George C. Marshall, the Chief of Staff of the U.S. Army, and later secretary of state, and then secretary of defense.

It was decided that the Russians would do the biggest part of the job, which was all the Japanese in Manchuria. The Russian and American sides had previously agreed that in Korea the Russians would take the surrender of the Japanese in the north half of the country, and the Americans in the south half. Two senior U.S. staff officers (using a National Geographic map) tried one night before the meeting to find a natural geographic line to propose as a boundary between the north zone of surrender and the south zone but could find none, and so agreed to suggest the 38th parallel as the line. When this line was proposed at the meeting, the Russians accepted.

This line was intended simply to indicate which Japanese were to be gathered up by the Russian Army, and which by our Army. Unexpectedly, the Russians left strong forces in the North, and after the Japanese were gone proceeded (no doubt on instructions from Stalin) to indoctrinate—with a club, so to speak—the population of the North with communism, in effect dividing the North, politically, from the South.

Nothing could be a worse dividing line between two nations (though much of our own borders with Canada and Mexico are such) than a parallel of latitude—particularly when it is specified for an already densely inhabited piece of terrain. Such a border may cut a winding river into several segments, and possibly do the same thing to a road, or railroad, or telephone line; it cuts farms and other bits of real estate in two or more pieces, and villages as well. Indeed, if you live there, it may split your house, putting your living room, one bedroom, and half your bathroom and half your kitchen in one country and the rest of your house in another.

I would emphasize, however, that the 38th parallel was *not* proposed by our side as a national boundary, but merely as a demarcation between the area in which the Russians were to take the surrender of the Japanese, and the area in which we were to do so. In both areas the Japanese soldiery was, in fact, subsequently gathered up, disarmed, and repatriated.

However, while we put two of our Army divisions into southern Korea as an occupation force, and while our military government and then the State Department made polite efforts to instruct the people of the south in the virtues and procedures of democracy—the Russians (again no doubt on the direct personal order of Josef Stalin) continued a strong military occupation of their half of the country while imposing communist doctrine with a brickbat—a forceful, savage indoctrination in the teachings, principles, and disciplines of Marx, Engels, and Lenin.

Thus were sown the seeds of the bloody, three-year-long Korean War. We, in our innocence, withdrew our two understrength divisions in 1948. Two years later a well-equipped North Korean Army, vigorously trained, motivated, and advised by their Soviet big brothers, attacked across that fateful 38th parallel.

For more than three decades Americans have read in their newspapers of the riotous students of South Korea—all of them protesting the undemocratic nature of the Korean government. It has indeed been undemocratic much of the time, but in the view of some, for a very good reason. South Korea has faced a bitter enemy, communist North Korea, on its north border since 1953. The international border is only about five minutes by modern jet combat aircraft from South Korea's capital, Seoul, and the North Korean Army has steadily maintained, for 48 years, a force on the ground superior to that of the ROK Army. One may call it self-serving, but the military men who have served (sometime via a coup) as the South Korean head of state have, in a sense, followed the U.S. example. We, as the reader well knows, suspend some of the democratic rights of our own people when we are at war—our citizens can't, for example, buy all the gas and meat they want to, our men may be drafted into military service, some industries are forced into production of military hardware, and the press is denied some of its accustomed freedom.

Syngmun Rhee, the Army Chief of Staff during the Korean War, was the first president; he lasted about seven years. After his ouster by student revolt, he was succeeded by a civilian, Chang Myun, for less than one year, that government being overturned by another soldier, Pak Chung Hui, who lasted until his assassination in 1979. Pak was replaced, via coup, by yet another soldier, Chun Do Hwan. Chun was a crook and a bum, as he ultimately admitted, so I can't defend him.

On the other hand, one may logically contend that despite their autocratic (but I would say generally patriotic and benevolent) ways, Syngmun Rhee and Pak Chung Hui led the Republic of Korea honestly and wisely enough to modernize it, to make it highly competitive in the world marketplace, to vastly increase its per-capita income and the educational level of its people, while at the same time keeping the country strong enough (with much U.S. help) to deter attack from its bitterly hostile northern neighbor. This was peace and progress—on a dramatic scale. Could a series of democratically elected presidents, each one opposed by an active, hostile political party—and therefore constantly at pains to maintain his popularity so he could be reelected—have done as well?

I am a firm believer (with some reservations) in democracy, but I would answer my question, above, as follows: *No.* Among other things, a politically sensitive president, with a legislature he was unable to control, might well have been unable to keep the country militarily strong enough to prevent a resumption of the war. As I write this, Korean students continue to riot—and maybe by now, given the overall weakening of world communism, a politically liberal government could keep the peace. But in the decades just past I'd guess such a government could not have done so.

But I'm biased.

The Koreans in my day had become very modern in many respects, but they had not relinquished all their ancient morals, one of which is ancestor worship. On a certain specified day each year—and on some unspecified ones—they forgo other obligations and interests to visit the graves of their forebears, going through certain specified rituals and then having a picnic. This is a matter of tradition and family solidarity, not to be lightly regarded. Actually, family graves, all of them hemispherical grassy mounds carefully tended year 'round, occupy a substantial part of the Korean terrain.

I had very frequent official meetings with my counterpart, the Korean Army Chief of Staff, General Song, during which we discussed multiple topics of common interest—all of them pertaining to the modernization and training of the Korean Army and its readiness for war. One time, however, I arrived at his office shortly after completing a helicopter flight over the area just south of Seoul, and began conversation by suggesting that much excellent arable land, now occupied by graves, could be recovered for agricultural purposes by moving thousands of said graves from the valleys onto hillsides, Korea being a very mountainous country. Tiger Song received this suggestion in silence, but after a time said to me, very solemnly, "Ham, you are my friend, so I shall give you some *very* good advice. Never, so long as you are in Korea, say that again." And I didn't.

Perhaps the nadir of my tour as Chief KMAG, however, came when Song asked that my wife and I be his guests at the Sunday service at the Korean Army Chapel, a Christian institution. Korea is mostly Buddhist, with a scattering of Confucianism and Shintoism, but Christianity, due to the longtime presence of American missionaries and the influence of U.S. Army chaplains, is pretty strong there. Well, I didn't tell my Korean aide, Capt. Pak Bo Hi, or Mary about the engagement, and I forgot. Pak Bo Hi, somehow alerted, came tearing into the service at the U.S. Army chapel about 11:30 A.M. of the appointed day to get us, informing us also that the Korean service had already been held up a half-hour pending our arrival; I also learned, for the first time, that Syngmun Rhee, the venerable Korean president, and Madame Rhee were among those waiting for us.

Well, we hurried over, and after the long-delayed service—in English, for our benefit—we had our pictures taken outside the chapel with the president and Mrs. Rhee (the latter an Austrian by birth) and General and Mrs. Song—and the chaplain. But it was not, for me, a very happy occasion—and poor Mary had to share my embarrassment.

Capt. Pak Bo Hi was a very capable and attentive aide, among other things giving me, in the first year of my tour, a daily half-hour lesson in Korean, a terribly difficult language. This never allowed me to converse in Korean or give a talk in it, but I did learn to enunciate, with an acceptable accent, the phonetic written language, Hangul, and could therefore read in Korean the introduction to the talks I gave to Korean military audiences. Incidentally, this Pak Bo Hi was—is—the same one who now is the Reverend Sun Young Moon's (head of the Unification Church, USA) right-hand man and the administrator of some few billion dollars' worth of church property and business interests in our country. Those interests include the ownership of the *Washington Times*.

Mary and I experienced two revolutions during our first two-year tour in Korea. In the spring of 1960 the outraged students simply threw themselves at the police barricades across the main street of Seoul; the police killed a great many, but not enough to stop them. The survivors did not manage to reach the Blue House (the Korean equivalent of our White House) but President Rhee, faced with the news of the revolt, simply walked out the front door, down the hill and around the corner to his own residence, and never went back.

Rhee and his Austrian wife were evacuated, courtesy of the U.S. Government, to Fort Shafter, near Honolulu, where they spent his remaining days, which were not many, under the friendly eyes of Gen. and Mrs. I. D. White, U.S. Army—old acquaintances of the Rhees. I recall seeing in at least one Korean newspaper the allegation that Rhee had escaped Korea with $25 million. The Whites, on the other hand, told Mary and me and others that the Rhees were almost penniless, needing the Whites' help in paying for their groceries.

When Rhee was overthrown, the Korean National Police practically disappeared. It had operated too much in the style of the earlier, much hated police in the forty years of Japanese domination of Korea and had forcibly opposed the student uprising. In all of Korea's cities, the students, in effect, simply stomped any police they encountered into the sidewalks. So most of the survivors, we learned, took off their uniforms, buried them, and sought other employment.

To replace Rhee, the National Assembly elected an interim president pending a general popular election. This new man was Chang Myun, a thoroughly well-educated, mild-mannered, apparently able man with an excellent command of English. He was fully accepted by our military and the State Department as a welcome replacement for Rhee, who by then had become very obviously senile. And Chang's accession to office had pacified the students.

The second revolution—or coup—came about eight months later, shortly before my scheduled departure from Korea. Mary woke me about 3 o'clock one morning to report that she heard machine-gun fire. I said that was silly, but I went to the window to see long strings of tracer bullets arcing across the night sky over Seoul. I apologized to Mary and got into my clothes. When I got to Gen. Carter B. Magruder's office he and his Chief of Staff, Maj. Gen. Pat Carter, were already there.

Magruder told me to go over to ROK Army headquarters, only five minutes away, to find out what was going on, but he cautioned me as follows: I was free to give the Korean staff any military advice it asked for, but I would stay entirely clear of all issues that had political implications.

The night was still pitch black. I found the headquarters building surrounded by ROK marines in scout cars, each of which carried two machine guns with belts of ammunition hanging from their sides. By this date, I should say, Tiger Song had retired from the Korean Army, his successor being one Gen. Chang Do Young, a man of lesser caliber.

In my day Korean offices included, always, not a high table that one could conveniently use to write notes on but what we'd call a coffee table: low and rectangular. In the Chief of Staff's office the Chief always sat at the head of his table and I at his immediate left, the place of honor in Korea; the rest of the Army general staff, at our meetings, sat further down the table, in order of rank.

When I came into the Chief's office all the chairs around the table were filled, my seat being occupied by Maj. Gen. Pak Chung Hui, whom I'd come to know only casually. He was in command of the large Korean Army supply depot in the port city of Pusan, on Korea's south coast. At the head of the table in his usual spot was Chang Do Young, the Army Chief of Staff, all slumped down and looking as though his last friend had left him.

Chang apparently told Pak that he had my seat, whereupon everybody except Chang Do Young stood up and moved down a notch to accommodate me. But then a long silence ensued. Eventually I turned to Pak, on my left, and asked, "Are you the leader of this revolt?" Pak said yes, he was. "Where," I asked, "is President Chang Myun?" Pak said he was alive and well, though in house arrest. Then, because of his limited English, Pak asked that an interpreter be provided, and a Korean corporal came in and stood behind him. Pak then turned to me, saying via the interpreter that he had instigated the revolt because the existing interim civilian government was manifestly too weak and indecisive to lead the country and would, in particular, be unable to defend it in case of communist invasion from the north. And then, to my astonishment, he said approximately this: "I have set up an interim Revolutionary Advisory Council to govern Korea until a new president is selected, and am here now to ask General Chang Do Young to be the Chairman of that Council. If he does not accept that proposal I am ready to submit to his arrest."

Well! After I digested this news I was for a time tempted to grab Pak's skinny little arm (he was a small man, but a tough one) and say to Chang—"Hey, we got him! The revolution's over!" But then I remembered General Magruder's strict admonition—I was free to give the Korean Army any military advice it asked for, but I was to stand strictly aside in all political matters. This was political, so I kept silent.

Conversation around the table was now stone dead—no one said anything. The G-3 (the Operations Officer, a major general) said in effect, "General Howze, this is a very difficult situation, and strictly Korean. We cannot freely discuss the problem facing us in your presence, and therefore request that you withdraw." Very naturally I did so, immediately, and went back in the breaking dawn to report to my boss, General Magruder.

Naturally both overthrows of government, briefly described above, involved some uncertainty and some pretty tense situations—one could not be certain as to where loyalties lay. For this reason some Korean Army forces had to be withdrawn (with U.S. acquiescence) from their reinforcing positions along the DMZ and sent to areas near Seoul for purposes of maintaining stability and public order. I tended to these matters, under Magruder's direction, and carefully kept abreast (via KMAG's U.S. military advisors present with each combat division, corps, and field army) of military sentiment. But though some senior commanders were shifted about for political reasons, we had no other serious trouble within the forces.

For about 72 hours I spent most of my time, day and night, either out in the field or in Magruder's office. Magruder, with the benefit (I hope) of my advice, had a number of decisions to make—in a very complex and ticklish situation. But I report this: he spent about three-quarters of his time formulating, often with my assistance, answers to the incessant queries from Washington and one-quarter in dealing with the complexities of a pretty uncertain and possibly dangerous situation in Korea. I came to think, in this period, that the overseas military commander had things better in the days when the sailing ship provided the only communication between the national government and its overseas commands. A military commander in times of stress cannot properly be forced to spend most of his time looking back over his shoulder.

Magruder had the reputation, throughout his last few years of service as a four-star general, of being very hard on his underlings. Indeed, his Chief of Staff in Korea, Maj. Gen. Pat Carter, a brilliant guy with a tremendous sense of humor, often had to use all his talents to keep the United Nations and Eighth Army general staffs (both under Magruder) reasonably happy. One of Pat's most useful gestures he copied from the pope: when staff members approached a state of rebellion Carter calmed them down with hand blessings and pronouncements of peace.

Once, after he had completed making out my efficiency report, Magruder called me in to say that he had given me a good report but that I was *rude*—apparently, in his mind, to him. This left me speechless—he had, by reputation, the Army's championship for rudeness. He was nevertheless smart and a good soldier, meriting not love, certainly, but high respect. I eventually came to get along well with him.

When he left Seoul for retirement, though, his action was pretty typical. To a gathering of his staff officers in the large briefing room of his headquarters he spoke approximately as follows: "In the last two years I've tried my best to make you young gentlemen into staff officers. Sometimes I may have been too severe. But I quote that famous philosopher, Leo Durocher, 'Nice guys finish last.'

"I wish you well. Good-bye."

He put on his hat and left.

I'll close this chapter with a few Korea incidentals.

In bringing up our two boys, by then 12 and 14, I had used the airborne training discipline: when they were guilty of small misdemeanors I made them do ten push-ups. Worked great. However, when the American school in our Yongsan Compound had a gymkhana Mary was embarrassed when they won first and second in push-ups and everyone wanted to know why.

Korea in the late fifties had, to my delight, what might have been the best pheasant shooting in the world—largely no doubt because native Koreans had no shotguns to hunt them with. Koreans sometimes used to poison them, though, with strychnine-laced corn kernels. They had to watch, however, from cover close by while the bird took the bait—grab him and bleed him immediately when he keeled over, else the poison would ruin the meat. We had pheasant even around our quarters—all the birds surviving the frantic two-year effort of my youngest son to shoot one with his bow and arrow.

Koreans in the early 1960s were pretty familiar with the sight of adult Americans—mostly in uniform—but American children were still subjects of great curiosity. Our youngest boy then was still very blond, in sharp contrast to the jet-black hair of every Korean—man, woman, and child. Sometimes Korean peasant women would run their hand through Guy's hair, chattering in wonderment. In those days Korea still had some of the characteristics of the Hermit Kingdom.

In the low wooded mountains near the city of Taegu, in central South Korea, is the Hain Sa Buddhist temple. "Sa" means "Temple." As Mary and I, on a weekend holiday, approached the temple on its narrow dirt road we found ourselves alongside a stream running among a great many large, very white boulders—apparently soft limestone, for the huge rocks had been softly rounded, over the centuries, by occasional high water. Many of the rocks had writing on them—not with paint, but by chiseling into the soft rock. And all of the carvings were in the form of Chinese characters, so that the names or messages or whatever were quite beautiful, fitting perfectly into the scene. It was the only instance of graffiti that I have thought to be anything but hideous.

At Hain Sa itself the temple was attractive, but we'd seen many of those. Nearby, however, were two rectangular heavy-walled wooden buildings, each about 100 by 30 feet, and about 20 feet high. They had to be that big to house the complete Buddhist Scripture—the Buddhist equivalent to the Christian Bible. The Scripture was (and, of course, still is) in the shape of ¾-inch-thick (about) wooden printing blocks, each block very black and about 8 by 14 inches in size. On each side of each block had been carved, by hand, the *raised* mirror-image of maybe 200 Chinese characters. As one of the monks explained, one could smear an ink on the surface of the raised characters, press the board onto rice paper, and thereupon read (if you were well versed in Korean and knew the meaning of Chinese characters) that bit of the Buddhist Scripture. The two buildings housed something like 50,000 boards—all of them, on the basis of the several we pulled out of their racks, in very workable shape.

These boards, with their exquisitely carved, perfectly preserved (as far as we could see) characters, were more than 300 years old and were total strangers to anything resembling a "controlled atmosphere." There was a foot of airspace between the top of the walls and the roof, in each building, but nothing more. And Korea has a climate approximating that of upper New York state—rain, snow, heat, and extreme cold.

We were told, in explanation, that the boards that one sees were manufactured and carved not near Hain Sa but near the coast west of Seoul. After cutting to size but prior to carving, the boards were soaked for three years in seawater and then boiled for three days in seawater. Apparently the salt and other minerals of the water served as a remarkably effective preservative: the boards we saw showed no signs of insect boring or of warping, and very little indication of cracking—after 300 years! Of that time they have been housed at Hain Sa less than 50 years.

Mary and I left Korea in June of 1961 with orders to the Army's Continental Army Command at Fort Monroe, Virginia. We had had an intensely interesting and pleasant time in the Land of the Morning Calm, broken by one joint trip, on holiday, to Okinawa and Hong Kong and several excursions by jeep around the beautiful (and sometimes a bit odiferous) Korean countryside. Mary took other trips to such places as Bangkok, Thailand, and Anghor Wat in Cambodia, but I had no time for those.

We had made countless friends among the Koreans, mostly officers and their wives. Indeed, almost my final act was to visit four generals in jail—put there by the ruling Revolutionary Advisory Council on the grounds that they had not been altogether sympathetic with the last revolution. I made the visits not simply to say goodbye but to indicate U.S. official approval of their integrity and disapproval of their imprisonment. All were released within weeks of our departure, and two became ambassadors to foreign countries after their retirement. All part of the game . . .

FORT BRAGG

18 Fort Monroe, Virginia, on the north shore of the entrance to Norfolk Harbor and the Norfolk Navy Base, was one of the Army's oldest and most historic ex–Coast Artillery posts, boasting a wide moat and lots of old cannon. It was in 1961 the home of the Continental Army Command, the headquarters commanding all Army combat forces within the lower forty-eight states and charged also with the formulation of Army combat doctrine and battle tactics. Its boss was Gen. Herbert Powell, a fine soldier. Because I found military tactics a fascinating study and because I was anxious to effect some modernization in the Army's battle doctrine, I was happy with my new assignment.

Very shortly after our arrival I was promoted in an impressive ceremony with the post band and honor guard, Mary joining the CG in pinning on the third star. I was much flattered—never before had any promotion been noted by more than a few handshakes and a hug and kiss from Mary.

Our assigned quarters, an enormous old-fashioned house surrounded with wide porches on both levels, was on the waterfront where we could see all the sea traffic entering and leaving Norfolk Harbor. I found this attractive—marred a bit by the soot-laden screens surrounding the porches, the soot put there by ships' smoke. Also, for reasons known only to the architect, the living room was on the second floor. Altogether, Mary wasn't too fond of the accommodations at Fort Monroe.

She need not have worried. Within weeks I had orders, I suppose because of an unexpected vacancy occurring somewhere within the Army's top echelons, to the command of the XVIII Airborne Corps at Fort Bragg, North Carolina, relieving Lt. Gen. Hall Trapnell. Trap was an old friend, once an All-American halfback at West Point and later a fellow member of that wonderful 26th Cavalry (Philippine Scouts) polo team. But shortly thereafter, as a major in that regiment, he was captured and imprisoned by the Japanese, thus missing the rapid promotion that came during the war years. He otherwise would surely have gotten a fourth star.

Mary and I got to Fort Bragg almost coincidental with the arrival of Pres. Jack Kennedy, there to have a look at my old division, the 82nd Airborne. It was the first time I met the president, but not the last. Trapnell, when he left Bragg, went down to Fort McPherson, in Atlanta, to command the Third Army. In that capacity he would be my boss, though a few hundred miles distant.

I had been brought up as a horse soldier, became a tanker when the war started, and now, with only one previous tour as an airborne soldier found myself now in command of our only airborne corps, including both of the Army's parachute divisions. With the exception of the Green Berets, these were all the airborne forces in the Army. I was immensely flattered, proud as a peacock, happy as a clam at high tide.

I was also the nominal commander of STRAC—the Strategic Army Corps—that being composed of my own corps and three other combat divisions within the United States—this loose organization being the forerunner of what became the Army's Strike Command with headquarters at McDill Air Force Base in Florida. My attached divisions—all distant from Fort Bragg—remained under the jurisdiction of one or another of the several Army commanders in the United States (their armies being composed mostly of reserve and national guard forces) but I sent the divisions my training directives with the admonition that their implementation was subject to the approval of said Army commanders. I think the directives had varying effect.

Within the Airborne Corps I continued, on a broader scale, the training practices I'd found useful in earlier commands—with special emphasis on weapons competitions, combat firing drills, and the 24-hour-long training inspection, all of these being made obligatory in both the airborne divisions. I demonstrated how the training inspection was to be done by doing one myself, in each division, under the observation of the division and brigade commanders.

Training directives in the Army are habitually issued "by direction of the commanding general" but are written in the third person—"units will do such and such"—and signed by the Adjutant General. They are therefore generally taken as the fulminations only of the staff operations officer, and though they are strictly on the side of motherhood they don't carry much punch.

I changed the pattern, drastically. The Airborne Corps Training Directive No. 32 was, as I believe all training directives should be, written by the corps commander—that being me—and directed specifically and personally to major subordinate commanders. It was written in the first person: "I require you" to conduct the following training exercises; and the document was signed not by the Adjutant General, as is customary, but by me, in big letters. This got everyone thinking about their efficiency reports and thereby got lots of attention. Commanders were advised to use the same format in their directives to their own subordinate units. I think that format had exceptionally good effect.

My tour as CG of the Airborne Corps was an eventful one. One midnight telephone call from Washington directed me (on orders of the president) to depart immediately for Oxford, Mississippi, where, the day before, a riot occurred to stop the matriculation of one James Meredith, a black, into the University of Mississippi, or "Ole Miss." The riot had injured several people and killed two, despite the efforts of a substantial number of U.S. marshals especially dispatched to Oxford to preserve order. Troops, I was informed, would follow my arrival. They sure did—to the tune of about 25,000, not including the Mississippi National Guard already on site, but much of the 82nd and 101st Airborne Divisions, my own people.

I flew myself down, landing on the strip belonging to the university just after dawn, and set up headquarters in a small building in Oxford belonging to and offered by the National Guard. I called on the city fathers and on the president of the university and certain of his staff. All greeted the arrival of federal troops with relief and gratitude. The situation earlier had apparently been a nasty one, particularly since the almost universal sentiment among students had been anti-Meredith and thus, at least in principle, supportive of the rioters.

Troops poured into Oxford via Air Force transports and Army aircraft—the latter mostly helicopters—all that day, and all landing on that tiny 5,000-foot strip, which had *no* tower, *no* taxiways, and only a very limited hardstand, already pretty full of parked civilian aircraft. Lieutenant General Moorer of the Air Force, an old friend of mine from our tour in Germany, turned up a bit after noon in his big command plane, and when I told him the situation he put his aircrew and his aircraft's communications into service as a tower. But before that, and even after that, Army and Air Force aircrews, in vastly differing aircraft (whose total number of landing and takeoffs on that date exceeded that of this country's busiest air terminal, Chicago's O'Hare) coordinated their operations with one another entirely via a military high-frequency radio channel. The sky near the strip was crowded with military aircraft, all in twin landing patterns (one for helos, onto the grass, one for planes) or in the process of joining one of the patterns—all pilots exhibiting the patience, discipline, and skill demanded by the incredibly dense traffic. And the day ended without so much as one scratch on an aircraft's paint.

One may see once more why I, as a part of it, took such pride in military service.

There were about 10,000 troopers in Oxford, and about 15,000 in Jackson, the state capital, where the proceedings of the Mississippi legislature had included some redneck speeches defying the authority of the government in Washington to put a Negro in the state university. I have no evidence that there was any expressed disloyalty to the Union, but I cannot rationalize the sending of 25,000 federal paratroopers into the state of Mississippi unless there was some fear, in the mind of the president, of radical action by the state government and/or the state's people. Secession sounds absurd, impractical, impossible—but 25,000 federal soldiers? What were they for—especially the 15,000 in Jackson?

My impression was not lessened by a daily telephone call to me from the Army's Chief of Staff, Gen. Buz Wheeler. As soon as I answered the phone Buz would tell me to wait—while I heard him put in a call for the president. I never heard Mr. Kennedy's voice, but Wheeler repeatedly interrupted his conversation with me to relay what I had just told him to the president, and to relay Kennedy's instructions for me. I found this process pretty ridiculous, but could do nothing about it. I naturally reported each day's events, none of them very exciting, and received in return amazingly detailed instructions. In the first few days, for example, our constant jeep patrols through the university grounds were to contain no blacks (I had already ordered that) but in later days they were to include them—without exception.

Nicholas Katzenbach, a very senior member of the national Attorney General's Office, also turned up in Oxford. I guess he was there for legal purposes; in any case I got along fine with him. I also made daily visits to the office of the president of the university, my relations with him and his staff being uniformly cordial, as they were with the mayor of Oxford. Both the president of Ole Miss and the mayor wrote me generous letters of appreciation and thanks after I returned to Bragg, both of them extremely complimentary as respects the disciplined behavior of the airborne troopers.

In my jeep travels around the outskirts of Oxford I noted that nearly every country crossroads boasted a store prominently displaying handguns for sale; also, a great many of the college students, though they never showed the slightest sign of active opposition to us, displayed the rebel flag very prominently on their automobiles. Of course the rebel flag was also the university flag. I nevertheless thought it prudent to do a little disarming, not by room search but by requesting the college president to ask the students to turn in their gats, for which we would give receipts. I was amazed by the results: several hundred students had pistols in their rooms, and most I believe turned them in.

I longed for President Kennedy's order withdrawing us from Mississippi—when young soldiers are kept too long in a strange civilian environment, trouble ensues. The order came after about 10 days—soon enough for us to get out with an unblemished reputation among the townsfolk of Oxford and the officials of the university. It had been a unique but not particularly entertaining experience.

In my files at home I had a large number of the letters written by my grandfather, for whom I was named, to his mother during the Civil War, in which he served as a lieutenant. One of his letters dealt with the battle of Chancellorsville and in that letter he was extremely critical of the leadership of the Union commanding general, one "Fighting Joe" Hooker.

During an earlier tour in Washington Mary and I had, on a weekend, gone down into Virginia with a camera to have a look at the beautifully maintained (and beautifully marked and explained, by the Park Service) battlefield at Chancellorsville—partly because of my grandfather's letter on that battle (see appendix). On the basis of our visit and the letter I developed a very elaborate presentation, supported by three assistants, two slide projectors and two screens—one screen for maps showing, day by day, troop dispositions; the other showing photographs of battle sites as they look now. I did all this because the battle was characterized by a large number of serious errors—errors of tactics and leadership—on the Union side, while the Confederate leadership was bold and effective. Moreover, the outcome of the battle was crucial: had the Union side with its much superior strength won that battle, Richmond, the Confederate capitol, would almost certainly have fallen and the war ended much sooner. The Battle of Chancellorsville, in sum, constitutes a magnificent object lesson in leadership and thus merits study by professional soldiers.

Using the large post theater I presented the lecture to all combat branch officers at Fort Bragg, I think with very good effect, and then found myself doing the same thing before civilian Civil War clubs as far away as Cleveland, Ohio—and even to the cadets at Sandhurst, in England, the British Army's equivalent of our West Point.

That last eventuated because I was appointed, while at Bragg, the 1962 American lecturer in a program under the auspices of the Kermit Roosevelt Lecture Foundation. The son of Pres. Theodore Roosevelt, Kermit was by this time deceased—but he had served, quite extraordinarily, in the British Army and the American Army both in World War I and World War II. For my lectures I was to go to England; my British opposite number, a General Hackett, was to come to the United States.

Mary (she being an official member of our party—the third one being my military aide) and I first went to New York to call on Mrs. Kermit Roosevelt in her handsome home on the East River; it was an interesting experience, for she was a highly intelligent and altogether delightful old lady.

In England we were met at plane-side by a British military aide, Capt. Tony Philippi of the Coldstream Guards, an attractive, highly polished young gentleman of the old school. Thereafter my *two* aides rendered more service than I could really use, but they were both fine fellows and enjoyed one another's company.

I lectured first at the British Army College of Science at Shrivenham, where the Commandant, who put us up for the night in his quarters, told us that Field Marshal Lord Bernard Montgomery, by then retired, had been my predecessor at the lectern. The Commandant added quite pointedly that Monty had said some "frightfully naughty" things to the students, upsetting the equilibrium of the little college.

Thereafter I talked at Camberley to the British Army Staff College and to the cadets at Sandhurst, where I gave that elaborately illustrated account of the Battle of Chancellorsville.

And finally I addressed the prestigious Imperial Defense College, in London, where I talked about the problems posed to uniformed forces by guerrillas, despite the fact that the British Army had far more extensive experience in guerrilla combat than we did. My rationale for doing what I did was that the introduction of the helicopter would make a big difference in tactics. This was, in fact, a correct notion.

I was meticulous, while in Britain, in seeing to it that my British host on each occasion was seated in the right side of the back seat of the car, that being in American government protocol the seat of the senior person present. Only too late did it dawn on me that in Britain, where they drive on the left side of the road and drivers therefore sit on the right side, I had consistently urged my British friends into the inferior spot.

And one more thing: our highly cultivated British hosts, when we dined with them and their wives, seemed to be much occupied with poltergeists. Some recounted experiences they'd had with them. Extraordinary!

I'd arranged for five days' leave, so Mary and I and my American aide, Capt. Cornelius Francis McGillicudy (the same moniker used by the erstwhile great baseball manager, Connie Mac, though he was not a relative), flew to Belfast, put on civilian clothes, rented a car, and set out to tour Ireland. We were in great spirits, all the lecturing behind us.

We first went south to Castlewellan, in County Down, where I'd spent five months in the summer and fall of 1942, before the onset of the campaign against the French and then the Germans and Italians in North Africa. We visited the castle itself, marveling at its size and the magnificence of its grounds, and then went up to Londonderry and along the north and west coasts of the island, spending nights at little country inns. We bought enough stout and victuals each morning to allow us to have a picnic lunch in the lush green—though pathetically poor—countryside, on each occasion welcoming to lunch with us one or more Irish countrymen who just stopped by to say hello.

Ireland, then and I presume now, had next to no trees outside the walls of the large once-British estates—other trees having long since been used up for firewood. Houses were mostly of stone, some few (in 1962) still with sod roofs—and many in ruins. Many families were much of the time without fathers because many Irishmen could find employment only in England. A substantial number of well-to-do English families have country homes in Ireland, but the typical native Irishman is not at all prosperous.

As we approached the city of Killarney, near the southwest corner of the island, Captain McGillicuddy (then on his first trip abroad) became increasingly excited—Killarney was the ancestral home of the very large McGillicuddy clan. Indeed, as he pointed out, the McGillicuddy Reeks (mountains) are just west of town, and *the* "McGillicuddy of the Reeks" had his ancestral home in Killarney. However, as we continued to drive in leisurely fashion down through the Irish countryside, stopping to talk to lots of people, my pronunciation of "McGillicuddy" had been strongly challenged: the proper way to say it, I was told, was "*Mo*clicuddy," with heavy accent on the first syllable. I of course started calling Mac "Moclicuddy"—until he pointed out that he had a wife and three kids at home and brothers and sisters, parents, grandparents, uncles, and aunts all in America, and he couldn't get them all to change their names. So I resumed the American pronunciation.

In Killarney Mac asked to be excused for a few hours while he paid his respects to the McGillicuddy of the Reeks, in his mind's eye expecting to see a large, imposing individual with a long grey beard. He rang the doorbell of a suitably large home surrounded by handsome lawns and gardens and was ushered by a maid into the presence of a very cordial, grey-haired old lady. Mac stated his desire to pay his respects to the McGillicuddy of the Reeks, but was told that was impossible: he was at Eton. *Eton?* Yes, she said, the McGillicuddy of the Reeks was only 12 years old.

This was such a shock to Mac that she gave him tea and crumpets to cheer him up. More shocks were to come when he discovered, later, that St. Patrick's Cathedral in Dublin was the Church of England, and that the mayor of Dublin was Jewish.

On our way to Dublin, via Cork, we stopped by to visit the parents of Tony Philippi on the south coast—they lived in a beautiful, not-very-little cottage with a productive salmon pool nearby, and were very pleasant to us.

And in Dublin, after some sightseeing, we got on an airplane for home.

THE HOWZE BOARD

19 The proper name was the U.S. Army Tactical Mobility Requirements Board, but USATMRB is not exactly a handy acronym, so people fell easily into the custom of calling the board by the name of its president, who is presumably the one to control its destiny. Actually, the Howze Board was out of control much of the time, for reasons I'll explain later.

This chapter talks about that board, but two preliminaries to its activities are worth mentioning.

In early 1957, I had marched around the corridors of the Pentagon with a briefing in the preparation of which I was helped by Col. Claude Sheppard—giving it to any and all of my superiors who would listen. I think we eventually got to the Chief of Staff, secretary of the Army level.

It was a pretty good briefing. With a bunch of Command and General Staff College maps and overlays, we were able to present Leavenworth's school plan of the delay, by one reinforced U.S. armored division, of an assault across Bavaria by three reinforced Soviet armored divisions. We then presented the problem again, using the same maps and the same sector, substituting a single small super-mobile U.S. air cavalry brigade for the armored division. The brigade was also reinforced by lots of conventional artillery and engineers.

Since the air cavalry brigade had no need for roads or bridges, we blew (in our solution) all bridges and big culverts forward of the artillery—which means we got 'em all, without worrying about disengagement of ground forces and the queuing up of many vehicles at the successive bottlenecks with all the delay and loss that that entails. Engineers also cratered roads wherever they could along a side hill, and liberally mined the roads and the fords at propitious points—all without regard to our own forward elements. The Soviet armor would have a sticky time, even if nobody shot at it.

But somebody would shoot at it.

We assumed the same Air Force fighter-bomber support allotted to the armored division. We thought, however, it would be more effective, partly because we removed the complication of close ground contact between our forces and the enemy's, partly because of the powers of observation of our scout helicopters, and partly because we thought we could make the enemy present better and fatter air targets.

We also left behind on high, rough, inaccessible ground lots of artillery forward observers easily recoverable by rescue helicopters. They should have had a succession of turkey shoots. Every jam point, every attempt at bridge-building, road repair, or mine removal, all easily observable by our artillery spotters on the hilltops or in the air, we would pound with artillery, itself protected from tank overrun by the multiple demolitions and mines. Actually, the greater part of the air cavalry brigade's strength came from its own observation, which could track enemy progress (and jam points) with speed and accuracy, and the combined effect of supporting fighter-bombers, artillery, and engineers.

Moreover, the brigade could deploy antitank missile helicopters (we had to imagine these things—there were none in the inventory, and no air cavalry brigades, either) to lurk in safe positions of ambush well off the roads. By attacking enemy columns in flank the brigade could inflict considerable damage on the enemy tanks and even more heartburn on their crews. Helicopter-borne riflemen, formed into tank-killer teams, could be put down well behind attacking enemy spearheads to do little jobs on the unwary.

Well, we wound up this little show with statements to the effect that the smaller air cavalry force, reinforced, could do a better job at far less cost in casualties than the much larger, also reinforced, armored division. As far as can be done on a map, I thought we proved the point convincingly.

In April of 1960, the Rogers Board (Lt. Gen. Gordon Rogers, president) had been convened. I was a member, coming back from Korea to attend. The board devoted itself largely to hardware, receiving from a number of small study teams that had been hard at work for many weeks recommendations for research, development, and procurement of aircraft in each of the primary fields of Army interest. Because the teams had done their work well, the board was able to perform a very worthwhile service by establishing practical guidelines for further aircraft development and purchase.

Because of its limited charter, the Rogers Board rejected, properly I suppose, my endeavor to insert into the basic report a few pungent thoughts about air fighting units, tactics, and doctrine. I was allowed only to add a short addendum marked, "Enclosure I to Section VII," called "The Requirement for Air Fighting Units." I quote from it:

> I invite the special attention of the board to another area of aircraft tactical employment, hitherto unexploited, which is of fundamental importance to the Army.
>
> MOMAR (Modern Mechanized Army, a CONARC plan) and DCSOPS Plans I, II, III and IV are all devoted to the purpose of enhancing the combat capability of infantry, tank and reconnaissance units through the device of assigning those units additional quantities of light aircraft.
>
> Substantial benefits will undoubtedly accrue from this, but it should be fully acknowledged that the assigned and attached aircraft will simply improve the ability of these units to execute their conventional missions, and that the employment of the aircraft will be restricted to those missions. A prime example exists in the Armored Cavalry regiments visualized in MOMAR and Plans I–IV: aerial reconnaissance companies will be very useful here, but the mission of the regiment, which has basically only wheeled mobility, will control and limit the employment of the aircraft. In the days when the horse provided the highest degree of battlefield mobility, it would have been a fundamental error to restrict the assignment of horses to the infantry divisions. While infantry divisions employed horses in considerable quantities, with benefit, it was necessary and desirable to group a substantial percentage of all the horses in cavalry units in order to take proper advantage of their mobility.
>
> I, therefore, submit that a new course of action, parallel to and of equal importance to the modernization of conventional type ground units, is urgently necessary. The Army should proceed vigorously and at once in the development of fighting units (which may be called air cavalry) whose mode of tactical employment will take

maximum advantage of the unique mobility and flexibility of light aircraft—aircraft which will be employed to provide, for the execution of the missions assigned these units, not only mobility for the relatively few riflemen and machine gunners, but also direct fire support, artillery and missile fire adjustment, command, communications, security, reconnaissance and supply.

Missions appropriate for assignment to air cavalry units are these: the seizure of critical terrain in advance of large forces, delaying action and cover for the withdrawal of larger forces, raids, penetration of shallow enemy positions and the disruption of enemy rear areas, pursuit and exploitation, the protection of a long flank and wide reconnaissance. New weapons developments will provide air cavalry units with very destructive firepower, and these forces will develop many targets for the employment of surface-to-surface missiles. Air cavalry would find particular applicability in any battle area in which the threat of area weapons forces wide troop dispersion—and hence, a porous battlefield—as well as in "brush fire" actions against relatively unsophisticated opponents.

This was submitted more than two years before the convocation of the Howze Board, but little if anything was done in those two years in response to this recommendation.

On 19 April, Secretary of Defense Robert S. McNamara wrote Secretary of the Army Elvis J. Stahr not one, but two memoranda on the subject of Army aviation. The first directed the Army to take a "bold new look" at land warfare mobility, conducting the examination "in an atmosphere divorced from traditional viewpoints and past policies." He said also that recommendations to be developed should "be protected from veto or dilution by conservative staff review."

The second paper was similar in tone. It outlined six areas for examination and said we should "seriously consider fresh, new concepts, and give unorthodox ideas a hearing."

Well, sir, there may have been in other fields other directives as good as those two, but none ever came to me for action. Only later did I learn that McNamara's directives were instigated largely by the efforts of Col. (later Lt. Gen.) Robert R. Williams, and carried through by Col. Spic Powell as members of McNamara's staff. Bob Williams was the first Master Army Aviator. He became a most valuable member of the board.

Mr. McNamara suggested that I be made a member of what he called a committee, and he named eight others as well. On 28 April, the Department of the Army wrote an implementing directive to Gen. Herbert Powell, Commander of Continental Army Command (CONARC). General Powell had earlier alerted me and Col. (later Lt. Gen.) John Norton, whom he appointed board secretary, and required us to submit a draft outline plan in which we listed the means—some units, some individual pilots, and aircraft—we would need. The CONARC directive, dated 3 May, told us to submit the final report by 20 August in order to meet Mr. McNamara's deadline of 1 September.

I could not begin to give the chronology of those first weeks. We knew we were in a great hurry: all the organization to be done, all the people and equipment to assemble—mostly from far away—all the tests and experiments and consultation and war games to be completed, all the debate and writing and rewriting and printing to be done, by 20 August.

In response to our question as to how big the report should be, the Department of the Army told us that one copy should fit into a standard Army footlocker, and that 300 copies were needed. The printers in the Adjutant General Department said that, if 300 footlockers worth of printing were necessary, we would have to let them have a final copy by 1 August. Jack Norton and I figured that practically all of May would be required for assembling people and things and for organizing, which left us only the two months of June and July to get the work done.

In the midst of the general confusion, I went irresponsibly off to England with my wife to do the Kermit Roosevelt lecture series, leaving Jack Norton to run everything. I do not know whether or not we asked him to, but Jack also moved into our house and ruled over our boys with all necessary firmness.

Now a retired lieutenant general, Colonel Norton entered into the job of secretary (and executive, as I appointed him) like a new bull released into the pasture, full of beans and looking for trouble. Always an idea man, Jack found full play for his boundless initiative and would have gone on forming committees and test groups and launching investigations forever had it not been for my occasional reminders that 1 August was just a few weeks away.

We could not have found a better executive and energizer. For one thing, he clung always to the belief that we would get through sometime and maybe even by the deadline—a thought I considered irrational. Maj. Jim Brockmyer was his capable and articulate assistant.

It was fortunate for us that the new Irving Elementary School building was formally turned over by the builder to the post of Fort Bragg shortly before the board assembled. We took it over, clean and shipshape and smelling strongly of plaster. We found that schoolrooms made fine committee rooms, and all that plumbing was mighty convenient even if some of the toilets and drinking fountains, particularly in the first- and second-grade areas, were just a touch low and added a little comedy when patronized by 6'3" board members.

We needed the whole school, what with some 100 (if my memory does not fail me) board members. The number seems ridiculous, and I guess it was. Part of the extraordinary size was due to representation; it was deemed desirable that every Army agency and office whose function might affect or be affected by Army aviation should provide a member or members. Since we had something to sell, we wanted the whole Army to associate itself with the concept.

There was much work to be done. For each major subject a separate committee was formed to do appropriate investigation and test and then write one of the fifteen annexes to the basic report. The committees were pretty independent and wrote too much, although we did not quite fill the footlocker.

In the general rush of things, the annexes had to be put in print with no more than cursory review by the steering committee; to this date, I have not read them all. One in particular I wish no one had ever read, for it was a bit visionary and gave the Air Force a stick to use on us.

As an aside, I find that I make a number of remarks critical of the Air Force. I regret it, for I am a very genuine admirer of that service. But in the 1950s and early 1960s, the Army and Air Force were almost diametrically opposed on the subject of who should do what with aircraft in support of ground forces. In fighting for its position, the Air Force did some unkind things to us and said some unkind things about us. I am tempted to say that we on our part maintained a uniformly fair, unbiased, and charitable attitude toward the Air Force, but that might not be altogether true.

The quality of board membership was excellent throughout, and although there was unquestionably much wheel-spinning, the members worked with great dedication to the task and the lights at Irving School burned through midnight every night. The steering committee (same membership as the board) usually had all eighteen members, plus members of the secretariat, at each meeting.

The number was too large; it generated too many ideas and variations in points of view and made meetings too long. Moreover, some members, because their active entry into debate would delay action even more, remained mostly silent—too bad. And too often, because of that inexorably approaching deadline, I had to close down debate and force a decision.

The Air Force sent down a brigadier general to act as monitor. He was privileged to see all the tests and exercises and could interview anyone he chose, but we did not invite him to sit with the steering committee, and all the subcommittees were privileged to exclude him. This, in retrospect, seems regrettable, but in some sensitive areas, frank debate would not have been possible in his presence. And, certainly what he reported would have alarmed the Air Force and that admirable establishment really needed no additional agitation.

We put many things in motion.

We requested and received from Army Intelligence a full report and briefing on the doctrine and armament of the Sino-Soviet bloc of nations; from a group of armament engineers and scientists we got a technological forecast of weapons developments in the period 1963–75; we did a certain amount of cross-fertilization with the newly established Combat Developments Command (CDC); we sent a team, led by Bob Williams, to visit the several countries of Southeast Asia (an area then only gradually warming up) to gain an appreciation of how the board's concepts for the use of Army aviation might apply there; and we assembled a team of Army logisticians, together with a civilian advisory panel representing twelve different civilian aircraft manufacturers and agencies, to do an extensive survey of the Army aircraft support system, appraising its current ability and its potential to satisfy much expanded requirements.

The logistics group explored many other matters pertaining to theater logistics, among them airfield construction criteria, petrol distribution, comparative efficiency and vulnerability of air and surface lines of communication (still a fertile and promising field of investigation), and logistics planning factors.

We wrote some 400 letters to ranking officers, active and retired, asking for opinions. The response was strong, indicating great interest and almost uniform support for a vigorous pursuit of air mobility. We sent over 300 letters to civilian firms of the airframe, engine, electronics, and armament industries, again asking for suggestions—and did we get 'em!

The response filled the floor of a fair-sized classroom about 18 inches deep. Nobody could read all that overwhelming volume of poop, but it served as a reference library to the board, particularly to its multiple committees, and later to the Department of the Army and the Combat Developments Command. And it served to pique further the curiosity and interest (in Army Aviation) of the leading companies in America's aviation and aviation-related industries.

Two agencies under contract to the Army, Research Analysis Corporation (RAC) and Technical Operations Incorporated (CORG), did studies and analysis for use as requested. Rand Corporation and Stanford Research Institute provided several analysts and scientists for consultation and evaluation of committee work.

RAC and CORG also did war games, balancing the operational effectiveness of several of our air mobile combat units against that of conventional infantry and armor. The enemy in most cases conformed to what was known of Soviet organization and doctrine, but some work was done against an irregular enemy force. The games were elaborate, difficult to set up and slow to get under way, and in the limited time available could usually not be run more than once each.

I did not doubt the gaming capacity of the agencies, but I did doubt the results, even though they were favorable. I felt that multiple gaming was very necessary for results to be at all convincing, because different sequential command decisions would modify the course of events each time. Moreover, I could not shake a lingering doubt that many human factors of decisive importance are not reflected in war games and the mathematical answers that are derived by them. I think it very possible that the French did indeed lose the battle at Waterloo because Napoleon had piles. How do you insert hemorrhoids into a war game?

I must nevertheless acknowledge that the war games were necessary—war-gaming was very fashionable at the time and had to be included to satisfy our superiors that every possibility to learn something was exploited. We did games at platoon, company, battalion, brigade, division, and theater levels. Actually, it gave us good answers to certain aspects of air mobile operations, particularly those problems relating to deployment, speed of intertheater movements, and character and quantity of air and sealift requirements.

To me, the work by RAC in analyzing—not war-gaming—the possibilities and problems to be encountered in the quick positioning of air mobile formations, under logically assumed situations, in four different world hot-spots was most illuminating; this alone was enough to make one believe in the applicability and effectiveness.

But it was, of course, the field tests that were the most valuable and convincing. We impressed several audiences, the most important of which consisted of ourselves. When we saw what could be accomplished by coordinating the speed, precision, maneuverability, and firepower of aircraft, heliborne infantry, and supporting artillery, we knew we had to be right, and everybody threw himself into the task of proving we were.

We had about 150 Army aircraft and their crews and the battle echelons of the 82nd Airborne Division with which to work. The Air Force helped us—with fighter-bombers and, for a week, 16 C-130s. To get the latter to land anywhere but on a concrete runway, I had to talk for most of two hours in my office to an accident-sensitive four-star Air Force general. The aircraft did splendidly, as Lockheed Aircraft Corporation promised they would. Lockheed test pilots made the first few landings, even so.

We were able to do some exercises for purposes of comparison, first by a conventionally equipped force and then one made mobile by the addition of aircraft. Other exercises, not practicable of execution at all by conventional forces, were done only by experimental organizations. Some forty formally identified tests were run, ranging from fairly elaborate live-fire exercises and three major week-long exercises against an assumed force of irregulars (one done in conjunction with the Air Force), down to auxiliary tests of a variety of new weapons and other equipment.

Seven scientists from Stanford Research Institute, RAC, CORG, and

Rand observed these tests and combined their judgments with those of the officers who developed the tests and observed them.

Brig. Gen. (later Lt. Gen.) Edward L. Rowny was in charge of what ought to have been called tactical experimentation. We actually made no real "tests" in a scientific sense but conducted rather a series of trials to see what would work and what would not. Trials were often short and sweet; say, a short attack problem (the enemy being assumed but not represented except perhaps by observers), repeated three or four times in a single day with organization, equipment, and tactics modified in each successive try.

It was exciting and great fun for the participants. We stressed precision, basing all movements on the time that a given air element crossed an initial line—a road or rail line or creek or small ridge. That time became H-Hour and was first estimated aloud by the element commander over his radio, and then, preceded by a countdown, announced precisely as he crossed the line. Other elements timed their actions and movements accordingly; artillery might fire at H+30 seconds, the gunships might deliver fires on the flank of the objective at H+50 seconds, and assault ships cross the initial line at H+60 seconds.

Such planning may sound complicated, but it is not; one simply has to know the characteristics and mobility of aircraft, of projectiles of various sorts, and of man himself, and that knowledge is simply a basic ingredient of professionalism. We used what I called the "Phase Plan," a simple and easily understood manner of writing an operational order in chronological, tabular form, each line being given a paragraph number, such as 4a(2).

If the action briefly described on that line was required, the commander simply ordered, "Execute Phase Four A Paren Two." The commander of the unit designated in the table to execute the action would at the proper time report, "Phase Four A Paren Two complete." The Phase Plan thus served not only as an excellent system of coordination but also as a simple, short-duration battle code. Later, in Vietnam, the Phase Plan was used by a very successful battle commander, Col. Leo E. Soucek, in many combat assaults.

We did the basic flying technique, small-unit and weapons trials at

Fort Bragg; when we needed cultivated farm areas, we used, with the generous permission of the owners, terrain in central and western North Carolina. For swamp and lowland woods and soft sandy soil, we used the ample but difficult acreage of Fort Stewart, Georgia; and for mountain jungle, we used the forests of western Virginia. Although the trees were mostly northern hardwoods, the last made pretty respectable jungle: double canopy, 75 feet high, and with tangled underbrush beneath. We did lots of long rappelling from hovering helicopters.

My function in all the trials was that of critiquer and the chief subject of my critique was usually time. One exercise done in farm terrain was a raid on a presumed enemy guerrilla headquarters in a group of farm buildings sequestered in a small hidden valley, with outposts on the surrounding hills. Our scouting and path finding was presumed done, at high altitude and very inconspicuously, we hoped, a day or so previously. The assault involved low-level formation flying, heavy suppressive fire, placement of a number of machine-gun crews on a ridge to cover the assault, and the assault by riflemen.

The first trial I saw took about 12 minutes. I established the goal of 90 seconds—from the time an observer posted on a hill guarding the objective first heard the approaching helicopters to the time all rocket and machine-gun fires had been delivered by gunships, other machine guns were on the ground and firing, and the riflemen were moving down the hill onto the objective itself. This was accomplished. It took only coordination and good flying in a large formation at very low level.

Our "combat assaults" into the heavy mountain forests of West Virginia were a mite hairy: UH-1s hovered for anxious minutes while riflemen rappelled down through the trees, sometimes entangling themselves badly in high branches. We practiced blowing down trees pretty successfully, but lacked a proper munitions. We also developed (and entered into the report) a need for a "fence" of some sort: a mechanical contrivance, perhaps electrical, perhaps utilizing explosives, which could be very quickly erected by riflemen as an effective barrier to prevent enemy escape through the jungle.

We could devise no sure tactic, without assuming the placement of such a barrier, to ensnare an enemy guerrilla force. From what I saw on a much later visit to Vietnam and from talking to many of our commanders there, I gather no sure tactic was ever developed; it was an apparently very rare thing for a Vietcong force to be surrounded and annihilated. I still believe that industry could have developed such a barrier had the Army made the demand and backed it by money.

One of the exercises at Fort Stewart involved the quick air movement of a sizable force and its supplies for two weeks down from Fort Bragg, about 250 air miles. Scout aircraft picked out a landing strip on a low sandy ridge and assault transport helicopters landed security elements. Caribous then landed on the totally unprepared soft sand, pretending to discharge light bulldozers. We actually had to bring the bulldozers in by land; no light dozers were in the Army inventory.

The dozers worked four hours smoothing and compacting the strip, at the end of which time the first C-130 landed, unloaded a small cargo, made a careful return to the downwind end of the strip, and took off in the damndest cloud of dust we ever saw.

We brought in about a half-dozen of the C-130s, removing each before the next one arrived. The dozers, however, had to do about 15 minutes of work between each ship and eventually the sand became so loose that the C-130s opted out, and we had to restrict landing to Caribous and helicopters.

This occurred at a time when a number of the Pentagon civilian "whiz kids" were maintaining that the C-130 was capable of anything that the Army's de Havilland Caribou could do. This position was maintained for some years after the board submitted its report, in spite of the Army's crying foul. I wish the whiz kids could have heard the Lockheed pilots on our exercise; looking at the Caribous landing and taking off without the benefit of any site preparation, they said, "We're not in competition with *that!*" This is not to say that the C-130 is not a splendid machine, but certainly it imposes considerable demands on a runway surface.

We did all weapons testing at Fort Bragg. The French SS11 antitank missile was difficult to score hits with, but we knew that demonstrating a launch capability with some hits resulting was a big start; better missiles and guidance systems would surely be forthcoming, and they were. The quad 7.62mm machine guns awkwardly hung on the cross-tubes of the UH-1Bs were great for that time and, of course, did splendidly in Vietnam.

The same was true of the 40mm grenade launcher in a nose turret. We dropped napalm out of the helicopters. We mounted Browning .50-calibers to shoot out the left rear door, also as in Vietnam, and even put a 20mm on a heavy steel plate to shoot out that door. Some of these were jury-rigged affairs, but our purpose was mostly to show that pretty formidable weapons could be used without blowing the helicopter out of the air.

We recommended in our report a number of new weapons development projects and the vigorous pursuit of some already under way. Some reached fruition, but some that we thought especially desirable for airmobile operations did not, notably armor-penetrating bomblets (to drop on the thin top decks of tanks in bivouac), light air-delivered antitank mines, and air-delivered antipersonnel mines and bomblets.

The board at the time believed, I think correctly, that STOL technology had arrived at a point that justified the Army's having organic to it a small portion of the close air support it needed. We drew a parallel to the indirect-fire support available to the infantry company commander. That gentleman had call on battalion 4.2mm mortars, brigade 105mm howitzers, division 155mm and eight-inch howitzers, and even corps eight-inch and 175mm guns and 240mm howitzers. Even so, he would not give up that crummy little platoon of three 81mm mortars that was part of his own company. For he had to ask no one's permission to use them—they were totally responsive, always available, a precious asset even though a small part of the total firepower backing up the infantry company.

We, therefore, wanted Mohawks and successors to Mohawks as close-support Army aviation. We recommended twenty-four fixed-wing attack aircraft in the assault division, twenty of the same in the special warfare aviation brigade, and eight in each of the other divisions in the Army. The Grumman Mohawk was recommended as the proper choice within the existing state of the art; events since would make the advanced helicopter (none then in service) a future choice for the role.

This sort of thinking, we knew, would put us on a collision course with the Air Force and many civilians in the Department of Defense.

The board report, therefore, addressed the possibility of conflict in this and similar matters carefully. I quote the report in some detail:

(S) VIII. Joint Consideration

The Board strongly supports the view that in the national interest the Army should take every advantage of aviation support which can be effectively furnished by the other services, the Air Force in particular. . . .

Army aircraft, fixed and rotary wing, armed with appropriate weapons, are capable of delivering a measure of fire support for conventional and air mobile forces, of escorting helicopter-borne forces, and of executing close-in visual, photographic, radar and IR reconnaissance. The Air Force also has capabilities in these fields, but there are many missions to be flown in each category which absolutely require for effectiveness the most intimate coordination with ground combat elements—infantry, tanks and armor—and this coordination, and the responsiveness also necessary, can only be achieved if the pilots are part of and under command of the ground elements, live with them and operate their aircraft from fields close to the headquarters they serve.

It is quite impossible for a commander or staff officer to brief a strange pilot, whom he has never met, by radio or telephone (in code perhaps) as well as he can a familiar face in a tent before a map; it is unrealistic to expect a stranger to understand the interrelation of artillery and missile fires, tank and infantry maneuver, air reconnaissance and air-delivered fires if he has not seen the plan of operation about to be placed in effect and has not detailed knowledge of the situation and terrain.

It is not a question of courage, or will—the Army pilot may be inferior in both to his Air Force counterpart, yet be infinitely more useful because his aircraft is of a type that permits him to live and work in the Army environment, and the chain of command which governs his action is direct and unequivocal. Having made that point, however, it is necessary to repeat that the Board holds firm the view that the Army should remain dependent on the Air Force for the far greater part of the weight of close air support.

The division of the function into two parts will permit the desirable concentration of Air Force fighter firepower in support of the primary objective which, according to the situation may be the destruction of enemy local airpower, deep interdiction, the attack of enemy ground forces opposing the main U.S. ground effort, or a combination of these.

As a subsequent action to the efforts of this Board, a detailed examination should be made of the operational and numerical requirements for intermediate performance fighter-bombers in joint operations. However, this examination should not delay incorporation of light attack aircraft in the Army structure.

That examination was finished before the ink on the report was dry. Obviously to short-circuit Army ambitions in this field, the Air Force formally submitted to the Department of Defense a request for four more squadrons of fighter-bombers for the specific purpose of close support of the Army. We were all for that, but it did not negate the logic of our argument for some close-support capability made organic to the Army itself.

Because of initial Marine participation in the development, funding, and design of the Mohawk, the wing structure of that airplane was built to accept heavy armament loads; one had simply to open a couple of panels on the wing's underside to hang on bomb shackles, and the electric wiring was all in place. But we did not know enough about these matters, so we went to the Navy for help; we did not ask the Air Force because it just did not seem like a good idea.

The Navy sent us not only technicians to show us how to load bombs and check out the system, they also lent us a highly enthusiastic lieutenant commander pilot to teach our boys the fine points of low-level bombing and even gave us a fair supply of napalm canisters and 500- and 1,000-pound bombs. All the bombs had 11-second delay fuses.

Those were gorgeous things, those bombs. Eleven seconds is a long time. When a Mohawk at about 175 knots dropped a couple of 1,000-pounders at a 50-foot altitude, those big black beauties bounded across the terrain like a pair of superfast charging buffalo, throwing up geysers of sand and flattening trees six inches through, finally going off with a most satisfactory crash that rattled the windows in Fayetteville, eight miles away.

The fact that we didn't know exactly where they would explode was of no great moment—we knew that their spectacular charge across the ground was enough to absorb the individual attention of any enemy in the vicinity, even if they did not go off at all. We invented the technique of indirect bombing. The Mohawk would drop the bombs at the base of a hill; they would gallop obediently and noisily up one side and down the other, blowing up somewhere in the bottom where, we solemnly confided to our visitors, the enemy would be likely to site his battalion headquarters and mortars.

Our Air Force liaison officer watched this circus performance just one time. "By God, I can't believe it," he said, and rushed off to the nearest telephone.

War games and field tests during the summer of 1962 were a necessary prelude to formulating the recommendations of the Howze Board. We had already impressed ourselves and others, and of course we had to have a demonstration for Secretary of Defense Robert McNamara.

Also coming down from Washington with him were Gen. Lyman Lemnitzer, then chairman of the Joint Chiefs; Gen. Maxwell Taylor, who was to follow him as chairman; Cyrus Vance, secretary of the Army; a general officer representing Gen. Curtis LeMay, the Air Force Chief of Staff and who didn't look particularly sympathetic; Gen. George Decker, Army Chief of Staff; Gen. Earle "Buz" Wheeler, soon to succeed General Decker; Gen. Herbert Powell, Commander of Continental Army Command, and a number of lesser lights.

We first sat these people on low benches, out in the woods facing a low ridge about 1,100 yards distant. As the board's mouthpiece, I first explained the general idea—the assault of a fixed enemy position on the ridge, a position assumed defended by barbed wire, interlocking bands of machine-gun fire, antipersonnel and antitank mines, and ample mortar and artillery prearranged fires. To get through all that stuff by conventional tank and infantry attack, I said, would take several hours, result in many casualties, and would require the expenditure of heavy quantities of artillery and other ammunition.

We were about to show an alternative, not because we thought this would be the preferred or normal attack in the future, but because the chore of defeating a strongly emplaced and ready enemy was the toughest tactical problem that the Army faced; if we could do that one, we could do most of the other, easier ones.

The show began with a quick three-round volley of three battalions of artillery. Each gun was allowed eight seconds to get off its three rounds. The sound of the guns was the first thing audible or visible, and the objective ridge disappeared completely in great billows of dust and smoke. Flying under the artillery trajectory, there appeared immediately four Mohawks which released those wonderful 1,000-pound bombs at the base of the slope. Up they galloped into all the corruption on the crest and down the far side, shaking the earth with their explosions— and wiping out the enemy mortars, of course.

Before the show started, I had carefully explained to Mr. McNamara that the demonstration was to have included an Air Force dive-bombing strike on the objective, but unfortunately, the existing 300-foot solid overcast ceiling, plainly visible above him, made it quite impossible for the jets to participate. The Mohawks and other Army aircraft would, of course, have no trouble. (I later commended the post chaplain for sending in all those clouds.)

On the tail of the Mohawks came four Sikorsky H-34s, each of which had four machine guns and lots of 2.75-inch rockets aboard, pouring fire onto the objective. Those big 34s had been fine troop transporters in their day, but now they looked less like attack ships than so many fat, brown grandmothers. Never mind; they were all we had available, and we said the development of a proper gunship would be one of the board's recommendations.

While the 34s were still firing, the air just over the treetops in the spectator area became filled with UH-1Bs helicopters—about thirty, as I remember, which were all we could scrape up—and their sudden roar overhead made everybody jump. They went straight onto the objective, so deep into the dust and smoke we lost sight of most of them. This was pretty hairy, in fact, but looked even worse from the spectator benches.

There were no mid-air collisions or any other mishaps, however, and two companies of infantry swarmed out of the choppers right onto the middle of the objective and went about the simulated job of rooting the enemy out of his holes. I turned to the secretary and said, "Sir, from the first moment an enemy could know an attack was coming to the time our infantry was dismounted and on top of him, was exactly 120 seconds. That's what we mean by air mobility."

Everybody was impressed; no one could help but be, and I maybe more than anyone else. It was the most convincing and, by all odds, the neatest and quickest demonstration I had ever seen. It was then he asked the question: "General," asked Mr. McNamara, "what do you estimate is the cost, in dollars, to put each of those infantrymen on the objective?"

All I could do for awhile was stare at him while I listened to my colleagues snickering away behind some trees. I finally told the secretary I didn't know, but that it would be cheaper than by conventional means, and I would figure it out and tell him. I never did.

We left that area for some heavy woods where we showed the technique of assaulting a guerrilla position in a jungle. The Mohawks dropped napalm and bombs and the gunships sprayed the place with machine-gun fire while infantrymen rappelled from hovering Hueys. They even let a dog down—whether it represented a tracker or was simply the first sergeant's own pooch I didn't know.

We moved again, this time onto a farmer's pasture, a very moderate-sized field with an irregular border of woods. The unmarked 30-inch-high weeds and grass showed that we had never practiced there. The soil was sandy and, unknown to us, had been soaked deeply by a localized thunderstorm the night before. My spiel said that what we were about to show would serve to demonstrate a major difference between Army and Air Force aircraft.

We did that, all right. Right on time, a Caribou made an approach low over the trees. The pilot must have intended to stop that ship in a distance about three times its own length. He was tottering through the air with full flaps and gear down, of course, and just as he cleared the trees, he chopped both throttles. The Caribou came down hard, the left wheel digging deep into the soggy sand, and the long gear strut providing all the necessary leverage to peel that wing off clean, right at the root. The big fuselage promptly laid over on its side, stuck its right wing about a mile up in the air and came sliding in nice, easy circles down the field toward us. When it stopped, I ran over to it, but the crew had cut the switches and was out in the weeds before I got there.

It was a funny thing. Up to that time, the secretary had been somewhat aloof and noncommittal, but because I was a bit upset at this unscheduled event, he instantly became cordial and sympathetic.

A Mohawk was airborne behind a mask waiting to come in, but that Caribou, with its right flipper pointing up in the sky, blocked the best approach. So, thinking that the secretary might not relish our tearing up in the same wet field two of his airplanes whose dollar value I didn't want to have to estimate for him, I sent the Mohawk home.

We now had to get up that report. Its biggest volume was comprised of all the annexes the committees wrote. We tried in the steering committee to make the basic report a joint venture, but that had limited success. I ended up writing or rewriting the bulk of it; it was the only way we could get it done in time.

The report included what we considered first-class argument in support of the concept of air mobility, analyzing briefly its applicability to the situations obtaining in the Korean War and to the kinds of combat the U.S. Army was apt to encounter in the future. I discussed all aspects of tactical employment, striking power, the greatly enlarged possibilities of surprise, the requirement for specially designed armed helicopters, and vulnerability—on the ground and in the air—to enemy fighters, artillery, missiles, and smaller weapons. I suggested that it would be mighty handy to be able to move helicopters quickly under cover and back out again.

Brig. Gen. Clifton von Kann and I formulated the air mobile battle unit organizations. Primary was the air assault division, comprised of three brigade headquarters, an air cavalry squadron, eight air mobile infantry battalions, and a divisional artillery of three battalions of helicopter-transportable 105s and an aerial rocket battalion (rocket-firing helicopters).

In the divisional aviation, we placed a surveillance-attack battalion (reconnaissance and shooting Mohawks), two assault helicopter battalions (UH-1s), and one battalion of Chinooks. This was the organization tested by the 11th Air Assault Division and used later in Vietnam, excepting only the armed Mohawks.

The air assault division (for a time called "air mobile") was a good one, but it is worth noting that three lifts of its organic aircraft were required to move the whole combat echelon of the division from one place to another.

The air cavalry combat brigade we advocated was provided full air mobility for its combat elements—every man had a seat in an aircraft. Thus was provided the mobility differential (over air assault infantry) essential to the performance of the cavalry mission. The brigade had three squadrons, and each of those squadrons had four troops. Each troop had its own reconnaissance helicopters plus helicopters carrying riflemen (for manning observation posts, patrolling, providing security, and, when an opportunity presented itself, making small raids) and a generous allocation of attack helicopters—twelve per troop.

I believe it a great pity that none of these brigades was ever organized; they would have a most exceptional and desirable capability against either a guerrilla force or a modern tank-heavy force. The air cavalry brigade now in service is very differently organized, not the equivalent at all.

In Vietnam, Maj. Gen. George Putnam commanded for a time what was close to our air cavalry brigade: 2⅔ divisional-type air cavalry squadrons he inherited from other commands during the phase-down of our troop strength there. It had lots of combat action, he says, and was extremely effective.

I fervently believe the Army needs some of these brigades now. The infantry-cavalry concept I do not defend *because* it is traditional, but I do say that the traditional relationship is as sound today as it was during the Civil War. The very widely held opinion among our most experienced battle commanders, that the air cavalry squadrons were among the most effective combat units in Vietnam, leads one to believe that they would be even better in such places as Europe or the Middle East.

We gave infantry, tank, and mechanized divisions a modest increase in organic aviation, notably eight attack aircraft (then Mohawks), eight attack helicopters, and twenty-three utility helicopters. We recommended formation of corps aviation brigades to enable the corps commander to provide troop and logistic lift on request to the divisions under his command; a total of eighty Hueys and forty-eight Chinooks, plus some Mohawk reconnaissance and a dozen attack helicopters.

We recommended a somewhat air mobile corps artillery, providing it with lightweight 105s to allow lift by sixty up-powered Hueys, and thirty-nine attack helicopters whose principal weapon was to be the rocket.

To the field army, we provided an air transport brigade of twelve medium helicopters and eighty fixed-wing transports and a support command. The latter included a headquarters to boss whatever air transport brigades might be assigned, a terminal command, and two transportation movements commands. In this, we got much guidance from the logisticians on the board.

A special warfare aviation brigade was to help the Green Berets (which furnished some of the most enthusiastic board members) do their traditional deep-behind-the-enemy-lines job, as distinguished from their actual, also very effective, role in Vietnam. We gave the brigade twenty attack Mohawks, twenty-one Chinooks, forty attack helicopters, and twenty-one Hueys. Also provided were twenty-three fixed-wing utility ships, the lads being extremely interested in the Helio-Porter and other super short-field jobs. We made careful estimates of the comparative costs of airmobile and conventional forces of approximately equal size. A simple table with figures in millions of 1962 dollars indicates costs over the years:

Division	Initial Investment	Five-year operating (CONUS)	Total five-year cost (CONUS)
Air Assault	$282	$705	$987
Armored	182	681	801
Infantry	111	582	693

The board's report said that the troop tests also left little doubt of the validity of the basic idea: that many operational tasks could be done better with than without Army aviation. It was certainly an understatement. But we also said that, when the board disbanded, another agency should take over the responsibility; our testing should constitute simply the start of a process that should never be allowed to die.

We presented five force structure alternatives, each of which was costed out. At the time, there were sixteen divisions in the active Army. We showed various mixes, the number of air assault divisions varying from three to six, air cavalry combat brigades from two to three, and air transport brigades (logistics outfits) from one to five. We recommended the third alternative, which would have provided five air assault divisions, three air cavalry combat brigades, and five air transport brigades.

The thought of five air assault divisions and three air cavalry combat brigades in a sixteen-division force curled a lot of hair among staff officers in the Pentagon. But consider: In 1962, there were some 200 divisions on our side of the Iron Curtain; a recommendation that only five of them be made air mobile was, we thought, very moderate.

The report mentioned briefly an analysis I had required in July of the commander and staff of the 101st Airborne Division which had, at the time (and almost had to execute in October), an actual exploitation mission in a Latin American country. I told the 101st to compare its ability to do the job, for which it had developed a full battle plan, first with its current organization and then with the air mobile organization the board had formulated. The answer was unequivocal: four days to completion (with the new configuration) instead of seven, a reduction of 23 percent in personnel, 34 percent in surface ships, 45 percent in vehicles, 55 percent in supplies, and an elimination of logistical depots and water terminals after initial landings.

Those were good estimates, but I don't think anyone paid any attention to them. The 82nd Airborne Division, probably the finest anywhere at this writing (largely because, unique in the current Army, it is at full strength in personnel), should now be air mobile, as well as the 101st.

The board in all its recommendations considered basic the idea that Army aviation, to achieve maximum effectiveness, had to be closely integrated into the structure of the combat branches—as low in the structure as it was possible to get. It was for that reason we dearly loved the reconnaissance helicopters and the Huey. All of these we kept during exercises under the trees and camouflaged, not difficult to do because they had only two blades, and we could move them by manpower.

The Huey was to our riflemen roughly what the horse was to the old cavalryman—close by and ready. I can't visualize altogether what influence the comparatively large UH-60 Black Hawk and AH-64 Apache, had they been available as our basic ships, would have had on our conclusions and recommendations. Certainly, they would have had an effect on our tactics and doctrine, lessening the close association of human and helicopter. I don't mean to wave an alarm flag here, but simply to point out that the Army will still need some varieties of aircraft small and simple enough, in the words of the CONARC endorsement to the report, to live "in the austere day-to-day environment of the troops it supports."

Sometime in late July, I believe it was, a horde of Air Force generals, headed up by the Air Force inspector general, Gen. William S. Blanchard, descended on us. We met their big shiny transport at Pope Air Force Base, gave them a briefing, watched them look curiously about (there was nothing to see since we were then struggling with the report only), and saw them off. They were obviously suspicious.

Lt. Gen. Jim Gavin, then ambassador to France, gave us in his reply to our letter some words we could use, so we included them in the report:

If there is one thing that stands out clearly in all recorded history of man's military endeavors, it is that innovation is essential to survival and is usually decisive in battle. . . . Regardless of the system employed, but assuming that it is employed with reasonable intelligence and direction, the final criterion of effectiveness is the product of both firepower and mobility. These may have exponential values, and in fact the mobility part usually does. It is in the thorough exploration of the field of mobility and the application of knowledge gained that we will find the greatest possibility for innovation in the future.

After the report was finished, I put at its beginning a fifteen-page "Brief by the President of the Board." The commanding general of CONARC, Gen. Herbert B. Powell, gave the report a very favorable endorsement and sent it on up to the Department of Defense "undiluted by conservative staff review."

Shortly after we had submitted the report, the Disosway Board was created by General LeMay, the Air Force Chief of Staff. We and the press assumed that this board, headed by Lt. Gen. Gabriel Disosway (later to get his fourth star and to become commanding general of the Tactical Air Force), was given the charter of proving the Howze Board wrong. I don't know how much good, or damage, it did.

It was also in this period that somebody thought up the idea of creating a special test air assault division to check out the Howze Board's organization. This was a progressive step, most people thought, but I didn't like it.

I spent two long sessions with Secretary of the Army Cyrus Vance and General Wheeler, Chief of Staff, seeking their approval to convert the 82nd Airborne Division to an air assault division that would retain a parachute capability in the line units. The 82nd and 101st Airborne Division commanders were convinced, as I was, that parachute proficiency could be easily maintained in an air assault division. But I couldn't sell this. Mr. Vance and General Wheeler were convinced that McNamara, although pleased with the board report, wanted more proof by test and would approve the formation of a test division and a large temporary overstrength to provide the bodies. I argued that it was an enormous waste of time and dollars; it took lots of the latter, certainly, to recruit, train, and pay some 14,000 additional men for two years. I said that enough testing had been done; the board was right and its judgment should be trusted, that a going division should be converted and, given the construction money and aviation means, the 82nd was ready to convert. But no.

In late 1962, the 11th Air Assault Division started forming at Fort Benning, Georgia, and was provided with a first-rate complement of officers and NCOs. Under Lt. Gen. Harry W. O. Kinnard, it did an exceptionally fine job and later, as the 1st Cavalry Division (Air Mobile), was outstanding in combat in Vietnam. I have nothing but admiration for that division, and I mean absolutely no derogation of it when I say the 82nd could have been converted much more easily.

As I write this, the Army has one very capable Air Assault Division, the 101st, but no air cavalry brigades as we envisioned them. It does, however, have in its new Aviation Branch a very considerable capacity for combat, anywhere. Because its aircraft are bigger and more difficult to maintain, however, Army aviation has lost some of its earlier close integration with the other combat branches of the Army. As a sort of postscript to this discussion of the doings of the Howze Board, I add this extract from an article by Barry Goldwater (then still a U.S. senator) in the November 1974 issue of the *Saturday Evening Post*:

With the establishment of a separate Air Force in 1947, the roles and missions of close air support were given to that new arm. I fully expected at that time that the Air Force would take over the flying of the services which would have included all military airlift whether fixed wing or rotary wing (and) all close air support whether that was to be used by the Marines or the ground troops. . . .

What the Air Force didn't reckon with, however, was a task force headed by General Hamilton H. Howze whom Defense Secretary McNamara ordered to investigate the possible uses of air for the benefits of ground troops. His report is probably one of the most brilliantly studied, written and put together papers that I have ever read, but there are times when I think that I was probably the only person interested in air power who took the trouble to read it. It clearly spelled out how the Army was going to take back part of the roles and missions, particularly in transport, of observation and close air support, which they did in Vietnam and did brilliantly. Because the Air Force did not pay attention to the role of close air support by developing an aircraft until too late, I believe that it will now share close air support missions with the Army, Marines and the Navy, so we are right back where we started. In effect, we have four tactical air forces today, each assigned a role in close air support.

I didn't but I should have written Mr. Goldwater, whom I admire: "But Senator, the Air Force flew away from the Army, and you, sir, watched it do so!"

CUBA

20 In the early fall of 1962, high-altitude aircraft photos of Cuba disclosed that the Soviet Union was building a substantial number of huge missile emplacements on that island, and indeed had large missiles, capable of carrying atomic warheads, and powerful radars positioned nearby ready for installation. The whole array was pointed at the United States, promising soon to threaten almost all of this country east of the Mississippi with devastating atomic attack. Pres. John Kennedy, of course, reacted very strongly to this development, ordering the Joint Chiefs to prepare for an invasion of Cuba, preceded by strong air attack of the island. He also began a series of urgent telephone calls to the Soviet premier, then Nikita Khrushchev, who on several previous occasions had made pretty belligerent threats against America, such as "We will bury you."

The XVIII Airborne Corps, which I commanded and which was to be augmented by one and one-third armored divisions (and after it was on Cuba, a Marine division), was to conduct the invasion. This news was conveyed to me as I attended, by direction, an urgent meeting of the Joint Chiefs of Staff in the Pentagon. I vividly remember the meeting, conducted by the Chairman of the JCS, Gen. Maxwell Taylor, and attended by Gen. Curtis LeMay of the Air Force, General Wheeler of the Army, the Chief of Naval Operations, and the Marine Commandant. When it came to a vote, everybody voted "aye"—even the stenographer nodded his head. This vote, of course, was a recommendation to be carried to President Kennedy by Defense Secretary McNamara—who arrived as the JCS meeting broke up—for decision, presumably after discussion within the Security Council and congressional leaders. General Taylor, however, said approximately the following to me as the JCS meeting broke up and he and McNamara left for the White House: "You will assume, with no room in your mind for doubt, that the invasion will take place—get your forces, in all respects, ready to go."

I at once called my Chief of Staff, telling him to assemble the pertinent division commanders (excepting that of the Marine division, for it was to come under command only after link-up in Cuba and was being separately alerted and made ready) and key staff officers at Fort Bragg at 8:00 A.M. the following morning. A waiting helo took me to Davidson Army Airfield at Fort Belvoir, and my own airplane back to Bragg.

At the meeting next morning, after briefing the commanders and key staff officers, I announced my estimate of the probability that the invasion would go as being 98 percent, but told them to proceed as if it were a certainty.

Within days, orders were issued, plans were complete, equipment was complete (all unserviceable having been replaced with new), troops were thoroughly briefed and "standing in the door," as paratroopers say, ready to go. Morale could not have been better. The 2nd Armored Division, with all its tanks and other equipment, was moved from Texas by many long trains to an area close to an East Coast port, ready to load on ships. Several days later, President Kennedy came down to look at it and talk to the tankers and their commander, Maj. Gen. Ralph Haines, and me. I went down to meet him. He gave no indication that the invasion might not take place. Homestead Air Force Base, in southern Florida, was being piled high with military supplies to be flown in to us as soon as Cuban airfields were secure.

During the period of preparation, lasting about ten days, an officer from Army Intelligence flew down from the Pentagon each day to bring us at Fort Bragg the latest photos produced by the Air Force in its daily reconnaissance sorties over Cuba. Many of the pictures were taken by jets flying at very low level. Plainly to be seen (in addition to the missile sites and other areas of interest) were a number of encampments identified as Soviet. Equipment was obviously of Soviet manufacture, but so, of course, was the Cuban Army's equipment; markings on the equipment in these camps were Soviet, and so were the uniforms of the soldiers. We had no positive information showing a brigade structure but thought that was the approximate size of the force and its likely organization.

Whatever the command arrangement, photographs indicated that several battalions (some of them equipped with tanks) of Soviet troops were encamped in a wide arc encircling Havana, the capital city, on the south or land side. We at Fort Bragg figured that this was a praetorian guard, constituting in itself no threat to the United States, but being instead charged primarily with the defense of the Cuban communist government against a possible attempt at overthrow by a counterrevolutionary Cuban insurrection, anti-Castro sentiment being high at the time, and secondarily being charged with the back-up protection of Soviet missile sites against the same potential Cuban enemy.

Our battle plans took the Soviet formations into full account. None of them were in proper position to block our scheme of maneuver. Our Air Force, however, did have the urgent mission of interdicting any possible Soviet troop movement; almost certainly it could have done so successfully.

Actually, we did not anticipate any attempt at such movement; the Soviets, we thought, would prefer to sit tight and uninvolved, in view of what would be the preponderant American military strength on the scene and what would have been, by that time, a badly battered and perhaps altogether extinct Cuban Air Force.

While we were urgently getting ready for the invasion, I was called up to Washington to see the president; also present were the Army Chief of Staff, General Wheeler, and Gen. Ted Parker of the Joint Staff. Sitting in his familiar rocking chair (because his back hurt), Mr. Kennedy asked how long it would take us to overrun Cuba. I said, "Two weeks, possibly only ten days." He seemed skeptical about that, in spite of my reasoning that, after a heavy preparatory air bombardment—strictly against military targets—and our initial landings in force, a large proportion of the Cuban population would probably greet us as deliverers; even some elements of the Cuban Army, I felt, would either defect or lay down their arms, perhaps within the first few days. Intelligence reports supported this view—all we had to do was to display (as the earlier unsuccessful Bay of Pigs operation could not) organization, plan, determination, and power, and that we most emphatically could and would do.

The president asked also about our casualties. I gave him our estimate of a maximum of 10,000 killed and wounded but added the hope and expectation that we might have many fewer. Mr. Kennedy, undoubtedly thinking of our experience in Korea, said U.S. commanders habitually underestimated the effectiveness of what he called an unsophisticated enemy, and then gave his estimate as 20,000. We'll never know who was right. I suspect, of course, that I was, if only because our forces—Army, Air Force, Marines, and Navy—were so well equipped and prepared, so thoroughly motivated and so altogether ready to go.

Our battle plan was simple: after seizure of the selected airheads by airborne attack, a quick movement into the city of Havana, on multiple routes, by one airborne and the Marine division, supported if necessary (it might not have been) by the tanks of the armored division; thereafter, leaving the Marines to occupy Havana, a rapid thrust down the long island by the second airborne division and the one and one-third armored divisions in combined-arms task forces, followed by the airborne division withdrawn from Havana in reserve. Using helicopters as means of quick and easy vertical envelopment (defending forces get *very* uncomfortable when some of the attacking forces get behind them), progress by the assault echelons should have been very rapid. Strong Cuban delaying positions—and we didn't expect more than one or two, perhaps none—would have been reduced by a combination of concentrated fighter-bomber attack, parachute landings behind the defenders, and the assault of an overwhelming number of tanks and accompanying parachute infantry.

No pacification or occupation of the countryside would have been necessary, nor would pursuit of residual enemy forces into the hills—we had only to get down the *Carratera Central* to the end of the island, seizing or isolating the population centers, and the show would have been over. For *Cuba* was not our enemy—just Castro and whatever Cuban forces supported him. After we had flushed out Castro, I hoped that our State Department could set a new provisional Cuban central government quickly in place to deal with the local problems, allowing all but a small fraction of the U.S. military forces to withdraw from the island very promptly and thus escape the distasteful and alienating chore of occupation.

Because fighting in cities has sometimes been very difficult (one always thinks of Stalingrad) some may—and in fact some did at the time—question our judgment that Havana would fall in a matter of days. The point is that, although a heavily defended city is hard to take, a lightly defended one is almost impossible to hold. The hundreds of streets and thousands of buildings greatly restrict fields of fire and thereby soak up defenders like a sponge, it being impracticable to cover all or even most of the manifold avenues of approach. Two examples, among many, are Paris and Rome in World War II: they were abandoned without a struggle by the German forces because the streets and alleys and buildings would have engulfed the defenders and yet would have permitted relatively easy Allied penetration.

Was there a real danger of a Soviet nuclear strike on the United States had we invaded Cuba? It is *very* doubtful. At the time, we had a plain nuclear advantage—when Khrushchev was criticized for backing down before the American "paper tiger," he responded that the paper tiger had nuclear teeth. Moreover, when we launched the invasion, our early warning system, our defenses, and our own counterstrike missile crews would all have been on the highest degree of alert, the worst possible time for the USSR to initiate the nuclear exchange.

Any military operation is beset with uncertainties and dangers and the possibility of failure. Even so, I am totally convinced that this one would have succeeded brilliantly. We were too well prepared and too strong for it to have ended otherwise.

But we didn't go, of course. On the phone with Mr. Kennedy, Khrushchev blinked.

It is interesting to speculate on what might have resulted internationally from a successful U.S. invasion of Cuba in the fall of 1962. It may be going a bit far to contend that the North Vietnamese subversion and invasion of South Vietnam may not have been attempted at all, and the

Vietnam War thereby averted. One might reason, however, that a quick and very decisive U.S. intervention into Cuba might have convinced communist world leadership that America would likely intervene also to stop forcible communist expansion in Southeast Asia. America, of course, did intervene there and failed; it is nonetheless possible that if Pres. Ho Chi Minh and General Giap of North Vietnam had anticipated active military opposition by the United States and the terrible punishment their country would in consequence have had to endure, they would not have attempted the conquest of the South.

But that is pure speculation, of course. Other results of a successful 1962 invasion of Cuba are more obvious.

Castro would have long since been deposed and exiled or imprisoned, and we may hope, a democratic government would have been installed in a Cuba once more friendly to the United States. Our trade with Cuba, before Castro profitable for both countries, would have long since been restored. Many thousand Cuban refugees now in the United States wouldn't be here. Cuban communist ideology would not, as it once did, exert a strong subversive influence in several Latin American countries. Cuba would not have provided the channel permitting Soviet arms to pour into Central America. Cuban troops, by the thousands, would not, as surrogates of the Soviet Union, have pursued their mischievous and damaging purposes in several of the countries of Africa.

The 27 September 1982 issue of *Time* magazine contained an article on "The Lessons of the Cuban Missile Crisis," written by Dean Rusk, Robert McNamara, McGeorge Bundy, George Ball, Roswell Gilpatrick, and Theodore Sorensen—all of them once very high in the national government. I quote from the article's Fourth Conclusion: "The decisive military element in the resolution of the crisis was our clearly available and applicable superiority in conventional weapons within the area of the crisis. US Naval forces, quickly deployable for the blockade of offensive weapons . . . and the availability of US ground and air forces sufficient to execute an invasion if necessary, made the difference."

What follows is by way of postscript. Most of us remember that, toward the end of President Carter's administration (1976–80), it was announced that a brigade of Soviet troops had been discovered in Cuba.

Mr. Carter promptly and forcefully proclaimed that such Soviet troop presence in Cuba was "unacceptable"—intimating plainly that he wanted the Soviet force withdrawn, at once, else the United States would somehow contrive to force it out. But then, of course, he did nothing about it (realistically, there was little he could do short of intervention), thereby accepting what he said was unacceptable.

Fidel Castro reacted to the bump and bustle in the White House with apparent amusement, stating quite accurately that the Soviet brigade had been in Cuba for (at that time) 17 years. But there was no public acknowledgment of Castro's statement by the American government.

The force was withdrawn after the breakup of the Soviet Union.

FOUR-STAR GENERAL

21 In the late spring of 1963 I received my fourth star and orders again to Korea, this time with three hats: Commander-in-Chief, United Nations Command, or CINCUNC (in this job my boss was to be the U.S. Joint Chiefs of Staff); Commander U.S. Forces Korea (my boss: the Commander-in-Chief, U.S. Pacific Command, a four-star admiral of the Navy, with headquarters in Hawaii); and Commanding General, Eighth Army (my boss, the U.S. Army's Chief of Staff). The three jobs required two separate staffs in Korea: a United Nations Command/U.S. Forces Korea Staff, whose Chief of Staff was a lieutenant general of the Air Force; and an Eighth Army staff, whose Chief was a major general of the Army.

This apparently complex arrangement really worked very well, though in respect to some problems one had to figure out which of my three bosses to appeal to. On the other hand the two chiefs of staff and I were occasionally guilty of a little sleight-of-hand: if we anticipated an adverse reaction on the part of one boss it was sometimes possible to put the decision in the hands of another.

I was relieving Gen. Stan Meloy, a fine soldier with a shot-up leg and a very attractive wife, the former a memento of World War II. There was an elaborate change-of-command ceremony, with smartly drilled Army, Navy, Air Force, and Marine contingents of both nationalities, and even a British contingent, representing the United Nations. The reviewing stand included most of the numerous ambassadors to Korea and other military and civilian dignitaries. Big show.

Shortly before leaving Fort Bragg I had a call from a Miss Daisy Beck, who had served as General Magruder's secretary while he was CIN-CUNC. After two years in the United States she wanted to go back to Korea as my secretary—that post being open, she said. I agreed immediately. She served very ably—served me and my fourteen successors. She may be said to know more about the United States and Korean high military command headquarters than anyone. She's still there, with the great-great-grandchild of her original cat.

Mary and I hadn't brought our two boys with us this time. While we were at Fort Bragg they had both attended St. James, an Episcopal boys school near Hagerstown, Maryland, and for their own good we left them there. This was a sadness. St. James did well by them, but we didn't like the separation at a time when both were at an age at which boys need some little direct parental guidance and, let's say, energizing. Of course, they came to Korea during their summer holiday.

The oldest boy, Bill, graduated from St. James in 1964 and entered Georgia Tech, having failed to score high enough in a competitive examination for West Point—possibly because he wasn't exactly wild about going there. At Georgia Tech he majored in Greek Letter Fraternity, the fact of being pledged by ΣAE obviously being a matter of greater importance than that of achieving passing grades at the university. His status in the latter respect varied, during his entire stay, between "Warning" and "Probation"—I forget, after all these years, which performance grade was the most complimentary.

In this situation I tried to enlist the assistance of the dean of men at Georgia Tech, the dean's last name being Dull. I addressed numerous letters to him—"Dear Dean Dull"—and though I informed him repeatedly that his reply to me had to carry an airmail stamp if it were to arrive in less than four weeks (the transocean mail system in 1963–65 being very different from what it is now) Dean Dull *never* caught on—never discovered that Korea was about 8,000 miles away from Atlanta, and so far as I could determine never gave Bill counseling of any useful sort.

At one time, Mary and I thought Bill would get his degree at Georgia Tech at about retirement age, but in actuality he took only five years—not an unusually long time at that university. Thereafter, he got a reserve commission as a second lieutenant in the Army and became a very capable helicopter pilot, serving, among other places, in Vietnam.

We had not large but very comfortable quarters in Yongsan Compound, in Seoul, with three servants and a nice garden in which the post garden nursery, during the growing season, managed to keep flowers in bloom—always: when any plant stopped blooming it was immediately replaced with one in full flower. The CINCUNC mess, under an American mess sergeant but with the benefit of an expert Korean staff and lovely china, glass, silverware, and napery, could put on a formal dinner for thirty which, I venture to say, the best restaurant or hotel in New York couldn't match.

On our arrival I found our quarters under a 24-hour guard by a detachment of the British Devonshire Light Infantry—this detachment helping to preserve the notion that our forces in Korea were representative of the UN Organization. My predecessors also had Secret Service people (in civilian clothes, but sometimes pretty evident) accompany them when they played golf at the Seoul Country Club or otherwise mixed with the local citizenry. I thought the necessity for all this had passed, stopping it except for the British sentry around our quarters—and even this vigil I had confined to the hours of darkness.

I also inherited the best Honor Guard anywhere in the American military establishment. It consisted of a fine U.S. Army band, a mixed color guard carrying the U.S., UN, and Korean flags, and four platoons: one American Army, one Korean Army, one Korean Navy, and one from the Devonshire Light Infantry Regiment. All, though in varying uniforms, were drilled to absolute perfection. I'd never been especially impressed by honor guards because all I'd known were not particularly smart in appearance or well drilled—but this one was, enough to knock your eye out. And it always made a big impression on visiting dignitaries—of which we had a great many, including occasionally a head of state. The Honor Guard incidentally served also as a security force for our double-staffed headquarters.

Mary and I inevitably became a part of the diplomatic social whirl, either doing the entertaining ourselves (with the benefit of the magnificent CINCUNC mess) or dining at various embassies or at one of the city's hotels. In the evenings we were out an average of five times weekly when I was in town. Actually, we didn't mind it, what with the official car and driver; moreover, to the great credit of Seoul's diplomatic community, a dinner party broke up promptly at 10 o'clock. And we were rarely more than 15 minutes from our quarters.

We had brought to Korea a venerable Hammond Chord organ. I am a musical idiot, but that organ was easy to play and its tones, at least to my ear, were really very good. After breakfast each day I would practice until my driver, a seasoned, tough American Army sergeant, arrived with the car to pick me up. I don't think he ever got over hearing CINCUNC practicing "I'm Forever Blowing Bubbles" and similar classics.

With the able assistance of the Deputy Commander, Eighth Army, Lt. Gen. Ted Conway (an exceptionally fine soldier who had commanded the 82nd Airborne Division for part of my tour as CG of the Airborne Corps), and that of the Korean high command, we continued the development of the Korean Army. We had, inevitably, a stream of congressional and other official visitors to Korea. Some of them were genuinely interested in the military and political situation in the Far East; some were on a boondoggle—but careful to get their pictures taken on every occasion while tending to "vital affairs overseas."

To all official visitors we showed a reinforced Korean infantry regiment drawn up in formation with all its weapons and other field gear. The regiment always made a strong impression on visitors and even on me, who saw it many times—they were, indeed, tough, first-class light infantry. And I was able to tell visitors that U.S. military aid money was supporting fifty-four such regiments across the north border of South Korea. It impressed them.

The Army was the biggest force in Korea and on that account the most important, but the Korean Air Force, Navy, and Marines were at least equally competent. It was not at all unusual to hear members of the several U.S. military advisory groups—one group for each service—debate the comparative combat quality of U.S. and Korean forces.

Since Mr. McNamara, the SecDef, was convinced that we could reduce our commitment to the defense of Korea, I repeatedly asked him to come see for himself, but he never came. I wrote him that I thought one U.S. division could, indeed, replace the two infantry divisions that we had, provided that the replacement division be one of the air-mobile type recommended by the Howze Board. I suggested that such a division, in central reserve, could serve not only as a commitment to Korea but also as a mobile reserve for the entire Far Eastern theater. I thought that a sound idea, but it didn't fly in Washington.

I had a two- or three-hour weekly conference, always very cordial and informative, at the U.S. embassy with the U.S. ambassador, first Sam Berger and then Win Brown. Usually present also were the chargé d'affaires, Ed Doherty, and Phil Habib, the political advisor. Years later Habib became the U.S. presidential special emissary to the Near East during much of the difficulty between Israel and its Arab neighbors. But given our continuing mistaken policy in that area—the unwavering, uncritical support of Israel, under all circumstances—he couldn't do much good.

From articles in North Korean newspapers I learned that I was dubbed by the indestructible North Korean Communist dictator, Kim Il Sung (he was in power for at least forty years), as the "Nine-Tailed Fox"—that being the ultimate Korean insult, earned I suppose by some of my remarks about North Korea and communism quoted in the South Korean press. More serious were some of the border incidents.

I'll recount only one of these: it involved a young Korean Army pilot, fresh out of flight school, who in a light artillery spotter plane took the heading of 345 degrees magnetic out of Wonju, a north-central Korean city, instead of the correct heading for his destination: 325 degrees (the cited bearings are approximate). When he crossed the DMZ, North Korean antiaircraft guns shot him down, and the North Korean press was immediately filled with invective against the United States and South Korea for "spying." At a special meeting of the Armistice

Commission, as usual at the tiny village of Panmunjon, in the DMZ, our people had to listen to all sorts of nonsense and eventually had to admit, in my name, to the false charge of spying on the part of the pilot. There was no other way we were going to get his body back, and the South Korean government (and his family, of course) very much wanted it back. So I lied—but all the Western press, including that in Europe, knew it was a lie and explained to its readers why I did it. No damage done.

Well, the time eventually came for the delivery of the body at Panmunjon. Both sides of the Armistice Commission were seated at the usual long, rectangular table, with a never-to-be-crossed line painted down the middle of the table and across the floor. Six North Korean soldiers appeared, carrying a large, rough wooden box. This was not handed across but thrown across the line. On hitting the floor it burst open, by design, the pilot's body, still in muddy uniform, rolling out for all to see.

Such were the relations between communism and freedom in the Far East.

For one six-month period our armistice commission was headed by one Lt. Gen. Bill Yarborough, a good friend of mine and the erstwhile head of the Army's Special Forces (Green Beret) Center at Fort Bragg. Through long study he had become something of an expert on the Marxist dialectic. At the Armistice Commission meetings at Panmunjon, Bill sometimes enlivened the usually dreary process of insult, charge, and countercharge by informing one or another of the North Korean or communist Chinese representatives that he, in the long statement just made, had his dogma all wrong—Bill pointing out, right in front of the culprit's fellow Commies and the electronic recorder, the details of his gross misinterpretation of communist theory and advising him that he had better brush up on things lest he be found guilty, officially, of serious dogmatic error and indiscretion—with what he knew very well could be dire results.

One day the Swedish admiral who was the senior member of our side of the long-standing Neutral Nations Armistice Supervisory Commission told me that he had been contacted by the Polish (communist) member of the same commission to the effect that Yarborough's charges were getting the communist side of the commission upset— making life in their compound near Pyongyang, the North Korean capital, really very unpleasant. Could anything be done, asked the Pole, to make Yarborough shut up? I, of course, told the Swede that I thought the situation hilarious and much to be preserved, and he fully agreed.

Unfortunately, this little matter had gotten into State Department channels, and our ambassador, Win Brown, was instructed by Washington to tell me to have Yarborough quit it. I was much dismayed—but State maintained that there could be only one point of ideological interface between the United States and the USSR—and that was to be, exclusively, the United Nations in New York. I thought State was stuffy, and told Brown so—and he agreed. But it was fun while it lasted.

The Korean Army and police picked up about 150 North Korean spies each year—some of them having sneaked across the DMZ at night, some being delivered by very fast naval speedboat (faster than any boat available to the United States in the South) to the east or west shore of the Republic of Korea. Each agent had been issued, apparently, exactly $4,000 in U.S. $100 bills and some Korean money. If our side caught the agent quickly enough, very little of the four grand had been spent. The intelligence people on my two staffs were given four days to interrogate each newly caught spy—but if at a later date they wanted to question him further he was declared, by the South Koreans, unavailable.

Parenthetically: where did that U.S. $4,000 in the possession of each enemy agent come from? We thought we knew: it came from money U.S. tourists to Hong Kong spent—though they were asked in writing not to do so—in certain Hong Kong shops selling goods manufactured in communist China. Apparently many American tourists, seeing a reduced-price communist-manufactured trinket, would buy it, and to hell with the consequences.

I don't think our side missed catching more than a few of the enemy's agents, but the other side was probably tighter still because it was North Korean law that every citizen was obliged always to report strangers— either in his town, if it were a small one, or in his neighborhood if he lived in a city. We were told that North Korean secret police checked the system regularly by inserting a stranger into the town or neighbor-hood—and if a citizen was detected as having seen the stranger, yet had not reported him, said citizen was himself punished, often cruelly.

In November of 1963 I flew back to Washington to attend an Army Commanders' Conference, at which the Army's business was discussed by major overseas and continental commanders with the Army's Chief of Staff and his primary general staff officers. President Kennedy did a good job of giving us, when our group visited the White House, his per-sonal view, in considerable detail, of the world's geopolitical situation. This was the normal and, for us, very useful thing for the president to do.

In November 1963, Mary and I were awakened at 3:00 A.M. by a phone call from the Army duty officer in the Pentagon: Kennedy had been very severely wounded by an assassin in Dallas. I was authorized, at my dis-cretion, to put U.S. troops in Korea on alert. I saw no reason to do that, but Mary and I were much distressed by the news about the president. I had gotten to know him somewhat in connection with the 1962 Cuban missile crisis and other matters.

Because of Kennedy's death the annual Commanders' Conference was postponed—we convened in January, as I remember, instead of No-vember. And one morning, as was customary, we went to the White House to be addressed by the president—in this case, Lyndon Johnson, Kennedy's successor. I'll never forget it.

We were seated, as before, around the huge oblong table in the Cab-inet Room. The president started by telling us of his life as a boy and a young man—how he was an elevator boy in a hotel, and later a truck driver for, as I remember, a mining or construction company. These and similar jobs, he said, taught him *humility*. And then he turned to another subject: us.

Oh, he said, he knew we were all brave (which we weren't, especially) but that we were *arrogant*—"I know what you do," he said, "you drive by in your sedans and splash muddy water on your soldiers!" And then he told us to quit it.

I almost fell out of my chair. If one added up all our responsibilities we—his visitors—had operational control over maybe 3 million soldiers,

American and allied; we controlled, to a great degree, the spending of billions of dollars annually in foreign military aid; and we had responsibility for the defense against communist aggression (not very improbable, in those days) of a major part of the earth's surface. And, of course, we faced lots of problems, some of them serious ones—yet here was our Commander-in-Chief telling us not to splash muddy water on people.

I had great respect for the Chairman of the Korean Joint Chiefs of Staff—in my time, an Army general—and for the Air Force Chief of Staff, for the Chief of Naval Operations, and for the Commandant of the Marine Corps. I had no respect whatever for the Korean Defense Minister, an ex-Marine, and not much regard for the first (in my tour as CINCUNC) Army Chief of Staff, a fat and not very bright little man who went about with his shoes untied. Also disturbing to me were stories about the sometimes successful attempt on the part of Korean politicians—especially certain members of the National Assembly—to influence the selection of armed forces officers for highly responsible jobs.

This situation led me to ask the president, Pak Chung Hui, to give me approval authority not over promotions but over the assignment of all senior military officers to positions of high command—Army, Navy, Air Force, and Marine. After all, I told him, I was the one responsible to my government and to his government for the defense of the Korean peninsula, should that be required by North Korean attack, and I should not find it necessary to fight that battle, if it came, with commanders who did not have my confidence.

Undoubtedly, President Pak had to overcome lots of opposition, especially in the Korean Defense Ministry and in the National Assembly, to bring about that arrangement, but it eventually came true. It had the effect of strengthening U.S. command authority and removing political and sometimes financial pressure (Korean) on military commanders. I, in turn, made the arrangement less onerous than it otherwise might have been.

Never, for example, did I turn down a recommendation formally submitted for my approval. But the U.S. MAAG (U.S. military advisory groups) Chiefs (each a senior experienced U.S. flag officer served by a competent staff) could, if necessary, when a new assignment to command was proposed, say to his respective Korean Chief of Staff, "General Howze, I know, wouldn't approve this"—and the nomination would be withdrawn. So, because the MAAG Chiefs kept me informed, I knew all the final nominations to high command long before they got to my office, and sent them back, approved, within a half-hour of their submission.

Mary and I took three days off to see the 1964 Olympic Games in Tokyo. There we encountered Gen. William Westmoreland—the well-known "Westy," a friend from my days with the 82nd Airborne Division—who was the newly appointed U.S. commander in Vietnam and who asked me about the approval arrangement just described. I described it, told of its advantages and workability, and suggested that he might try for the same arrangement in Vietnam—where the real war hadn't even begun yet.

I don't know whether or not he made the attempt, but I do know the arrangement never came about there. Perhaps it shouldn't have, but perhaps it should; perhaps also it wasn't possible. I also know, through a postretirement visit to Vietnam in 1967, that many U.S. corps and division commanders were very distrustful of the security in the various headquarters of the Vietnamese Army—conceivably because of political influence in the appointment of commanders.

There was a substantial number of U.S. and foreign official visitors to Korea whom I had to receive in my office, brief on our situation, and entertain. And I made, in turn, several such visits to countries along the western periphery of Asia, including the Philippines, Taiwan, Okinawa (a territory of Japan), Indonesia, Hong Kong, Australia, and New Zealand. It was a worthwhile liaison because all these governments, to some degree, were threatened by the expansion of world communism.

I've only an anecdote to report on the Philippines, which for many years tried for nationalistic purposes to substitute Tagalog for English. Tagalog was one native dialect among scores of native dialects and known only to a few Filipinos—and certainly to no one else on earth. English, because of the school system installed under American direction during the colonial days, was the only language common to most Filipino citizens.

Well, at the Philippine Army headquarters, on my visit, I was greeted by the Chief of Staff and an honor guard—the commander of which was, no doubt as required, giving his orders to the honor guard in Tagalog. He said something to make the soldiers come to attention, then to present arms as the band played the two national anthems, then order arms—and then, I figured, to do squads right and pass in review. But apparently the platoon wasn't doing it correctly, upon which the commander shouted, at the top of his lungs, "Hold it! Hold it! Hold it!"—in crisis, obviously, employing a language he could use and his people could really understand.

On one mostly protocol visit to Taiwan, I made long and very informative calls on the American ambassador, the president's (Chiang Kai-shek's) son and the Army's Chief of Staff—with whom I also played golf. And then Mary and I called on the "Generalisimo" himself, Chiang Kai-shek, and his wife, and were entertained formally at tea. Chiang is now dead, and I am aware that by now his name is in history's doghouse. To this I can only say that in the early 1960s he seemed to be a highly intelligent man, very friendly toward America and, with Madame Chiang, a gracious host and a most interesting person to talk to.

On a second visit to Taiwan I flew across the straits to the islands of Matsu and Quemoy, just a few miles offshore from the city of Amoy on the communist Chinese mainland. The Nationalist Chinese artillery had in former years exchanged gunfire, frequently, with the Chinese artillery on the mainland—gunfire meant to destroy things and kill people. This was why most of the military installations I visited on the island were underground. But over the years the two military forces reached, independently, the conclusion that this was a ridiculous practice instituted by politicians for political purposes—an expression of hate.

So by the time of my visit the Nationalists weren't shooting at all, thus conserving ammunition. The Communist Army, however, had an illusion to preserve: it was shooting still, but only three days a week at precisely the same time each day, and its fire was always directed at the same barren, uninhabited spot on each of the two islands. Sometimes soldiers aren't too dumb.

With my small party I had an elaborate, fifteen-course luncheon—in a cave on Quemoy—with about a dozen Chinese generals, Air Force and Army. Each of us had a not-too-small porcelain hot wine cup at our place, and when each new course (of the fifteen) was served it had to be toasted, bottoms-up, with the salute, "Gambei!" which I was told means "New Dish!" The cup was then refilled. I learned from this that one should not make a habit of attending a formal Chinese luncheon every day.

The most extensive trip for Mary and me was to Australia and New Zealand: we were the U.S. president's representatives at the quadrennial celebration of the Battle of the Coral Sea—this battle being the one that, in 1943, marked the limit of Japanese expansion in the Southwest Pacific. As a result of the battle a large convoy of Japanese troopships bound for Port Moresby, in Papua, New Guinea—this being Australian territory—turned around in mid-course.

Coral Sea is notable as the first major naval engagement in which the capital ships of each side did not come within sight or range of each other—all combat action pitted aircraft against aircraft, or aircraft against ship, never ship against ship.

But the battle itself, I discovered by reading up on it, was not exactly perfect in execution. Some Japanese airplanes tried to land on American carriers, and some U.S. aircraft attempted to land on Japanese carriers, in each case being frantically waved off by an indignant landing officer on the fantail; one Japanese oiler was reported by our aircraft observers as an enemy carrier; several American naval aircraft made a determined attack on four Australian cruisers, and others on a coral reef that they identified, through low-hanging cloud, as a Japanese carrier.

As an Army guy I had always suspected that our Navy was immune to error; it was nice to learn that it could mess things up, too. But I guess it won the battle, for the great Japanese thrust south across the western Pacific was halted. But it took lots more fighting to turn it around.

In the course of our visit I made thirty-eight speeches in 18 days, and Mary made three. We visited all the major Australian cities and even Alice Springs, in those days no more than a little oasis in the gigantic desert that constitutes most of Australia. And we went also to Tasmania, a huge island off the southern Australian coast. I have always been good at geography, but I confess that I had previously regarded Tasmania as fictional.

The Australians were extremely nice to us, in all respects. I discovered how anxious were its politicians to present, for the benefit of their constituents, a plebeian aspect—on each formal occasion I was introduced grandly as an "American four-star general," usually by a lord mayor who then hastened to assure the audience (usually falsely, I began to suspect) that "in the war I was only a corporal, myself."

At a huge reception in a Sydney hotel, after the receiving line was finished our host, again the lord mayor, suggested a cocktail. I ordered a scotch and soda, he a scotch and milk. "And be sure," he told the waiter, "to put plenty of scotch in that milk!" Well, shortly thereafter the photographers swarmed us so I, being in uniform, started to put down my drink. "Oh, don't do that," said the mayor, "Let's make this informal." The rat. I took back my drink, and next morning on the front page of every newspaper in Sydney there appeared a photograph of "General Howze with his scotch, and the Lord-Mayor with his *milk*."

Lord love the politicians!

We encountered a limited-occupancy heaven in Australia. the vice-regal governor-general, who lives in Canberra, and the governors of the six provinces were—and presumably still are—all retired senior officers of the British Army. Each one lives in a mansion so huge that it has a separate in-house telephone system, a large staff of servants, and grounds big enough to accommodate about a six-hole golf course. Each incumbent's position is largely ceremonial with very little political power, true, but it's a nice way to spend one's declining years.

The runway of the airport in Wellington, New Zealand, in 1964 ran from one part of the ocean to another—across a low sandy spit connecting two land masses. We had a very bumpy approach, and when Mary came out the aircraft door onto the little platform atop the ladder she was seized by two husky New Zealand Air Force officers to keep her from blowing off: The wind was at something like 75 knots.

The cities of New Zealand, to our eyes, looked like none other, for there seemed to be little else but single family dwellings. I suppose there were, somewhere, an adequate number of hotels, apartments, stores, and office buildings, but at the time of our visit they were hard to find.

In New Zealand we again participated in the accustomed cere-monies—parade-viewing, wreath-laying, and speech-making, all ap-propriate to the Battle of the Coral Sea and well handled. We also did some sight-seeing and successful, if brief, trout fishing, particularly near Rotarua, the source of much underground geothermal energy. But we saw only North Island, not the spectacularly beautiful South Island.

New Zealand is inhabited by large quantities of fine big deer whose progenitors were imported from North America. But New Zealanders have little taste for venison, so a visitor sometimes sees large stake-bod-ied trucks, piled high with deer carcasses, on the way to canning facto-ries and eventual shipment to other countries in the Far East.

For all its beauty, New Zealand is very socialist—somehow an odd persuasion for an apparently prosperous people of British origin. On one occasion, my uniform cap, which I had laid down in the vestibule of a museum, was stolen, almost certainly by college students. It ap-peared a few days later in the grounds of the U.S. ambassador's resi-dence, where Mary and I were staying. It had been ripped, disgustingly soiled, and, with a vulgar message attached, thrown over the fence. Some years later Pres. Lyndon Johnson was treated somewhat similarly in the same country.

We went back to Korea via Fiji and Guam. It was an uneventful flight.

My weekly routine in Korea included, unless it was interrupted, three days in the field looking at the troops, U.S. and Korean, Army, Navy, Air Force, and Marine. Believe me, they were worth looking at: the MAAGs did a fine job, and uniformly admired the forces they were helping to supply and train. I remember the U.S. Air MAAG Chief telling me that Korean air fighter squadrons (taking into account some differences in equipment) were absolutely on a par with those in our Air Force. Other (Army, Navy, and Marine) MAAG Chiefs had similar views.

I did practically all my visits in a helicopter, and thus came to know the terrain of the southern half of the Korean peninsula better than anyone alive, Korean or American. I once took three days to fly the en-tire periphery of South Korea by helicopter in order to gain a reasonably good understanding of the cargo-handling capacity of the various ports, most of them small.

We landed at each of the little towns, and each time were surrounded instantly by a sea of children—all ecstatic at having a close-up view of that magic bird, the helo, and all cheerful and uniformly well behaved. Once we landed on what I thought was a remote mountaintop for a lunch of iced tea and sandwiches: we ended it with a giggling audience of about a hundred kids. They had literally run up the mountain.

Korea has its full share of bad weather, so I had the Eighth Army Aviation Section publish foul-weather flight-route maps of the U.S. I Corps operational area, down to the outskirts of Seoul. On these maps every obstacle more than 50 feet high along the valley-bottom flight routes was shown, so a helo could get at least to most of the headquarters location even under very low ceilings. With a copilot, always, I flew these routes often in such weather, sometimes going under the power lines and river bridges. I imposed a $100 fine on any pilot who flew a helicopter, anywhere in Korea, without one of the obstacle maps aboard.

Mary did a lot of good in Korea—on one occasion, with the help of trucks and other things furnished by my headquarters commandant, greatly easing the suffering of the Koreans in a village badly damaged by a heavy thunderstorm. She also managed to involve the wives of senior Korean officers in "grey lady" work at Korean military hospitals—for them, a hitherto unheard-of activity. And with other American women she had some liberalizing effect on the social status of Korean wives.

From our point of view, that status needed improving. When we first came to the country in 1959, wives even of some high-ranking military officers tended to follow their husbands around at a distance of three paces, even on social occasions. They were always behind him in receiving lines.

By custom, among Koreans a wife was known as "the mother of Kyong"—"Kyong" in this example being the name of her oldest son—her own given name relegated to little or no importance. Indeed, within the family the husband usually called her "Yobo"—translated as "Hey, you." When I or any other American male addressed a Korean woman, she—unless she was already accustomed to international society—put a fan or her hand across her face and dissolved in a paroxysm of embarrassed giggles.

I can't say that my wife was able to bring the Korean married women we knew out of their positions as distinctly second-class citizens, but by her warmth and friendliness, and with the help of other U.S. military wives, she did make very apparent progress in that direction—at least in the city of Seoul.

On one summer weekend Mary and I and our younger boy took a jeep trip (no other motor vehicle could get far out of town in 1964) across the northern mountains of South Korea to the east coast, where the tides are only two feet instead of the 25 feet normal on the west, China Sea coast—so the east coast has lovely sandy beaches, not the wide mud flats common to the west.

We had tried to avoid it but the Korean Army insisted, because the North Korean border was only a few miles away, that a guard accompany us. As we drove, we noted a jeep full of soldiers in front of us and another behind—in a way, sort of violating our little private holiday. But after we settled into a little, apparently never-used government-owned cabin on the beautiful, totally deserted beach Mary and Guy decided to go swimming; I had a cold and decided not to get wet.

So help me, as Mary and Guy in their swimsuits started picking their way into the gorgeous, clear, shallow blue water there was a lot of ruckus in the brush behind the beach and here came at double-time a complete Korean infantry platoon, armed to the teeth and carrying live ammunition. As I watched, goggle-eyed, the platoon leader sent one squad tearing off to positions on the right, another to the left; he put his two machine guns in the center and posted the third squad in reserve. The situation was now in hand: the swim could proceed. I thought all this was a bit much, and later told the Korean Army so; well, they said, the corps commander of the Sixth Corps, General Suh, on the east coast, didn't want a North Korean patrol scooping up the CINCUNC or his family.

I awoke one morning to learn that the Chief of Staff of the UN Command, Lt. Gen. Ed Broadhurst of the Air Force, an outstanding airman and a great friend, had just been taken to the little Army hospital in our compound with a heart attack. I went there at once, learned that he was dead, and then had the heartbreaking experience of telling his wife so. It was a big loss, also, to our headquarters.

His replacement as Chief of Staff, one Lt. Gen. Benjamin Davis of the Air Force, was equally capable. His father was, I believe—though I can't be sure of it—the first and for perhaps three decades the only black officer in the Regular Army, becoming a colonel and the commander of a cavalry regiment. He, it was said, hung his cap and saber on a hook immediately behind his desk so that while officers who might not want to salute a black man saluted instead his emblems of rank—the cap and saber. But those days were long past. The Ben Davis coming to me had commanded, in World War II, a fighter squadron comprising all black pilots.

I was most impressed, before Davis's arrival, by the number of letters I received from my acquaintances in the Air Force praising Davis and his wife, Aggie. Blacks in those days weren't very widespread in the officer ranks, and all the letters were from people who wanted to make damned sure that I gave Davis a fair break. It was easy for me to do so— he was a fine man. Coincidentally, I write this only an hour after Ben Davis appeared on the ABC evening news as the "Man of the Week."

In the midwinter of my second year as CINCUNC, Korea, I elected to retire from the Army—unquestionably the stupidest decision I ever made. I had several reasons, one of them being that Westmoreland had only nine months previously been appointed to command in Vietnam, a job I'd like to have had; I was also told by the Army's Chief of Staff, Gen. Harold Johnson, that my prospects were to continue in Korea for an extra nine months or so and then to go to the Panama Canal Zone as CINCSOUTH—a command of lesser importance than the one I already had.

This was bad news for Mary and me—we had been separated for two years from our two teenaged boys, and preferred not to extend the separation for almost three more years. And, I must confess, that although

I loved the Army—as I should, considering how good it had been to me—I was very curious about what civilian life was like, no relative of mine having ever experienced it except in retirement. And I thought that I could probably get an interesting job with some aircraft manufacturing company. These reasons seemed cogent enough at the time, but I shall always regret, nevertheless, that I didn't stay the four more years I could have.

Our second tour in Korea had been a peaceful one—no revolutions, no very serious border incidents, only a few moderately severe riots by the ever-rioting students. It was a happy, interesting time and certainly a rewarding one, for the armed forces of Korea made much progress, and so did the battle readiness of the two U.S. divisions and the fighter wing, down at Osan, of the U.S. Air Force.

We elected to go home the long way, via Manila, Bangkok, New Delhi, and Madrid. We paid that part of the fare that was greater than what it would have cost the government to bring us back via San Francisco.

When the time came to leave, Mary and I made a large number of official goodbye calls—on the president and Mrs. Pak Chung Hui, among others. The Paks presented us with a lovely, tall eight-panel silkscreen—which according to U.S. regulations I should have refused. But, of course, I didn't—it would have been very offensive to the president and his wife.

I would talk a bit more about the president. He was autocratic, sure enough, but there is little doubt that he was a devoted patriot and very capable—a firm but generally benevolent and far-sighted leader of his country. He was stubborn, withdrawn, and not very popular with the people in our embassy. But he presided over an amazingly productive era of social as well as industrial progress in Korea—even while sometimes getting a very bad press in the United States.

On a return visit to Korea a few years after my retirement I had a two-hour visit with Pak in his office, and mentioned that bad press and what effect it might have on American support for his government. He thought a long time before answering that he knew about, and greatly regretted, that bad press. But, he said, he had to make the decisions that were best for his country, no matter what U.S. newspapers said about him—so he did that.

Pak's wife, who knew a little English, was younger (and taller) than he and an absolutely beautiful woman—her beauty set off by the lovely, long, high-collar dresses traditional in Korea. But Pak was hated, all right, by some rednecked Koreans—they murdered her. And later on they murdered him, while he was still in office.

After the usual formal change-of-command ceremony (Gen. Dwight Beach, an old friend, being my successor) we started home on a USAF passenger aircraft, the Paks, Ambassador Win Brown and Mrs. Brown, and a large delegation of Korean and American officialdom and foreign ambassadors seeing us off. The ROK Army's new Chief of Staff, of whom I thought very highly, presented us with a brass statue (of the Goddess of Liberty, or some lady) on top of a tall column rising from a large square base all decorated up with miniature cannons and chain fences. All of this I conservatively estimated to have weighed about 75 pounds. After I thanked the donor very profusely, my aide and I lugged the present onto the aircraft that was taking us only partway home, via New Delhi and Madrid—the rest of our trip being at our own expense via commercial aircraft.

I hope my friend the (then) Korean C/S doesn't read this (and I'm sure he won't) because with the assistance of my aide I dismantled his gift in Manila, our first stop—removed the inscription and dumped the remains in the torpid green Pasig River as it flowed under a bridge. I felt awful, as the reader probably thinks I should have. But how could we have gotten that enormous thing home via a succession of civilian aircraft? And where could we put it in our home?

After Manila and Bangkok, one of the airplane's engines developed trouble shortly before our arrival in New Delhi. We used our accrued leave time to spend eight days in India, visiting the huge old palace at Jaipur and the incomparable Taj Mahal in Agra. We traveled to these places overnight by train, an interesting experience inasmuch as my wife and I shared cabin space with my aide and an Indian gentleman who unabashedly stripped to his underdrawers—stopping there, fortunately—before climbing into bed.

And outside New Delhi I went partridge shooting (lots of birds) with a distinguished-looking Sikh businessman, our host, and Col. Paul

Tibbets of the U.S. Air Force, then stationed with our military advisory group, who had been the pilot of the *Enola Gay,* a B-29 bomber, when it dropped the atomic bomb on Hiroshima.

Our week in India was, of course, fascinating in most respects, but we also found offensive the profusion of skinny cattle, even in some city streets—and of pigeons, which in their tens of thousands looked as though they'd break down the telephone and power lines. All this potential food was protected against human consumption by the Hindu religion; said humans, meanwhile, were in large part undernourished and in rural areas housed mostly in tiny huts made of cow dung. I would advise my readers that if they anticipate reincarnation in India each should elect to be a cow.

In 1965 both the United States and the USSR maintained military advisory groups in India: about half of the combat divisions of the Army and combat wings of the air force were provided U.S.-made arms and equipment, the other half with Soviet. In consequence, officers assigned to the respective MAAGs were strictly limited as to what units they could visit. I suppose all this made sense from a political point of view, but I should hate to be the logistician who would have to support such a force in time of war.

My retirement ceremony and parade was conducted by the 3rd Infantry Regiment at Fort Myer, Virginia, across the Potomac from Washington. The secretary of the Army and the Chief of Staff did the honors and said nice things about me. I was flattered also by the presence of the redoubtable Gen. Omar Bradley, long since retired, who came even to the reception following the ceremony.

So I was out.

VISITS AND VIEWS

22 I'm not sure, but I rather think that the military service is a profession more personal and more emotionally charged than most of the others: a professional soldier, sailor, or airman, though he may on some occasions be disgusted with his current job—and his job changes constantly—is more inclined to be sentimentally inclined in respect to his career than would, say, a lawyer or shopkeeper. I don't think lawyers, for instance, have songs about regimental exploits—good, bad, and ridiculous—or about the virtues of dying on the field of honor, or, when they die, going to some special place "halfway down to hell" where there are a lot of good horses and whiskey. At least I hope they don't.

In any case, leaving the Army was very hard on me and on Mary—for her lineage in the military service is as long as mine. As beforesaid, my retirement three or four years before I had to do it was just plain dumb.

I wrote two or three aviation companies I knew to ask for a job, was not overwhelmed with the response, but took the best, deciding to join Bell Helicopter in Fort Worth as a vice-president and at a modest salary. The Bell president who made the offer was Harvey Gaylord, whose handsome wife, Anne, made sure that we met the right people in Fort Worth and got us into the right country club. But when we showed up in early July, 1965, Gaylord had been replaced by E. J. Ducayet—"Duke."

I was made vice-president for "product planning"—obviously a made job, my job description commissioning me to look into the future as respects U.S. (and by extension some foreign) military helicopter type requirements. This meant, within the company, that I was a member of all the company planning boards and the chairman of one or two, but taken all in all I was sadly unemployed. There were only four other VPs—and the executive VP—besides myself, and there had already been divided, among the four, executive responsibility for all company activities. I suppose I could have elbowed my way into a position of control over some of these activities but that would have caused much disruption, so I didn't do it.

Having not enough to do while feeling obliged to spend full time at "work" is a very unsettling state. This was mitigated, however, by the cordiality displayed by the company personnel, at all levels, and by the privilege of keeping up my helicopter proficiency in the Bell Jet Ranger.

Bell was and is a fine company, with great entrepreneurial ability, superb engineering, and no-nonsense, courageous management—all of these being necessities in the aviation field. I would mention a prime example of what they can do. In view of the complexities of government military aircraft procurement (proposal, counterproposal, contractual procedures, engineering, development, X-model and Y-model construction and test)—all of which for a new aircraft always takes several years to complete—I think Bell's own development of the Cobra, a military attack helicopter, was an extraordinary accomplishment.

Bell had already made thousands of UH-1 Hueys, of course. But during the Vietnam War, Bell engineering, Bart Kelly presiding, took the Huey powertrain (engine, transmission, blade, and control system—some requiring adaptation) and in the course of about a year built around them a new narrow shark-like body with a gun turret under the nose and provisions for other weapons on each side, and offered it to the Army as a complete, aeronautically proven combat attack helicopter—the first in the world. After military testing this craft, the Cobra, was ready for production—and, indeed, the Army needed it right then in Vietnam, where it did yeoman service. In a succession of models, each an improvement of the previous one, Bell sold several thousands of these to our services and others around the world. A great many of them are still flying.

Early in my stay at Bell I did a sort of recruiting job for the Army, visiting and lecturing to a number of university Army ROTC units on the subjects of the Army and the new developments underway therein. With a copilot I flew a Huey to the several locations: Texas A&M, Texas, TCU, Rice, and LSU. I think I did some good in my talks, and the helo did lots of advertising for the Army ROTC.

In 1966 I went to Vietnam on a visit, General Westmoreland putting me up in a guest house in the grounds of the very substantial mansion that he lived in in Saigon—as had his predecessors. Westy was very generous, making available for my use an airplane for long trips and a Huey for short ones. I did a certain amount of liaison with the several Bell Helicopter representatives in country, but spent most of my time in visits—to every major ground force headquarters in country, down to include separate brigades. Without exception I found every commander—and I knew them all, save the Marine—upbeat and very proud of U.S. troop performance.

I was startled, however, by the huge, walled and otherwise fortified encampments positioned at various spots within the combat area—that area being all of the jungle, and in the south, the rice paddies. The major cities, though known to harbor dissidents, were quiet.

To this minute I am unsure about the desirability of those elaborate semipermanent garrisons, which provided our combat units two-story wooden barracks, beds, and ice cream and movies at night. No doubt service in the tropical jungles and paddies was onerous and difficult, but the tour in Vietnam was only for a year, and I wonder at the advantages to our enemy of so precisely locating our strength and to some extent limiting our freedom of action.

I was also surprised and dismayed by the lack of trust, among our senior commanders, of the South Vietnamese Army; those U.S. commanders (somewhat unlike our military advisory personnel working on a daily basis with Vietnamese units) considered the Vietnamese poorly trained and unreliable in combat. They were also outspoken in the belief that the staffs of the Vietnamese divisions were seriously penetrated by communist agents who alerted Vietcong or North Vietnamese headquarters to any military operation planned against them, allowing the enemy to clear out of the target area. The attitude of most U.S. commanders, therefore, was that a combined operation with South Vietnamese troops was impractical—unwise to attempt. This to me meant that we had taken over too much of the job of fighting the war.

There were a thousand other things of interest to me in my ten-day visit, but I shall speak of only one other: the unrestricted use, by the enemy, of Cambodian soil for troop movement, reinforcement, and resupply, while U.S. ground forces were by executive order barred from entry into Cambodia to cut that line of supply. There was, in Vietnam, no identifiable "front": no line with our forces on one side and the enemy (which were the Vietcong—black-pajama guerrillas—plus several divisions of the North Vietnamese Army) on the other. However, though it was possible for our troops to clean the enemy out of a given area of South Vietnam to some reasonable extent, there was no way to keep it sanitized against new infiltration via Cambodia. Westmoreland was confronted with a problem he couldn't solve with the forces on hand. Even in 1966 no route to victory, no winning strategy, was apparent under the constraint inflicted by that long, impossible flank—which the enemy could cross at will and we couldn't cross at all.

I concluded my visit by typing out an eight-page, single-space, multicopy memorandum to Westmoreland, suggesting improvements in some tactical procedures, and a procedure by which I thought South Vietnamese divisions could be safely used in combined operations with our forces—in general by giving them, very late in the planning stage, limited blocking functions without any information as to what U.S. forces were to do.

Mind you, it is easy for a visitor to find, in any very large military operation, things to fault. I found many, and thought that my report would be helpful to Westy and his staff. But as I reread the report I realized that it was critical in many respects and therefore gave him all five copies, telling him that I retained none. I hope the report was helpful to his staff, but wish very much, only as a matter of my own record, that I had retained a copy.

Before I leave the subject of Vietnam I would comment on the role of the helicopter there. It is true that the war wasn't won, despite the very extensive use of the small troop transport helo and the helicopter gunship; moreover, after the enemy got used to the helo he shot a lot of them down. But it is also true that without the helicopter our troops in Viet Nam would have been relatively helpless in that gigantic "triple canopy" jungle. And I was told by more than one division commander that his aerial reconnaissance elements inflicted more casualties on the enemy than any infantry battalion in the division. The point is simply this: off the trail the thick tropical jungle reduces the mobility of a uniformed soldier, with his rifle, ammunition, and pack, to not much above zero.

The Marines like to tell stories about the Army, and the Army about the Marines. I was told about a commercial airplane jammed with returning Marines about to take off from Tan Son Nhut Airport in Saigon for the United States. Saith the stewardess to the passengers, as the engines were starting: "It's a very hot, high-humidity day; we have a heavy load, and the runway's not very long. So! To lighten the load at takeoff, just before we lift off the runway I want you all to *lift your feet off the floor!*" So they did, and the airplane got off in fine shape.

I had met Gen. Moshe Dayan, one of the great soldiers of Israel, at a U.S. infantry division's field headquarters in Vietnam: despite his distinguished military record he was there, black eyepatch and all, as a civilian reporter for the Israeli press. In August of 1967 I took advantage of that earlier meeting to ask him—he was by then the Israeli defense minister—if I might visit Israel to learn more about the June 1967 Six Day War against the Arabs. He said to come ahead.

I first had a two-hour talk with him in his office, and learned much. For example, the Israeli government, when the Egyptians, Jordanians, and Syrians had massed troops on Israeli borders and fervently promised to destroy it utterly, called all reservists, whose ranks include virtually every able-bodied man in Israel except the religious zealots, to their assigned military units. I said I could not see how the business of everyday living, and the economy, could survive that long absence from work of virtually all the country's males. Dayan gave me that twisted little grin and said, "Well, there's always the United Jewish Appeal!"

Dayan made available to me an automobile and driver, an escort officer, and a beat-up old German Dornier single-engine airplane—the latter for a trip, with stops, across the Sinai Desert to the Suez Canal, down the canal and back via the Gulf of Acaba and the Negev. Near one stop, el Arish, we saw a deserted Egyptian trench whose bottom contained numerous abandoned shoes and messkits. You'd leave a messkit, maybe, if you were in a great hurry to leave, but why your shoes?

Altogether I had a fascinating ten-day visit, talking extensively to the Chiefs of Staff of the Army and Air Force and to several battle commanders, and visiting all of the battlefields—many of them still littered with destroyed Arab tanks and other motorized equipment, essentially all of Soviet manufacture. And I thus came to admire, very much, the armed forces of Israel. Their battle accomplishments were classic.

I'll mention only a few features of that war, which started only after the three Arab nations had formed for attack (the Syrians actually shooting artillery at Israeli kibbutzim in the Vale of Hula) and had threatened, openly and repeatedly, to wipe Israel right off the earth. Very justifiably the Israelis, after mobilizing, attacked first.

The jet fighter aircraft of the Israeli Air Force (this as told me by Gen. Mordecai Hod, the Air Force Chief) took off shortly after daybreak the first day. Most of them, leveling off at *50 feet,* flew across the southern corner of the Mediterranean, turned south at the same altitude across the north Egyptian desert, and rose to about 1,200 feet over the Egyptian airfields at a time they knew that most of the Egyptian pilots, according to routine, had had their early morning stand-to and had gone to breakfast. Other Israeli fighters had flown a high southwesterly route across the almost uninhabited desert from Israel to the southern Egyptian airfields. All the strike aircraft arrived over their targets at virtually the same time.

Bombs and heavy-caliber machine-gun fire took care of the several hundred Egyptian combat aircraft parked on the hardstands and in the hangars, and so-called concrete dibber bombs cratered the runways. The Egyptian air force, to all intents and purposes, died within the hour.

I would, with my background, also mention the use of maybe a dozen Israeli Air Force light two-seater Bell OH-13 helicopters, made available to the Army. The Middle East desert, almost everywhere, has a roll to it. Flying only a very few feet off the ground these little choppers, with tank battalion commanders aboard, allowed the Israelis to scout the location and formations of the opposing Arab tanks, and then pathfind for the Israeli tanks across the wadis (deep, dry ditches) and other terrain so that the Israelis could catch their Arab opponents by surprise and from an unexpected direction—the flank or rear. The Arabs had no helos, and without them suffered a towering disadvantage: their tank formations were largely blind. Israeli tank units knew Arab strength, dispositions, and in what direction they were faced, and therefore could (and did) first surprise them, in direction and timing, and then clobber them.

In Tel Aviv one evening I had dinner with a group of perhaps eight Israeli civilian men, all of whom had served in uniform during the war—one of them with a moderately severe heart condition. He said that he had told the military doctor, on being called to duty, about the condition in the expectation that he would be excused. But the doctor had said, "Well, just bring it with you. It won't kill you any deader than an Arab bullet." Not a bad point.

I also asked a number of Israelis, military and civilian, and including the fellow assigned to the U.S. desk of the Israeli Foreign Ministry, why the victorious Israeli forces were still, three months after the war's end, in possession of all the captured territory—from the Suez Canal in Egypt to the Jordan river and the Syrian city of Qunetra. The answer was pretty uniform: "Oh, that's strictly temporary—they'll all soon be back in Israel." And except for those in the Sinai they're not all back yet. And Ben Gurion, the first president and the George Washington of Israel, said soon after the war, "What Israel needs now is peace. For that we should return all the captured territories."

On the basis of this visit to the Six Day War, not long after it was done, I lectured on the subject to the U.S. Army general staff, and to the Army and sometimes Air Force general staffs of perhaps a dozen countries of Europe and the Far East. The story of that extraordinary war, as I had learned it, was exciting and instructive to every military professional. It confirmed once more the overwhelming advantages afforded by surprise and mobility—and highly professional execution.

I made a visit to Okanagan Helicopters of British Columbia, whose headquarters were in Vancouver. Okanagan has very professional pilots, many of whom during my visit were busy flying on behalf of a power company engaged in the construction of high-capacity high-voltage power lines from power sources (river dams) in the big mountains of British Columbia. Helos were of enormous utility in the transport of supplies and personnel and in building the towers and stringing the heavy lines—but the helos were always held in an ancillary position, much of the transport being done over super-rough precipitous roads hacked, by enormous effort, out of the wilderness. I tried to persuade the Canadians that a *total* dependence on the helo for transport would bring all sorts of additional savings. It would be possible not only not to build the roads at all, but also to lay out much shorter routes for the power lines to follow across that terribly rough terrain. My arguments didn't take, and of course those people were pros. I still believe that the first job done, in very rough topography, with total dependence on the helo will startle everybody by its efficiency and economies.

A particularly interesting event was one of the Paris Air Shows—interesting largely because of the excitement engendered by our (Bell) flight demonstrations and display of the Cobra, the world's first helicopter gunship. The Soviets couldn't get over that Cobra—photographing, from every angle, each part they could see from the outside.

During the show several Bell people—including Joe Mashman, at the time perhaps the world's finest helo pilot and whom the Russians knew well—were invited to ride in a commercially configured Soviet heli copter which boasted the unbelievable total of ninety-three upholstered passenger seats. This enormous machine had recently come in to land alongside another similar Russian ship configured as an aerial firefighter. Each of them had an identical set of nine rotor blades, all of them so long and limber that as engine power was cut and the rotor slowed to a stop the blades drooped unbelievably—from a mast height of maybe 20 feet to a blade-tip height of perhaps six feet. This bending reduced the overall diameter of each ship's main rotor while at rest.

But though the two ships had *parked* at different times they both, with our party in one of them, started engines at the same time, with the result that as all those eighteen blades were straightened up by centrifugal force they, with a dreadful rattling sound, intermeshed, clipping the blade tips off one another. Well—the engines were shut down and our thoroughly embarrassed hosts apologized: no ride, then or later. We were sorry to have missed the ride and the opportunity to compare, if only superficially, a Soviet product with our own. We also speculated on how long it took for the Soviet crews to compose a message back to Moscow explaining why the Soviet ships couldn't participate in the demonstration scheduled for the next day.

Iran under the shah was an excellent customer of Bell Helicopter Company, the relationship eventually taking the shape of Bell's construction and manning, with a complete range of instructors, of a large, permanent helicopter pilot and mechanic school—including quarters for a large number of American families—as well as Bell's construction of a very large rebuild facility for damaged helicopters, of an elaborate helicopter logistic complex, and of a helicopter manufacturing facility. The entire contracted business of Bell with the Iranian government—including aircraft sales, came to something like three billion U.S. bucks, but all of the project was not completed because of the Islamic revolution. I had nothing to do with the all-important business end of all this, but I did a lot of preliminary visiting and talking, and along with other Bell personnel got to know some Iranians—and a part of the countryside—pretty well.

One of my jobs was to put on, for the benefit of the commanders and general staff of the Iranian Army, a live fire demonstration that would illustrate the tactical advantages of having a few helicopters on your side of a battle. Preparation for this required our leaving Teheran every morning for about ten days to go onto the barren desert south of town. I'm reminded of two incidental events.

On the way around a traffic circle one day our bus crushed the fender of a little Volkswagen. The reader knows what that would mean in

America—tickets, appearances in court, possible suit, lawyers, and expense. On this occasion a cop strolled over from the center of the circle, looked at the damage, questioned both drivers, and within a few minutes directed the bus driver to give the auto driver so many rials. Our driver took out a pretty big roll, peeled off the required number of bills—I couldn't see how many—and everybody was underway again within ten minutes, the matter rectified. Could that happen in the United States? I'm afraid we're far too far down another path.

But "on the other hand": our bus went south out of Teheran, each day, via a street that crossed a railroad track. Maybe twice each week our street was cut by an outgoing or incoming freight train. And each time, without exception, the Iranian traffic on the near side *and* the far side of the train filled the not-very-wide street absolutely from curb to curb, ten cars deep. When the train was past there we were, in deadlock, everybody honking his horn. Eventually a cop would show up, and maybe a half hour later we could get underway again.

We had shipped from Fort Worth to Iran, for the Iranian Army to examine, a single new, improved, more powerful Huey troop-carrier helicopter of the type we wanted to sell them. In the demonstration it had to represent what should have been a little fleet of troop-carriers. We also had available a single Bell-manufactured Cobra attack helicopter—an Iranian-owned ship flown by our pilots—and several Iranian-owned (and flown) Bell two-seater scout choppers. For infantrymen we had a dozen Iranian paratroopers—all that would fit in the Huey, and for artillery an Iranian field battery.

As one can see, it was not possible to put on a full-scale show, but simply to demonstrate tactical principles by sample, asking the audience (practically the entire Iranian Army general staff, and much of the Air Force's) to use their imaginations a bit.

At the actual demo the artillery provided most of the excitement because (as was true during the rehearsals) although I had prescribed its target areas precisely, it was virtually impossible to know where it actually was going to shoot—or if it would shoot into only one area at a time, as intended, or two or three simultaneously. This was of considerable concern to the participating American pilots and scared the pants off me, at the microphone. But everybody survived and the Iranian brass was convinced of what helicopters could do—for those enormous contracts, previously mentioned, eventuated not long thereafter.

Two other things. When we got out in the early mornings to exercise, we were shocked to see some Iranians still asleep on the sidewalks—that had not yet become common in the United States. And when Bell personnel called on the very influential Iranian Minister of Defense General Toufanian in his office, usually with a paper on which we needed executive Iranian decision, we stalled around and stalled around until we saw him put our paper not in his desk drawer and not in his out-basket but in a baby-blue briefcase he kept on his credenza—for that briefcase, we had discovered, contained the papers he would bring to the shah for decision. That's where the action lay in those days.

As a matter of record, the enormous Bell activity in Iran died with the arrival, from Paris, of the Ayatollah Khomeini and the revolution that ousted the shah. We in Bell were able to recognize, in U.S. newspaper photographs, some of our friends among the Iranian military laid out on slabs on the roof of the huge Teheran prison where they had been summarily executed.

In the days of the shah, Iraq's Saddam Hussein would not have dared attack Iran: its Army, Navy, and Air Force would have eaten him up. The arrival of the ayatollah spelled the end of the U.S. Military Aid Mission and of Bell and virtually all other U.S. military contractors in Iran, and the heavy qualitative decline of all the Iranian military forces. The chanting, fist-shaking Revolutionary Guards became the force by which Islam maintained its dominance—the situation that encouraged Iraqi attack. I must say that Iran, partly by throwing masses of practically untrained Iranian youth at the enemy, did better than the West expected.

I should note here that the enormous Bell activity in Iran was under the control of two retired U.S. Army aviators, Lt. Gen. Bob Williams and Maj. Gen. Bob McKinnon. Their military background and judgment came into full play on the occasion of Khomeini's seizure of power in Iran, which put at risk hundreds of Bell employees and their families.

While with Bell I traveled much, repeatedly crossing the two oceans, because Bell agencies are scattered all over the world. Such travel is especially pleasant because one is always met at planeside by company representatives, who ease all the difficulties of baggage, immigration, and customs, and who know what is interesting to do and see on off-time. And what could be more pleasant, say, than a helicopter ride around the island of Singapore or over Paris?

I enjoyed much of my time with Bell, especially when I was overseas in its service. The company was very kind to me, in all respects, but after five years I changed status, on my request, to that of "consultant," coming to work only twice weekly at a much reduced salary. This arrangement made me much happier when I was in Fort Worth, and I continued, as consultant, on overseas missions.

At five-year intervals, since retirement, I've gone to the reunion of my class, 1930, at West Point. It is fashionable, historically, for old grads to remark that the "place [the Military Academy] has gone to hell." But now I think it has. I would dearly love to think that members of Congress would find out why so many experienced professionals believe this.

It costs the taxpayer about $300,000 to put a cadet through West Point. This means, I submit, that each cadet space, each three-hundred-thousand bucks, should produce, after seasoning in the Army, a *combat officer—not* a dentist or chaplain or a logistics or administrative person, for it is the combat officer whose skill is unique: not necessarily noble or admirable, but unique and uniquely valuable. All the other skills can come from among officers procured from the civilian universities. So, too, can the military skills capable of being performed by women—who I hasten to add, I do not suggest be banned altogether from military service.

Now, of course, a guy like me will always be held suspect when he talks like this. I have great respect and admiration and liking for women, but I would frankly state that women have no place in active military combat, and that only prospective combat branch officers should be trained at West Point. Lots of millions of dollars could be saved annually, without damage to our military strength, by adopting that philosophy—shared, I venture to say, by most other experienced military professionals.

Next: the cadet corps at West Point now looks terrible on parade. One may assume that the nation won't collapse on this account, but every military thing the cadets do should be done well—if it is not, it is very counterproductive.

Three recent decisions have caused this poor appearance: the admission of women, the practice of assigning cadets to companies regardless of individual height, and the abandonment of the marching line in favor of the marching blob. These practices have prevented uniformity, utterly destroyed style, and most important, buried the individual in the blob.

And finally, I at least suspect that the policy of offering too great a variety of academic instruction at West Point is damaging. At the broadcast of a recent Army-versus-Somebody football game some Army players were identified as majoring in "industrial management," "business administration," and several other similar fields. Are those the abilities the taxpayer is paying $300,000-plus a copy, at the *Military Academy,* to develop? I find it absurd. Instruction at West Point should be mind-developing: mathematics, English, history, natural and experimental philosophy, geography (since high schools seem to have abandoned the subject), and certain selected foreign languages. The *mind* is the thing, as it used to be in the old days. That, plus character and discipline.

The Army—not just the present administration at West Point— should, I earnestly submit, take a new hard look at the Military Academy, in the process talking to some retired officers of long service and good repute. I realize that Congress legislated some of what I complain of, but I venture to say that it would be willing to reconsider a failed policy. Among other things, it would save money, and Congress might like that.

With Mary I continued travel after leaving Bell, visiting again Western Europe, the Balkans, the Mediterranean islands including Crete, Greece, Egypt, Israel, and the Levant, the western periphery of Asia, the African game areas—a fascinating experience—the Caribbean, Alaska, and South America.

A trip worth mentioning (one without Mary) was that to Pakistan, as the guest of the president, then Zia ul-Haq. The trip was engineered by an elderly civilian named Lou Perlman who apparently had close rapport with the Department of the Army in Washington. I didn't know him, but retired Lt. Gen. Harry Kinnard did, and to my delight suggested to him that I and two other retired Army blokes go along. The Pakistani government paid the round-trip airfare, first class, from New York to Karachi. In Karachi, the largest city and on the Arabian Sea, we were met by an escort officer who put us on the presidential plane to go to Islamabad, the specially constructed capital city—all shiny and new-looking.

We were put up at a good hotel and taken to a very handsome dinner at the presidential mansion, where to our surprise the president threw his arms around our Mr. Perlman and kissed him on both cheeks. They *were* old friends, indeed.

As presidential guests (the memory of all this luxury shames me a bit) we flew on the presidential plane pretty much over all Pakistan, seeing much of the countryside including the Himalayas, the Hindu Kush range, and the great sprawling Indus River, and visiting Peshawar and Quetta. We also saw the countryside and people by car. In each city we stayed at the governor's palace—and I mean palace—structures built in the days of the British Raj, each of maybe seventy-five rooms and with a spectacularly uniformed staff of about 100. Every governor was an immaculately uniformed lieutenant general of the Pakistani Army, this being a military government. Every governor, like the president, was highly educated, cordial, urbane, and fluent in British English. This government was eventually ousted by election after Zia ul-Haq was lost in a highly suspicious airplane crash—the ship simply exploded and fell out of the air, killing the president and, among many others, the U.S. military attaché, an Army BG.

Pakistan was once much bigger, of course, incorporating the separate, pathetically poor, terribly overcrowded area far across the Indian peninsula, now the nation of Bangladesh. What remains of Pakistan looks less poor, by far, than India or Bangladesh, but that's not saying much. The country is fascinating to visit and very remindful of Kipling, who wrote extensively of the Northwest Frontier and the Kyber pass near Peshawar, and less fulsomely of the British Staff College and other things at Quetta.

When we were there, Pakistan was harboring about 3 million refugees from the Soviet invasion of Afghanistan. We saw several of their sprawling camps and visited one pretty extensively. The crowds of Afghans, mostly women and children, were housed in tents and appeared adequately fed and clothed and attended-to medically, but not exactly happy. Most of the few men were either aged or wounded. Pakistan, we felt, was much to be complimented for accepting and caring for these masses of helpless people.

Kharachi is a great modern city on the Arabian Sea, full of skyscrapers and traffic. We went crabbing in the harbor, on a sailboat—a rather silly-seeming endeavor after our grand tour and stays in the palaces of the governors. We caught too many crabs and ate too many—though they were delicious as cooked on a little iron stove in the bottom of our sailboat.

Perhaps as a result, Mr. Perlman, the very amiable, witty, and kindly person responsible for our being in Pakistan, complained of a chill a few hours before we got to Cairo, on our way home—our next stop after Dubai on the Persian Gulf. He said he was quite well enough to continue, however, but got worse (with what a doctor aboard now identified as a heart attack) over the Med on the way to Paris. I asked the pilot to make an unscheduled stop in Athens—which he did, no doubt at great expense to the airline. The rest of us continued on home, only Kinnard staying with the sick man, who unfortunately died in an Athens hospital. I called his wife from Paris to tell her that he—at that time still alive—was ill.

In Fort Worth Mary and I got all mixed up in a lot of boards and other charitable endeavors, as most retired folk do, and in the case of the Museum of Science and History she ended up as a volunteer member of its guild and I as the president of the Board of Trustees. This was most satisfying because of what we felt was the eye-opening educational value of the excellent museum—which had much earlier been a children's museum—for the thousands of schoolchildren who poured through it each year on tours conducted by our thirty-odd docents.

In 1982 I think it was, long after I had left Bell, that Jim Atkins, by then Bell's president, appointed me the head of an informal board of four retired Army officers (the other three being Generals Bob Williams, George Blanchard, and Jack Walker) to study and report on the prospective military applications of the tilt-rotor aircraft—the one designed by Bell engineering that can take off vertically like a helicopter and, by tilting its engines and rotors, convert to an airplane capable of a speed of about 300 knots.

We worked ten-hour days for nearly a month on that project, and evolved what I thought was an excellent document forecasting extensive military utilization of the design and extensive civilian use, too—as a city-center to city-center short haul (up to about 400 miles) transport, one that would do much to ease the increasing, and increasingly difficult to accommodate, load on the nation's airports.

And we also, in that report, had some advice for the Department of Defense. The Marines had shown much interest in the tilt-rotor design for use as a ship-to-shore troop-carrier for amphibious landings—its speed would allow the surface ships to stay further out to sea and therefore be less vulnerable to attack, and the Marine force ashore could be built up more rapidly.

We had no argument with that, but if the big aircraft the Marines wanted were to travel on a carrier they'd have to fit on the elevator that moves aircraft between the flight deck and the hangar deck below—and for that the aircraft would have to fold.

Well, I'll not go into detail, but I would say that folding a very large tilt-rotor aircraft approaches in complexity the folding of a grand piano. We said that in the report, and advised strongly that the Department of Defense make the Army the proponent service for the first prototype military aircraft. As an argument for our view we pointed out that World War III (which at that time everybody thought would, if it came, be fought out either by a general nuclear exchange, which would kill most everybody, or alternately by conventional combat on the continent of Europe) would in all probability be fought from beginning to end without a *single* Marine amphibious landing.

Bell made our report available to the military, I know, but I don't know whether it got up to the Department of Defense. In any case, the Marines were chosen as the proponent service, and the prototype aircraft is extra-complicated, extra-heavy, and extra-expensive. It was not the best way to get a new type aircraft into production.

For about 15 years I was a regular contributor of a biweekly column on national and international affairs to one and then another local Fort

Worth newspaper. Perhaps because I am by nature pessimistic (and somebody has to be—we can't all wear rose-colored glasses) I often wrote critically and pessimistically about this beloved nation we call the United States—particularly its state and national governments, which I believe don't function as they should.

For 14 years Mary and I spent four wonderful months each year in a condo we owned on a golf course in Gunnison, Colorado. Gunnison is not a resort town and therefore does not have the resort atmosphere we don't particularly like. The mountain half of Colorado is lovely— particularly in the early fall, when the yellow aspen is spectacularly beautiful.

And if anybody is interested, my golf handicap, which used to be pretty good, has gone up since I turned 86, to 21. It would be better if I could keep my head down.

L'envoi

I owe my God much—I have had a long and pleasant life with a beloved wife who controls my behavior and destiny and two fine sons who now have families of their own. Who could be any luckier?

APPENDIX A
FAMILY LETTERS

Letter of Col. Robert E. Lee, in 1852 the Superintendent of the U.S. Military Academy, West Point, to Mrs. A. A. Draper the widow of my great-grandfather Hawkins, who died as an Army doctor near Vera Cruz, Mexico, during the Mexican War, 1846. The letter is dated "21 Decr 1852."

I can well understand my dear Mrs. Draper your anxiety about your son, & Sympathize in your feelings. I shall be most happy at all times to give you any information calculated to allay them, & hope what I have to say at the present will not be without some portion of Comfort.

I have watched the course of your son from my first arrival here with much interest, & have every week questioned his Profs—as to his proficiency in his studies. It has been a source of regret to me that his progress in mathematics has not been better, which is owing I fear to want of *hard study*, although he does tell you that "he does his best." Lately he has been doing better, & I think now, unless he does *badly* at the examination that he will pass in Mathematics. I do not think there is any danger in reference to his other Studies, & his Conduct, though he has accumulated no greater amount of demerits than he ought, is good and *improving*. Upon the whole then I think he will get through the Jany Examination, and you must urge him to apply himself with *greater* diligence or he may fail in June, which will be equally mortifying to you and injurious to himself. Cadets deceive themselves sometimes by thinking they study, when in reality they do not, & are satisfied by reading over or devoting a reasonable time to their lessons. You know the difference between that and *understanding* it, & nothing but the last will *answer*, & with nothing less ought they to be *satisfied*.

It gave me great pain to deny him permission yesterday to attend his Sister's wedding, although I knew it would give him so much pleasure & her so much gratitude. Yet as his examination was so close at hand, & his position so hazardous, I thought every moment was of vital importance to him, & It might prove an unremediable injury to him, to distract his thoughts from his studies even for the short time required for this purpose. So at the risk of being considered by both *harsh* and *unreasonable,* I refused him from what I considered was for his benefit. I hope therefore you and they will excuse me.

    Mrs. Lee joins me in kind regards, & I remain

        Very truly yours,

        R. E. Lee

Letter (dated 15 January 1865) of Gen. William Tecumseh Sherman, U.S. Army, to Mrs. A. A. Draper, my great-grandmother. By many penciled interlineations on the original letter she showed bitter disapproval of what she considered to be Sherman's apologia for his famous (or infamous) "March to the Sea."

    My dear Mrs. Draper,

    I was much pleased to receive at the hand of your Son Hamilton Hawkins your kind letter of Jan 4. I had not seen him since he was a little fair haired boy of 10 years in 1845, and now he is a tall fine handsome looking officer. I saw him but for a few minutes and hope to see him again as he is with Mr. Draper now about at Port Royal. Indeed it feels strange to me to lead a large army through this Land, and ride through the streets of Savannah as its Enemy! But I wipe my hands of all unkindness for how mad, how Senseless . . . to arouse the Demon Spirit "War" in our Land. You & I remember how Bragg used to ridicule the pretensions of the "Mac tabs" of Charleston to dominion over us, how he resented their pretensions to excellence over us of ruder habits and born in distant lands and now forsooth he joins his fortunes to them & demands that our Country shall sink into ignominy at the demand of those Self Same, Self Constituted Rulers. How would you or I feel had we let Toombs, Slidell, Benjamin Davis, etc Crush up our Government because they could not rule. But I know when the truth is made manifest, that our Country will rejoice at its escape from the doom prepared for us. And that even our Old Charleston friends, the McBeths, the Hayes, Barksdales, . . . etc. will praise us for rescuing them. So terrible however is the Animosity to [*sic*] South Carolina that I fear my old attachment to Mary Lamb, Mary Johnson, the pretty Miss North and others of the Charleston girls will not hold back the Strong Arms and Eager Minds that led to her destruction. But how Strange! is it not? that I who used to ride all night to dream with Hardy or Sally Quash up on the Cooper or to hunt all day with Jim Rogers should now be the Leader of the bandit horde that has made its Mark from the Mississippi to the Atlantic. I feel little Changed but must be more than I realize; yet if the present dream could vanish, and the Night Spring should place us amid the sweet Jassamine of Mount Pleasant I could forget the Shouts of battle and the hissing shell and ever more gather the Magonolia blossom for some fair girl or drape the scene to make a picnic. But I forget, you are no longer the good kind Mrs. Hawkins whose dream I used to borrow. . . . Nor am I the red headed Sherman of Sullivans Island. I am now the father of five children living—and two dead—My eldest boy who was the best Companion I ever had, fearless, kind, and manly, but he died during a short visit he paid me down the Mississippi. Another baby I never saw And only know of him from his mother who thought him even better than any of the rest. I have one boy Tom 8 years old, also a manly firm child but less of the Sherman than the other two. My eldest girl Minnie bids fair to make a splendid woman. 2nd Lizzie more delicate from a scare at sea on our way to California—and two little girls almost twins Elly and Rachael who are pronounced by judges a real "Pony team." I could tell you a long tale, but my sheet is nearly full and leaves me only room to assure you that I never have or can forget you . . . or the noble gentle man now no more, Dr. Hawkins.

In his book *The Rough Riders,* Theodore Roosevelt makes several references to my grandfather, who led the infantry of Kent's division in the charge up San Juan Hill in Cuba during the Spanish American War. On pages 140, 188, and 189 are these references to my father:

While I was reforming the troops on the chain of hills, one of General Sumner's aides, Captain Robert Howze—as dashing and gallant an officer as there was in the whole gallant cavalry division, by the way—came up with orders for me to halt where I was, not advancing farther, but to hold the hill at all hazards. Howze had his horse, and I had some difficulty in making him take proper shelter; he stayed with us for quite a time, unable to make up his mind to leave the extreme front, and mean-while jumping at the chance to render any service, of risk or otherwise, which the moment developed.

On pages 188–89 this paragraph:

I also saw a good deal of the excellent officers on the staffs of Generals Wheeler and Sumner, especially Colonel Dorst, Colonel Garlington, Captain Howze, Captain Steele, Lieutenant Andrews, and Captain Astor Chanler, who, like myself, was a vol-unteer. Chanler was an old friend and a fellow big-game hunter, who had done some good exploring work in Africa. I always wished I could have had him in my regiment. As for Dorst, he was peculiarly fitted to command a regiment. Although Howze and Andrews were not in my brigade, I saw a good deal of them, especially Howze, who would have made a nearly ideal regimental commander. They were both natural cav-alrymen and of the most enterprising natures, ever desirous of pushing to the front and of taking the boldest course. The view Howze took of every emergency (a view which found prompt expression in his actions when the opportunity offered) made me feel like an elderly conservative.

APPENDIX B
THE HOWZE BOARD

STEERING COMMITTEE

Lt. Gen. Hamilton H. Howze, President
  CG, XVIII Airborne Corps
Edward H. Heinemann
  Aviation Consultant, Los Angeles
Frank A. Parker Jr.
  President, Research Analysis Corp.
Dr. Edwin W. Paxson
  RAND Corporation
Eugene Vidal
  Army Scientific Advisory Panel
Fred W. Wolcott
  Aeronutronics Division of Ford
Maj. Gen. Norman Vissering
  CG, Army Transportation Training Center
Maj. Gen. Ben Harrell
  CG, Army Infantry Center
Maj. Gen. Clifton F. von Kann
  Asst. C/ST, J-3
  U.S. Strike Command
Maj. Gen. William B. Rosson
  Special Assistant to the Chief of Staff for Special Warfare
Brig. Gen. John J. Lane
  Office DCSLOG
Brig. Gen. Beverly E. Powell
  CG, XVIII Airborne Corps Artillery
Brig. Gen. Edward L. Rowny
  Assistant Division Commander, 82nd Airborne Division

Brig. Gen. Frederic W. Boye Jr.
  Assistant Commandant Armor School
Brig. Gen. Delk M. Oden
  Director, Army Aviation
Brig. Gen. Ben Sternberg
  Office DCSPERS, DA
Brig. Gen. Robert R. Williams
  CG, Army Aviation Center
Brig. Gen. William E. Lyon Jr.
  Assistant Division Commander, 4th U.S. Infantry Division

ADVISORY PANEL

Lt. Gen. Arthur G. Trudeau, Retired
  President, Gulf Research and Development
Dr. Jacob A. Stockfisch
  Office of the Secretary of Defense

SECRETARIAT

Col. John Norton, GS (Inf) CONARC
  Executive to President of Board
Col. George W. Putnam Jr., Deputy
  Office DCSOPS, DA
Col. George S. Beatty Jr., GS (Inf)
  Army Aviation Center
Col. Alexander J. Rankin
  Army Aviation Board
Col. Franklin M. Davis Jr., Armor, Editor
  Army War College

APPENDIX C
LEGION OF MERIT AWARD

The President of the United States of America, authorized by Act of Congress, July 20, 1962, has awarded the Legion of Merit (Second Oak Leaf Cluster) to

LIEUTENANT GENERAL HAMILTON H. HOWZE
United States Army

for exceptionally meritorious conduct
in the performance of outstanding services:

Lieutenant General Hamilton H. Howze distinguished himself by exceptionally meritorious achievement in developing a plan of operation to be used in conjunction with the recent Cuban crisis. Despite the extremely short time span allowed for the development of this plan and the large and varied forces involved, he succeeded in developing a plan which was complete, accurate and covered every contingency. The specific planning included provision for the introduction of Army combat forces into an objective area, their subsequent employment, as well as all combat, administrative and logistical support required to support effectively the force and insure ultimate victory. By his forceful personality, intimate knowledge of the tactical and logistical problems involved, and decisive leadership, he was able to develop successfully a plan involving forces exceeding those normally assigned to an Army Corps and involving all types of Army combat forces and supporting units. Despite the time limitation, the large number of units and the size of the force involved, the plan substantially reduced the reaction time of these units, increased their state of readiness, and resulted in a combat ready force able to meet any contingency in the plan. By his military knowledge, sound judgment and unceasing efforts, he contributed directly and materially to the improvement of the defense posture of Army units based in the continental United States. During the initial stages in the development of the plan, he personally coordinated with Naval and Air Force representatives to insure that all aspects of the plan were reviewed and meshed with the plans of other services. After development of the plan, he conducted briefings personally at Fort Bragg, North Carolina, for commanders of all major elements so as to enable them to prepare supporting plans in accordance with his personal guidance and direction. When the Cuban crisis developed it became necessary to implement certain portions of the plan that he had devised. The implementation of these portions proceeded without difficulty and demonstrated that, under his superlative leadership, an effective, thorough and completely workable plan had been developed. General Howze's distinguished performance of duty in this sensitive and complex operation represented a significant achievement in the most honored and cherished traditions of the United States Army and reflects great credit upon himself and the military service.

INDEX